WITCH OF KODAKERY

WITCH OF KODAKERY

The Photography of Myra Albert Wiggins 1869-1956

CAROLE GLAUBER

FOREWORD BY TERRY TOEDTEMEIER

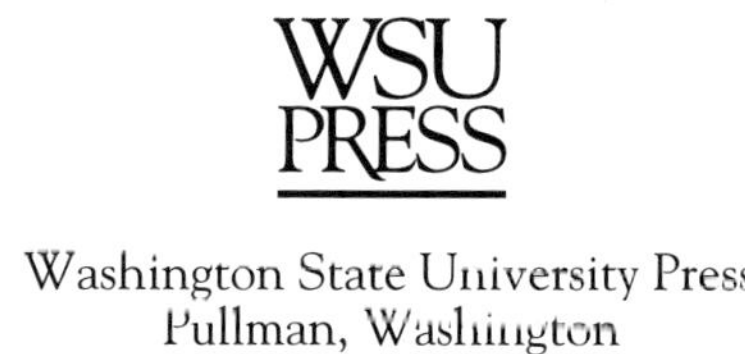

Washington State University Press
Pullman, Washington

The Washington State University Press gratefully acknowledges
the support and assistance from the following individuals and organizations
that made the publication of this book possible.

Robert and Shirley Benz

Josephine Albert Spaulding

Betty Smithberg

Regional Arts and Culture Council (Portland)

Northwest Women's History Project (Portland)

Oregon Council for the Humanities

Portland Art Museum

Washington State University Press, PO Box 645910, Pullman, WA 99164-5910
Phone 800-354-7360; FAX 509-335-8568

First printing 1997

Printed and bound in the United States of America on pH neutral, acid-free paper.

Library of Congress Cataloging-in-Publication Data

Glauber, Carole, 1951-
Witch of Kodakery : the photography of Myra Albert Wiggins, 1869-1956 / by Carole Glauber ; foreword by Terry Toedtemeier.
p. cm.
Includes bibliographical references and index.
ISBN 0-87422-149-8 (hdb. : alk. paper). — ISBN 0-87422-148-X (pbk. : alk. paper)
1. Wiggins, Myra Albert, 1869-1956. 2. Women photographers—United States—Biography. 3. Photography, Artistic. I. Wiggins, Myra Albert, 1869-1956. II. Title.
TR140.W474G55 1997
770' .92—dc21
[B] 97-16180
CIP

Contents

Acknowledgments

The existence of this book is due to the generosity of Robert Benz (Myra Wiggins' grandson) and his wife Shirley. They always welcomed me into their home, where I spent days sorting through letters, photographs, albums, and all the miscellaneous documents that can encompass a family's long and colorful history. Robert and Shirley Benz's donation of the Wiggins collection to the Portland Art Museum in Portland, Oregon, ensures that the legacy of Myra Albert Wiggins will forever be available to scholars, students, and other researchers. Robert Benz's personal memories of his grandparents also added immeasurably to this story, as did those of his mother, Mildred Wiggins Benz (Myra and Fred Wiggins' daughter and only child).

I likewise am deeply indebted to Josephine Albert Spaulding with whom I passed many hours in her lovely home asking questions regarding her "Aunt Myra." Josephine's enthusiasm, support, and encouragement in bringing this project to fruition deserve special recognition. Her son-in-law, Gary White, made my initial connections to the family possible, and, for that, I am grateful.

Along the way, many other people shared their knowledge and information. I owe special thanks to: Toby Quitslund for sending me her research notes on early women photographers; Gillian Marrah for her thesis on Seattle area photographers; Tom Robinson, whose ability to uncover obscure information never ceases to amaze me; Barbara Michaels for her scholarly review of my early manuscript; Lee and Steve Spratt, who read my initial work and made valuable suggestions; and Becky Simmons at the George Eastman House, who diligently researched and responded to my requests. I likewise am deeply grateful to Peter Palmquist for supplying me with items from periodicals unavailable through inter-library loan, for his inspiration, and, most of all, for his ardent passion for photographic history.

I also wish to thank: Robert Joki of the Sovereign Gallery, Portland; Marion Ross of the Toppenish Museum; Jack Cleaver, Susan Seyl, and the staff at the Oregon Historical Society; Judge Charles Crookham; Merridawn Duckler; Susan Fillin-Yeh of Reed College; Christian Peterson of the Minneapolis Institute of Art; Sharon Long Baerny; David Martin of Martin-Zambito Fine Art, Seattle; Susan Feldman; Sherry Brown; Judith Guheen; Kathy Wolkowicz of the George Eastman House; Lois Gauch and Robert Yokel of the Eastman Kodak Company; Steven King of the M.H. De Young Memorial Museum; Naomi Rosenblum; John Bernstein; Jill Quasha; Rod Slemmons; Roger Hull of Willamette University; Brian Booth; Charlie Kamerman; Bob Tompkins and Al Jones of the Marion County Historical Society; and Betty Smithberg for her special support.

Special recognition also goes to Lorna Robertson, Lillian Rehbock, Peggy Jacobs, Doris Jenson Carmin, Margaret Crookham Parr, Yvonne Twining Humber, Beaumont Newhall, and Jack McLauchlan who shared their memories of Myra Wiggins.

Other assistance came from: Mark Pence and Ann Eichelberg, registrars at the Portland Art Museum; Peggy Kendellen, who transcribed hours of interview tapes; Kim Smith, who planted the idea for this book; and David Trappe. A number of years ago, David was the person who introduced me to Myra Wiggins' work. He arrived at my house with an armful of Wiggins' copy prints, which we spread out on my dining room table.

I am especially grateful to Terry Toedtemeier of the Portland Art Museum, whose friendship, curatorial expertise, and generosity with his time are deeply appreciated.

A research fellowship from the Oregon Council for the Humanities (OCH) enabled me to visit the Library of Congress in Washington, D.C., and the Beinecke Library at Yale University, where I combed through the Alfred Stieglitz Archives. I wish to thank the OCH for believing in my project. Their support opened many doors for me. In addition, grants from the Regional Arts and Culture Council and the Northwest Women's History Project provided essential support for this book.

At the Washington State University Press, the collective skills of many professionals brought this book to completion. I wish to thank my editor, Glen Lindeman, for his encouragement, sound advice, and attention to details, Dave Hoyt for his superb design of the book, and Jean Taylor, Beth DeWeese, Director Tom Sanders, and Associate Director Mary Read for their enthusiasm and interest in my project.

I am especially grateful to my husband, Harry Glauber, who read my manuscript countless times, offered excellent editorial suggestions, and provided me with the gift of time, enabling me to research and write this book. It is to Harry and my sons, Benjamin and Sam, that I dedicate this book.

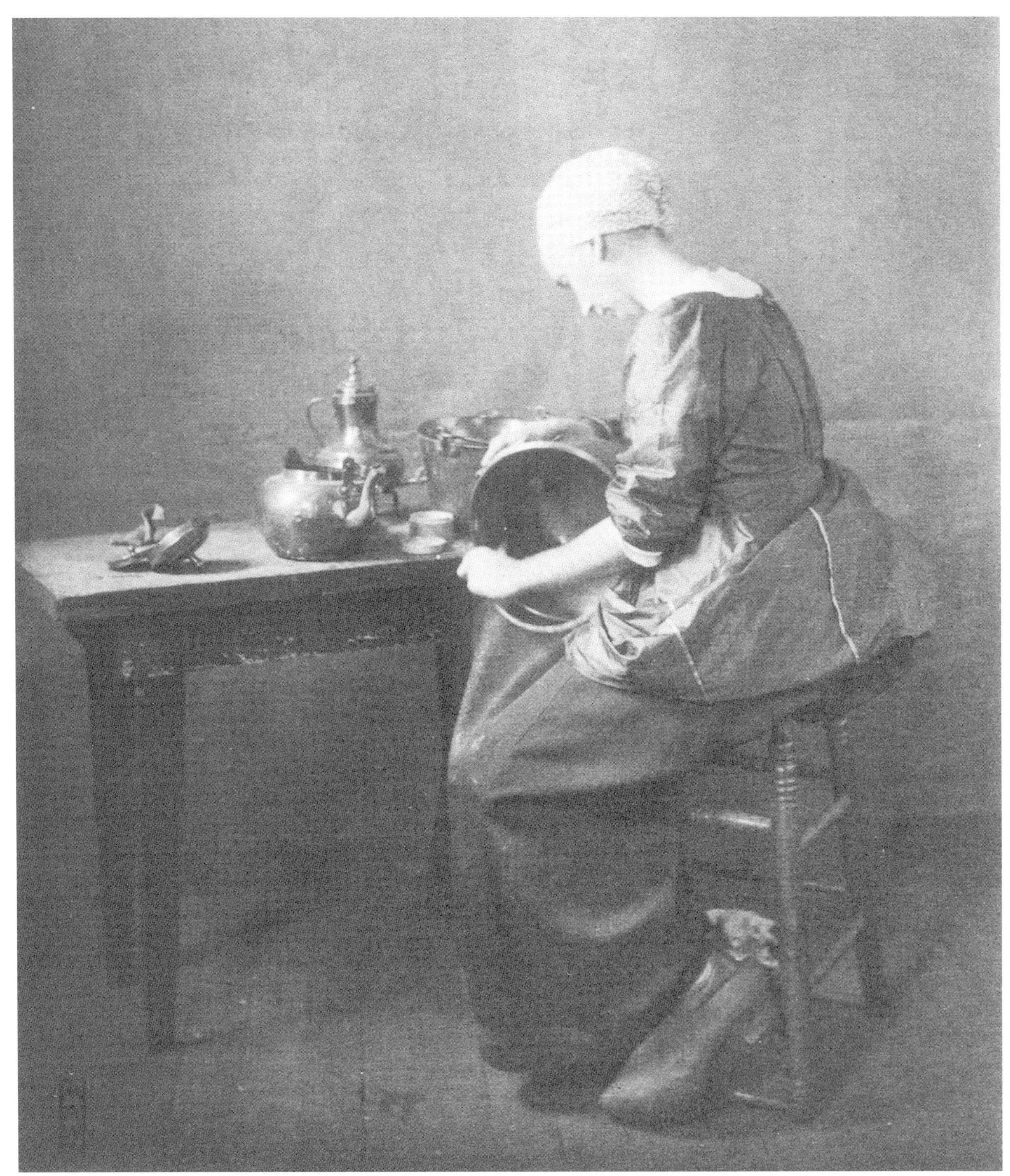

FOREWORD

MYRA WIGGINS, LILY WHITE, AND SARAH LADD: OREGON PHOTO-SECESSIONISTS

by Terry Toedtemeier
Curator of Photography, Portland Art Museum

We take for granted that photographs accurately resemble what the human eye sees. Where this phenomenon once carried an unequivocal aura of fact, the photographic image, particularly in the cinema, is now a vehicle for all kinds of popular fiction. Amazingly, even in the most fantastic of films, the image continues to affect us with a kind of believability that is remarkable—we are, at least for a moment, convinced by images of things we have never seen: aliens from outer space, Jurassic beasts, and rulers of ancient Egypt. Though the cinema had not yet been invented when Myra Wiggins began making photographs, an understanding of photography's verity was not lost on her. In addition to making fine portraits and landscape views, Wiggins became accomplished in the art of choreographing images in the studio. From an inheritance that included wooden clogs, copper and brass cooking ware, and traditional Dutch costumes, she fashioned reenactments of a domestic setting she had never witnessed—vignettes of eighteenth-century Holland.

Just as a nineteenth-century photograph of a person dressed to look like Thomas Jefferson might well be believed by many people today to be an actual photograph of Jefferson (even though he died in 1826, many years before the practical invention of photography), Wiggins' fabrications of Dutch genre scenes carried an aura of fact. Reminiscent of colonial reenactment photographs popularized in 1876 during the nation's centennial celebration, Wiggins' images struck a romantic chord in her public. A similar photographic approach proved effective for Wiggins' contemporary, Edward Sheriff Curtis, whose monumental, twenty-volume project *The North American Indian* attempted to simulate American Indians' lives in a time before white contact. From the virtual beginning of photography, the plasticity of camera representation has been put to the fascinating task of recording, on the one hand, what the eye sees, and on the other, of simulating what the mind envisions. Myra Wiggins and her colleagues were both fascinated and challenged by this duality.

By the 1880s, the implications of photography's dual capacity to simulate as well as record were being enthusiastically explored as vehicles for artistic production. The effort to create art with a camera was most often taken up by self-directed amateurs rather than by professional photographers.

MYRA A. WIGGINS,
POLISHING BRASS
1903, platinum print
Portland Art Museum

Unencumbered by the constraints of a commercial marketplace, amateurs could take creative risks and more freely direct their passion for photography. In fact, amateur photography, both in Europe and the United States, was gaining tremendous popularity with substantial followings in pursuit of each side of the camera's dual personality. Inevitably a philosophic division evolved.

Two notable photographers, Henry Peach Robinson and Dr. Peter Henry Emerson, both working in England, personified an ongoing debate as to which made better art: images produced directly from life or those crafted in the studio. Robinson advocated the posed, pictorial aesthetic of the studio, while Dr. Emerson preferred a more naturalistic approach, emphasizing selective focus. Emerson detailed the specifics of his philosophy in what became a very influential book entitled *Naturalistic Photography.* At roughly the same time, a young, American engineering student in Berlin happened to take note of a camera in a shop window.

The student was Alfred Stieglitz and the camera became his passion. Stieglitz enrolled in a photochemistry class and quickly became an avid amateur, making photographs from his European travels. He submitted work to a competition sponsored by the English journal *The Amateur Photographer,* where his photography caught the eye of Dr. Emerson. Shortly thereafter, the two began to correspond. Emerson praised the spontaneity of Stieglitz's images and encouraged an ongoing dialogue. Now in communication with one of the most powerful voices in Europe's photographic community, Stieglitz found the course of his life turning with increasing commitment to the practice and advocacy of the art of photography.

Upon his return to the United States in 1890, Stieglitz distinguished himself first as the editor of *American Amateur Photographer* and, a few years later, as the founding editor of the prestigious *Camera Notes*, the mouthpiece of the Camera Club of New York. Amateur photography in America had now come into full bloom with ample numbers of pictorial photographers working from coast to coast. Yet, at the turn of the century, American artists in all media were struggling to achieve recognition in an arena historically dominated by Europeans. In New York, Philadelphia, and elsewhere on the East Coast, issues of standards and excellence began to create divisions in the pictorial photographic community. Stieglitz, among others, felt a strong need to pull away from the all-embracing populist milieu of the camera clubs. Holding only the highest standards for their art, Stieglitz and a number of dedicated colleagues merged with a sense of common cause to shape a vanguard movement called the Photo-Secession.

Founded on February 17, 1902, with the bold, clear vision Stieglitz had long championed, the Photo-Secession came together in the form of an exhibition at the National Arts Club.

With the advent of the Photo-Secession, pictorial photography came into focus on the cutting edge of contemporary art in America. Broadcasting their influence far beyond Manhattan, the Secessionists produced and distributed to their members a state-of-the-art, quarterly publication entitled *Camera Work,* again edited by Alfred Stieglitz. For the quality of original-negative, hand-pulled tissue photogravure prints that were tipped in to each issue, *Camera Work* has remained unequaled to this day. A font of fresh criticism and dialogue, the is-

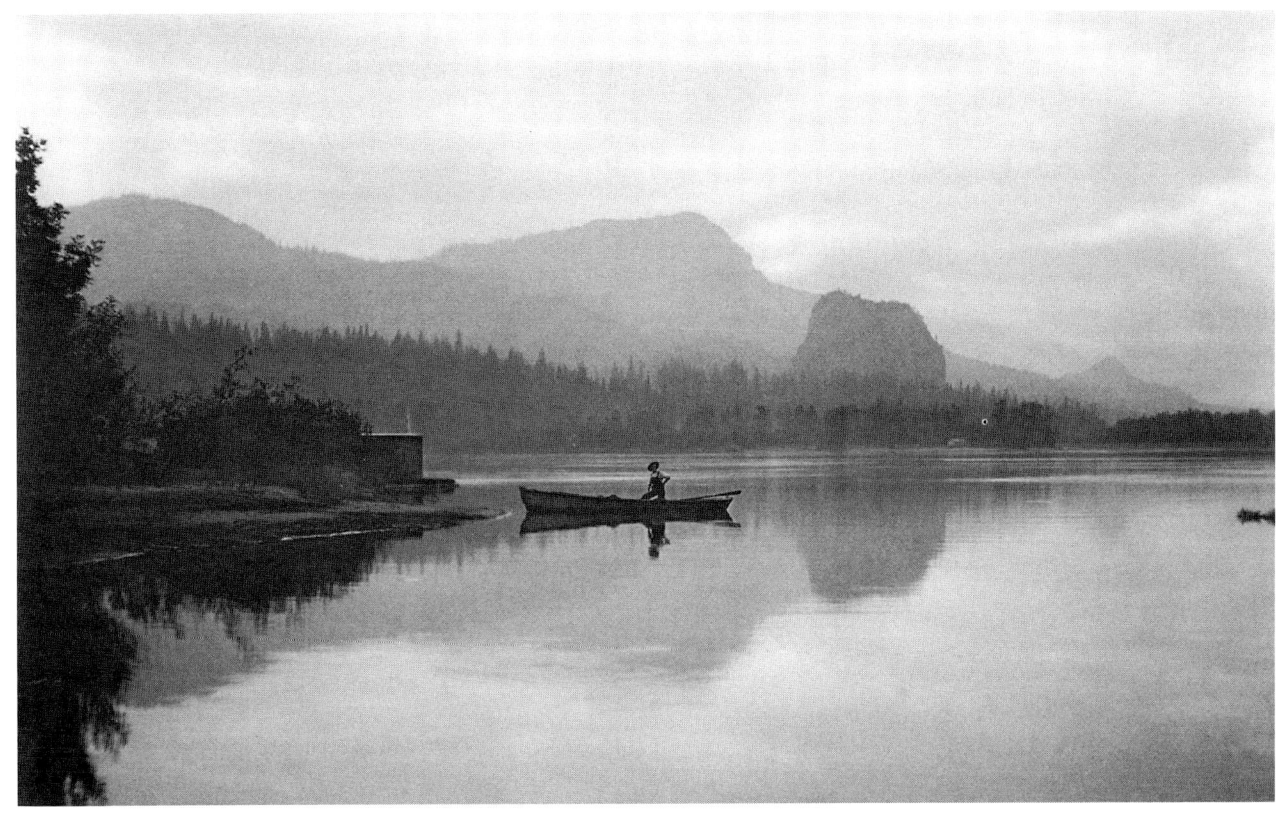

Lily E. White, Twilight on the Columbia - Castle Rock in the Distance
c. 1902, platinum print
Portland Art Museum

sues of *Camera Work* were the pride of Stieglitz and his 105 associate members nationwide. Yet the movement needed a home; on the 24th of November, 1905, with an exhibition of members' work, the Little Galleries of the Photo-Secession opened.

The Little Galleries of the Photo-Secession not only exhibited the work of Stieglitz and his associates, it also showed influential European photographers such as Frederick Evans, Thomas Annan, Heinrich Kühn, and Robert Demachy. Believing photography to be the equal of other creative arts, the gallery provided a venue, often for the first time in America, for paintings, drawings, and sculpture by such defining masters of modernism as Constantine Brancusi, Auguste Rodin, Claude Monet, Arthur Dove, John Marin, Marsden Hartley, Max Weber, Elie Nadelman, Henri Matisse, Paul Cézanne, Francis Picabia, Georges Braque, and Pablo Picasso.

It could be reasonably said that Alfred Stieglitz and his following were the detonators of modern art in this country. The charge they shaped and triggered, though centered in New York, was felt nationwide. Although dominated by an East Coast membership, there were six associate members of the Photo-Secession from the Pacific Coast—Francis Bruguiere and Oscar Maurer of San Francisco and Annie Brigman of Oakland, California; Sarah Ladd and Lily White of Portland and Myra Wiggins of Salem, Oregon.

It has been conjectured that the nineteenth-century American West provided a kind of psychological environment more open and conducive to individual pursuits than existed on the East Coast. If the criterion for this was a measurement of involvement in the arts, then it could be argued that this was even more the case for women than men. It has appeared to this writer that the creative accomplishments in photography in Oregon at the turn of the century were far and away led by women. A list of names would include not only White, Ladd, and Wiggins, but their colleagues Maude Ainsworth, Helen Gatch (a member of Rudolph Eickemeyer's Philadelphia Salon), and Julia Hoffman (founder of the Portland Society of Arts and Crafts and influential in the founding of the Portland Art Museum and Museum Art School). As important as the contributions of these women have been, the historic record of their lives is often weak or virtually nonexistent, as is the case with Lily White, Sarah Ladd, and Maude Ainsworth. Fortunately, Myra Wiggins was near-to-obsessive in her autobiographic habits, leaving an archive of hundreds of original prints, publications, and annotated materials. This legacy, a biographer's dream come true, was handed down to Wiggins' grandson Bob Benz and has become the source for Carole Glauber's much-needed book, *Witch of Kodakery*.

In 1990, Bob and Shirley Benz donated the majority of the Wiggins material to the permanent collection of the Portland Art Museum. One of the largest single gifts to the museum's holdings in photography, the Wiggins archive, in concert with the works of White, Ladd, Ainsworth, and Hoffman, completes a picture of the artistic initiatives championed by women photographers at a seminal time in the state's cultural history. Carole Glauber was instrumental in encouraging and facilitating this generous and most important gift and, struck by the magnitude and ambition of Wiggins' accomplishments, began to piece together the artist's story. It is a story that links a pioneer past to a machine age future, a life in the rural West with influences in the urban East.

At the time of Myra Wiggins' birth in 1869, Oregon had held statehood for only ten years. Salem, Myra's birthplace and the state capital, had become a hub of commerce, but was still very much a pioneer Willamette Valley town tied to its agrarian roots. As Wiggins came of age, the social and economic engines of her native state continued to be fueled by a unique form of pioneer spiritedness and zeal. Oregonians, it seems, held a kind of dual patriotism—one, distinctly American, the other, inherently Western. Beyond the physical prospects and possibilities that had lured people West was a sense of personal freedom that, for many, simply did not exist in the East. Yet, the vision of the future embraced by Oregon's captains of industry was informed by Eastern values. For the enterprising individual, freedom in Oregon meant the freedom to claim for yourself the opportunities that might already have been claimed in the East. For some it was a freedom that meant peace of

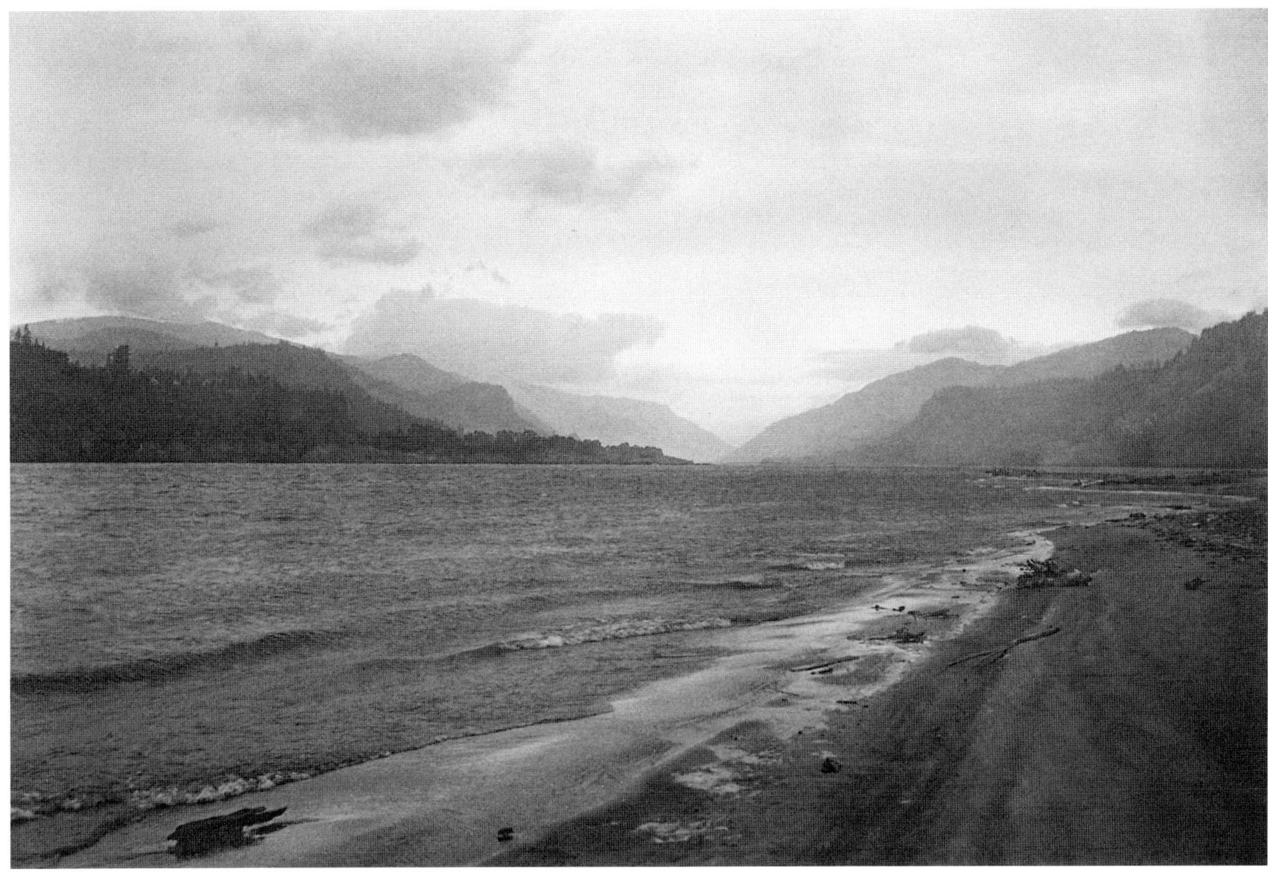

Sarah H. Ladd, Gateway to the Inland Empire
c. 1902, platinum print
Portland Art Museum

mind, for others it was a freedom that meant the opportunity to compete.

Less constrained by Victorian ideas, Oregon was the kind of place where a person could, as Naomi Rosenblum once characterized life in the West, "be as wacky as you want to be." In its beauty and openness, even the landscape itself echoed a sense of freedom. For Sarah Ladd and Lily White, that freedom existed on the deck of a houseboat called the "Raysark"—miles up the Columbia River Gorge. Here, for weeks on end, they translated the changing light and moods of a place they dearly loved into some of the most elegant platinum photographs of their time. Where White and Ladd's camera verified the miracles of beauty their eyes beheld, for Wiggins, in a studio that had been a barn, the camera was like a dream that could transport her across oceans and back through time. We can be thankful for what they saw and for what they envisioned—the gifts left us by these sisters of the light.

Portrait of Myra Albert Wiggins
age 35
Robert and Shirley Benz Collection

Preface

Myra Albert Wiggins is typical of so many American artists who, despite productive lives and careers, have been lost from our histories. Born in Salem, Oregon, in 1869, and later living in Toppenish and Seattle, Washington, Wiggins achieved creative success in a range of media that included photography, painting, music, poetry, and writing. This book is the first comprehensive look at her life and work.

My efforts to document Myra's life followed my contacts with her grandson, Robert Benz, and his wife Shirley. In their home in Yakima, Washington, the Benzes allowed me to sift through stacks of seldom touched boxes filled with a life-long assortment of Myra's manuscripts, letters, photographs, and diaries. They drove me to the home of his mother, Mildred Wiggins Benz (Myra's daughter and only child), who in her basement had created a "museum" of Wiggins memorabilia.

Within their homes were the treasures of a remarkable life. I found large black photograph albums with Wiggins' name embossed on front in gold letters, and filled with images of the Middle East in 1904, newspaper clippings, exhibition catalogues, and award certificates. I saw her Dutch shoes, melodeon, palette and brushes, and wooden glass plate camera with boxes of glass negatives. The walls of the homes were covered with her paintings. It did not take me long to realize that Myra Wiggins was a tireless woman with abundant creative energy and talent. After reading some of her letters and diaries, I knew I had found a vibrant artist, loyal to friends and family, but independent with a sense of adventure. The Benz family generously donated much of the photographic portion of the Wiggins estate to the Portland Art Museum in Portland, Oregon.

As an early twentieth-century artist, Wiggins exemplified the growing number of women entering professional fields and challenging the deeply rooted concepts of separate spheres of activity for men and women. Her ambition and the national renown she earned were almost unheard of for a married woman with a young child. While a network of colleagues assisted her advancement, Wiggins' lifetime achievements resulted from her artistic talent, energy, and acumen for self-promotion. Her prize-winning photographs appeared in major newspapers and photography magazines, and were viewed in exhibitions by thousands of people. Historically, Wiggins' connection to Alfred Stieglitz,

In thus combining the art of picture making with art of picture taking is found the true "Witchery of Kodakery."

—*The Witchery of Kodakery*, 1899 products catalogue, Eastman Kodak Company.

> The subtle charm of Art, the invigorating influence of active recreation, the joys of delving in the mysteries of chemistry and unveiling its photographic secrets—all or any of these are in store for the Kodaker. In them is the Witchery of Kodakery.
>
> —Eastman Kodak advertisement, *Ladies Home Journal*, 1900.

the founding force behind the Photo-Secession, and her admission to this association in 1903, served to reinforce her stature and link her with the photographic avant-garde, although by this time her national renown already was secure.

As Wiggins' life spanned the long era from stagecoach to commercial airlines, she adapted to a wide range of circumstances. She was equally comfortable exploring Oregon's largely unknown Mt. Jefferson wilderness, the Tomb of the Kings in Jerusalem, or Paris and Holland. In many ways, she embodied the emergence of the "New Woman," independent, energetic, and ambitious, as was the "Kodak Girl" created and promoted by the Eastman Kodak Company. Overlapping this promotion, Kodak utilized a witch or witchery metaphor for advertising purposes, implying the magical power of photography and its ability to charm or fascinate viewers.

Social, cultural, and technological developments impacted Wiggins' work. Her early life intertwined with photographic innovations and new marketing techniques, the Arts and Crafts movement, expanding educational opportunities, the rise of corporations, and the changing attitudes toward women and their work. Myra Wiggins used these changes to her advantage.

The biography of a woman who was a mother with a livelihood inevitably becomes a mix of her public and private sides. Wiggins had to balance the demands of marriage and motherhood with her career and did so ingeniously, by incorporating her private life into her art. While in many ways her domestic environment shaped her work, the men in her life—her father, brother, and husband—influenced her independence.

Later in her life, at a time when most people contemplate retirement, Wiggins embarked upon a second career as a painter. Her still lifes, portraits, interiors, and landscapes won many commissions and awards. Throughout her long life, Myra Wiggins' poetry rang from her soul and her singing touched many. Hers is a story that needs to be told.

> No wonder where the camera is
> A witchery is nigh:
> For see! the witch approaches
> With enchantment in her eye.
> And I feel the luring magic
> Of each dainty, rose-crowned curl
> As I view the pictured features
> of the
> Ko-
> dak
> Girl.
>
> —1904 newspaper advertisement (printed by permission of Eastman Kodak Company).

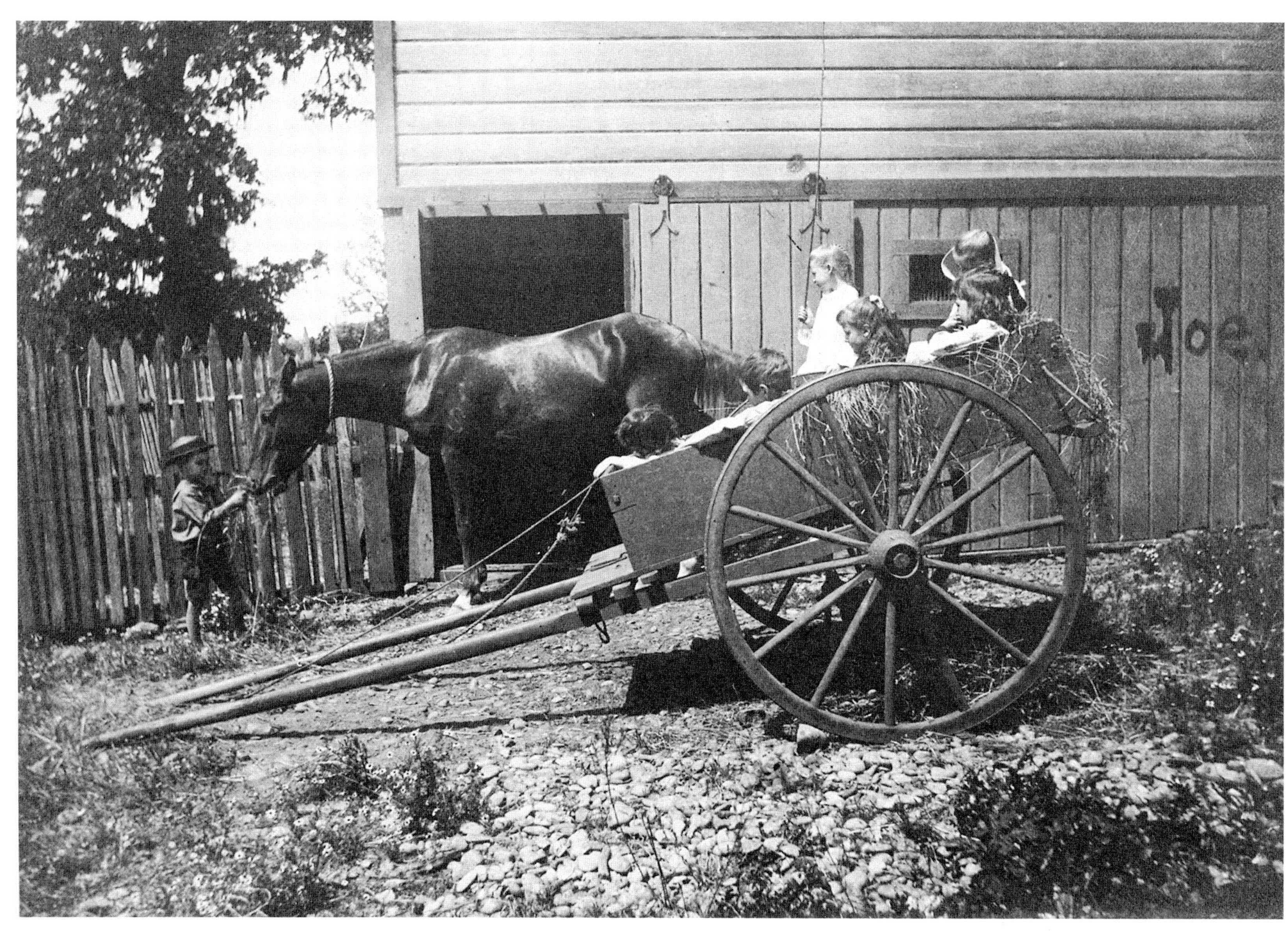

The Old Albert Barn
gelatin silver print
7¾" x 6½"
Robert and Shirley Benz Collection
"about 1889, Klein children, Ryth Gatch, and others."

Part One
1869 - 1890

Myra Albert Wiggins invented her life. She did so at an uncanny speed that might have left others breathless. She moved in a hurry by running in little steps on her toes; friends had to keep up with Myra rather than Myra keep up with her friends. During her long life, she was many things: a gifted photographer, diligent painter, sensitive poet, talented singer, opinionated lecturer, and devoted mother, wife, and grandmother. Tiny, energetic, courageous, confident, eccentric and self-promoting, loyal, elitist, and clever all describe Myra Wiggins.

Her story begins with her grandparents, who migrated West, infused with the enterprising spirit of pioneers. Myra's maternal grandmother, Almira Phelps, born in Westfield, Massachusetts, in 1814, said good-bye to her family in October, 1839, and boarded the ship *Lausanne*. The ship carried forty-eight adults, including four single women and sixteen children, plus twenty-four crew members. The Oregon Trail did not yet exist, so Almira Phelps braved the sea voyage around Cape Horn and survived the crowded living conditions and terrible food for eight months. This small group of missionaries, called the "Great Reinforcement," was on its way to the Oregon Country to assist Methodist missionary, Jason Lee, in educating and converting the Calapooya Indians near the Willamette River.

Dark haired and bearded, powerfully built and stoop shouldered, Reverend Lee stood an imposing six-feet three-inches tall. The mission he built comprised a small log compound divided into two or three sections. Almira Phelps possessed a sense of adventure and strong religious convictions that equipped her to pioneer in the Oregon Country, where few people besides Native Americans had ventured, and civilized life, as she knew it, was just a hope for the future. This area of the Northwest lacked formal government. With territorial ownership still undecided, both Great Britain and the United States claimed the area.

Myra's maternal grandfather, Joseph Holman, came west at age 25 as a member of the "Peoria Party," a group of eighteen trappers and tradesmen who followed Jason Lee's message from Peoria, Illinois, in 1838. These men were among the first to journey overland with the intent of settling permanently in the Oregon Country. With Thomas J. Farnham as their leader, they swore an oath that they would never desert one another, and set out

---

Amateur photography has the great advantage that its followers are confined to no age, sex, or conditions of servitude. The question of sex especially is becoming a past issue. It never should have been raised at all.

—Catharine Weed Ward, "Amateur Photography," *American Amateur Photographer*, 1893.

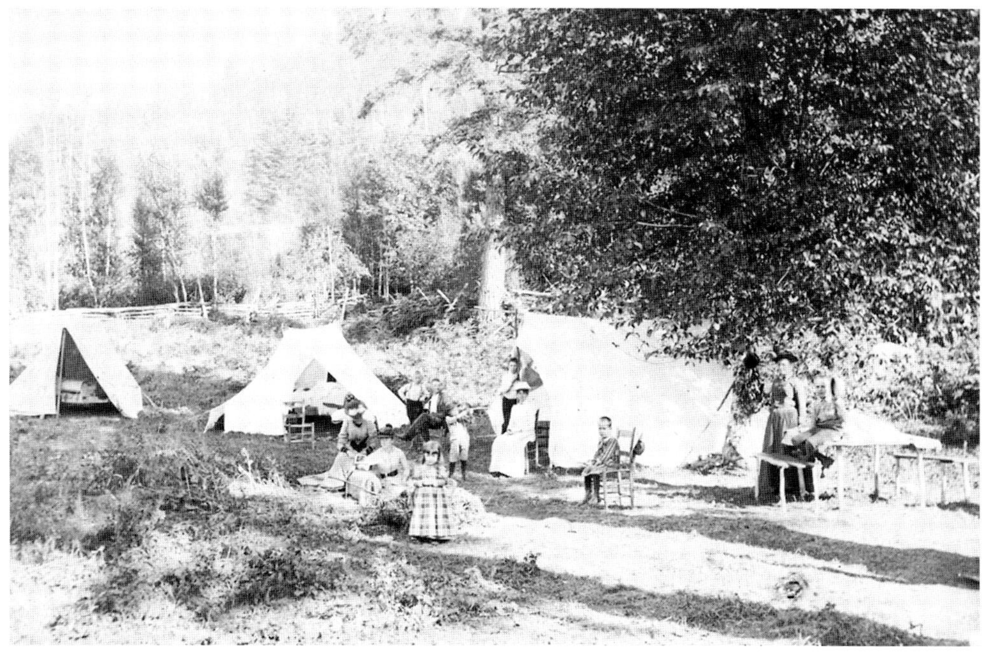

Camping Out
1889, gelatin silver print
8" x 6"
Portland Art Museum

under a banner embossed with the motto, "Oregon or the Grave."

The Peoria Party traveled with horses and wagons until they reached Independence, Missouri, where they sold the wagons and bought mules to carry packs. From there they headed to the Arkansas River and then to Fort Bent on the Platte River where, by then feuding and demoralized, several of the members turned back and Farnham and some of the men went to Santa Fe. Five men, including Holman, went on to Brown's Hole in the Rocky Mountains where they planned to winter with the trapper Joe Meek. Against better advice, four of the men including Holman left in February, 1840, were caught in a blizzard, and nearly perished after going four days without food. They traveled to Fort Boise, then to The Dalles on the Columbia River. After having to hand lead their horses over the bluffs of the Columbia River Gorge, Holman thought this terrain—from The Dalles to Fort Vancouver—was the most difficult part of their journey.

After thirteen months of struggle crossing the country, and just a few hours before the *Lausanne* landed on June 1, 1840, after sailing 22,111 miles in 236 days, Joseph Holman reached Fort Vancouver on the banks of the Columbia River. He had a heavy beard, long hair, and was dressed in buckskins—later traded for "civilized" clothes. When Holman saw Almira Phelps walking down the plank from the ship, he exclaimed, "That's the girl I'm going to marry!"

Almira Phelps and Joseph Holman indeed married "in less than a year" and settled near Lee's Methodist Mission, close to present-day Salem, Oregon. In 1842, Almira Phelps Holman gave birth to George Holman, the first white child born in the area. Their next child, Mary Elizabeth, was born in 1844.

Joseph Holman proved his mettle when in 1843 he joined a meeting in a grain warehouse owned by the Hudson's Bay Company to debate forming a provisional government. As the story goes, after much arguing between the British and American factions, Joe Meek, the burly, black-haired mountaineer, trapper, and hunter, proposed a vote. Meek drew a line in the dirt with a stick and shouted, "Who's for a divide? All for the report of the committee and an organization follow me." Fifty-two of the one hundred and two men in the room, including Holman, crossed the line, thereby establishing Oregon's first formal government.

As Jason Lee's efforts to educate and convert the Indians floundered, the missionaries put their energy into selling plots of land to finance the new

Oregon Institute for the education of white children and laying out a town. The town was first named Chemeketa, a Calapooya Indian word meaning "place of peace," but the missionaries settled on a Biblical word, Salem, with a comparable intent. Around 1846, Joseph Holman "cut the first stick of timber" in Salem, and built a home for his family. By 1853, Salem had grown to about 500 people and the Oregon Institute was incorporated into Willamette University with Joseph Holman as a trustee. Mary Holman became the University's first art teacher. Joseph Holman devoted his lifetime to business and community improvements in Salem.

Just as Myra's maternal grandparents met and survived the challenges of their new lives, so did her paternal grandparents. Ebin Albert, born in 1816, had lived in West Virginia, Iowa, and Ohio, and had run a hotel, sold lumber, and worked in the shoe business. He married Jane Gilchrest, the oldest of seventeen children. Ebin and Jane Albert's oldest son, John Henry Albert, was born in February, 1839, the same year Louis Jacques Mandé Daguerre's invention of the daguerreotype was announced in France. Thanks to his father's varied business interests, John Albert had an early introduction to the world of commerce. He came to Salem in 1865 and worked for G.W. Gray & Company, linseed oil manufacturers.

In April, 1867, Mary Elizabeth Holman married John Henry Albert. The merging of the Holman and Albert families combined their traits of courage, a sense of adventure, a love of education, and a capacity for pioneering in business. The Holmans and Alberts had proved themselves sturdy survivors with solid ideals to contribute to their community and family.

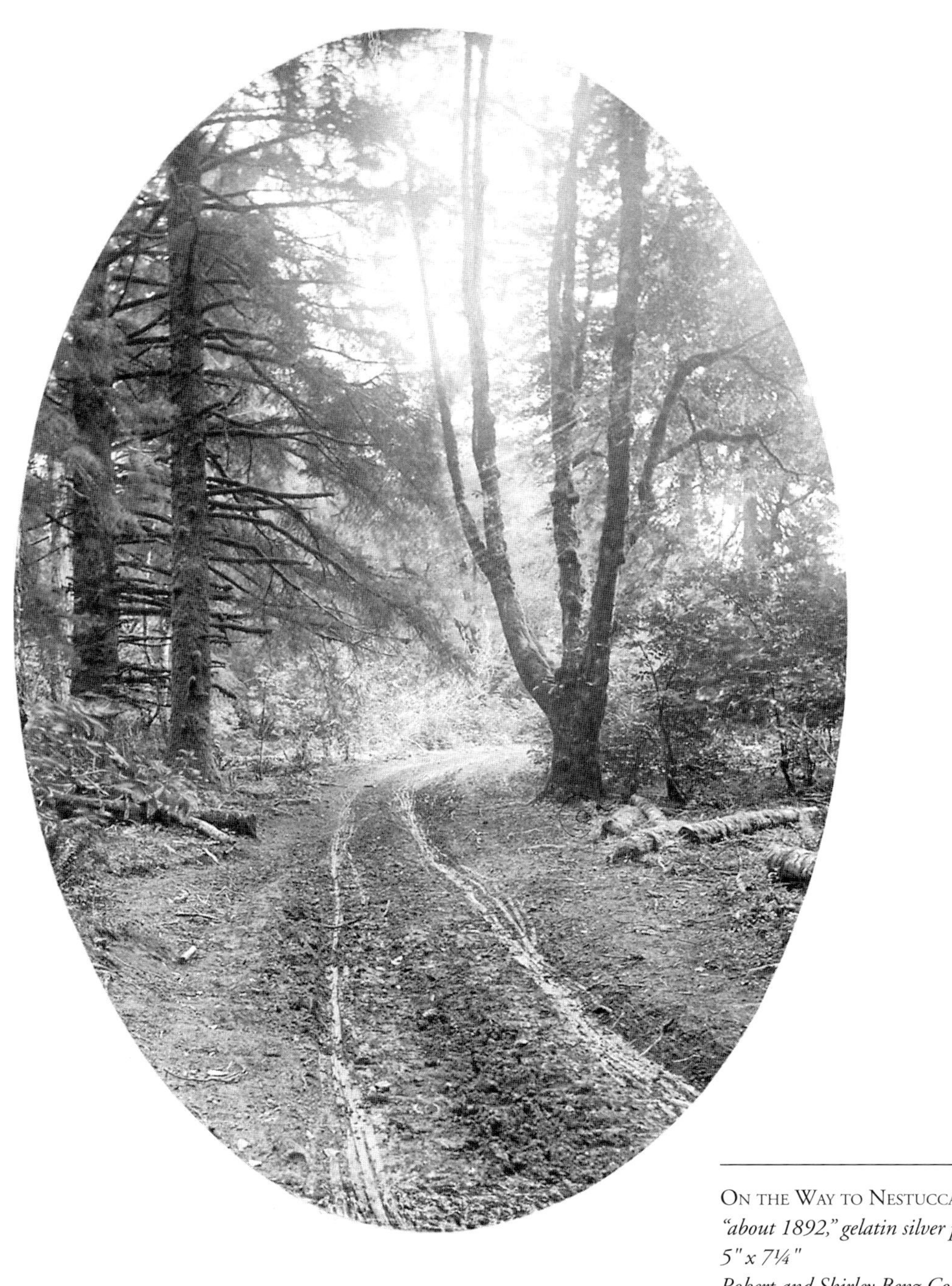

On the Way to Nestucca
"about 1892," gelatin silver print
5" x 7¼"
Robert and Shirley Benz Collection

Their community, Salem, the city of peace, lay in the midst of the fertile and picturesque Willamette Valley of Oregon, stretching sixty miles between the Coast Range on the west and the Cascade Range to the east. The length of the valley extends from the source of the Willamette River, about one hundred miles south of Salem, to the river's junction with the Columbia River, another sixty miles north. Native Americans had lived for centuries in the valley and along the Pacific shoreline west of the Coast Range. A series of volcanoes that dot the Cascade Range's skyline for hundreds of miles inspired reverence from both the Native Americans and settlers. About seventy miles northeast of Salem, as the crow flies, Mt. Hood, one of the largest of these snow-bound peaks, rises over eleven thousand feet. Fifty miles down the spiny range stands ten-thousand-feet-high Mt. Jefferson. The mountains take the brunt of the snowfall, leaving rain and mild winter temperatures for the lower elevations. On many days, finger-tipped mists sit quietly on the ridges and peaks.

In the late nineteenth century, vast forests supplied the raw materials for construction and fuel, and fed the growing lumber industry. Fifty miles north of Salem, the city of Portland grew near the junction of the Willamette and Columbia rivers, providing a safe haven for ships that survived passage through the treacherous and turbulent mouth of the Columbia River.

It was little wonder that Salem residents referred to their area as Eden. By 1869, with a population of about one thousand, Salem was on the verge of frontier sophistication. A water system, gas for illumination, and plank sidewalks appeared in the next few years. George Holman had lit the first street lamp on an ornate post in front of the Holman Building and requested one hundred maple trees to be planted on the streets around town. By 1880, Salem would be called "The City of Maples." The Reed Opera House opened in 1870, and accommodated hotel rooms, a theater, a state library, and a "supreme court room."

People traveled by horseback, wagon, or river steamer. The first train from Portland arrived in 1870, loaded with passengers for the state fair. That year, the Chemeketa House opened, where for the first time the people of Salem would see indoor plumbing and rooms with an electric bell for service. Salem residents benefited from the town's two flour mills, three sawmills, a woolen mill, two machine shops, four newspapers, three sash and door factories, a chair factory, a sock factory, and a linseed oil mill. But Salem also had public hangings, gambling, saloons, brothels, opium dens, and overt racial prejudice. When the state constitution was ratified by popular vote in 1859, it barred slavery, but also excluded African-Americans from residing in the state. In spite of the modern amenities in Salem, rainy, cold winters and hot, dusty summers challenged even the sturdiest citizens. Smallpox and typhoid fever took their toll and in March, 1869, a measles epidemic ravaged the town.

In the December 15, 1869, issue of Salem's newspaper, the *Daily Oregon-Statesman*, Lobdell's Photography Gallery advertised "sun" pictures, an early technique for making photographs. The Oregon and California Stage Company promoted a five-day trip to San Francisco and an eleven-day connection to New York (via the Union Pacific railroad), combining "pleasure, comfort, and speed." On that day, Myra Jane Albert was born, the first daughter of John Henry and Mary Elizabeth Holman Albert. Myra's brother, Joseph, preceded her

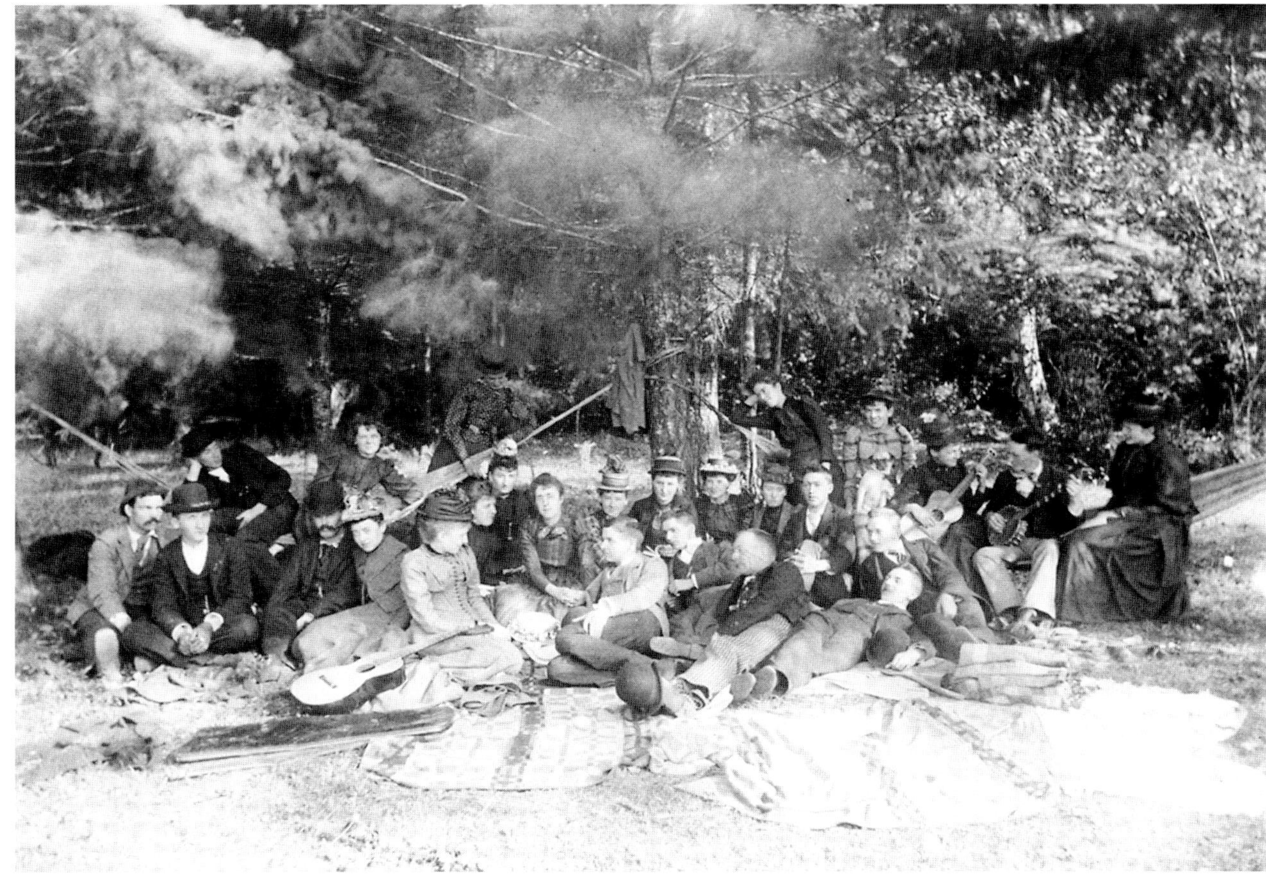

Drift Creek,
Memorial Day Weekend
"1890 or 1891," gelatin silver print
8⅜" x 6⅛"
Portland Art Museum

by two years. Two more siblings, Harry and Blanche, were born during the next four years.

John Albert served as cashier, bookkeeper, and teller of the Ladd and Bush bank when it opened on State and Commercial Street on March 29, 1869. He worked there until 1885, when he became cashier and later president of the new Capital National Bank. As John Albert prospered, his affluence grew. His wealth was probably unmatched in the community. In his children, John Albert instilled his belief in hard work and the value of money. Myra's older brother, Joseph, recalled spending a day of back-breaking work in the hot sun, hoeing tough thistles embedded in the hard ground. "Money so earned," he said, "represented sweat and labor." Beginning at the age of ten, Joseph attended school in the preparatory department of Willamette University, as his sisters and brother probably did. Mary Albert worked as a homemaker. John Albert dabbled in the new pastime, photography.

As a young girl, Myra loved the outdoors and later wrote in her diary that "no boy or man in my

Pink Greenaway Party
c. 1890, gelatin silver print
8⅜"x 5½"
Robert and Shirley Benz Collection

Myra is on the far right, third person back and wearing a bonnet.

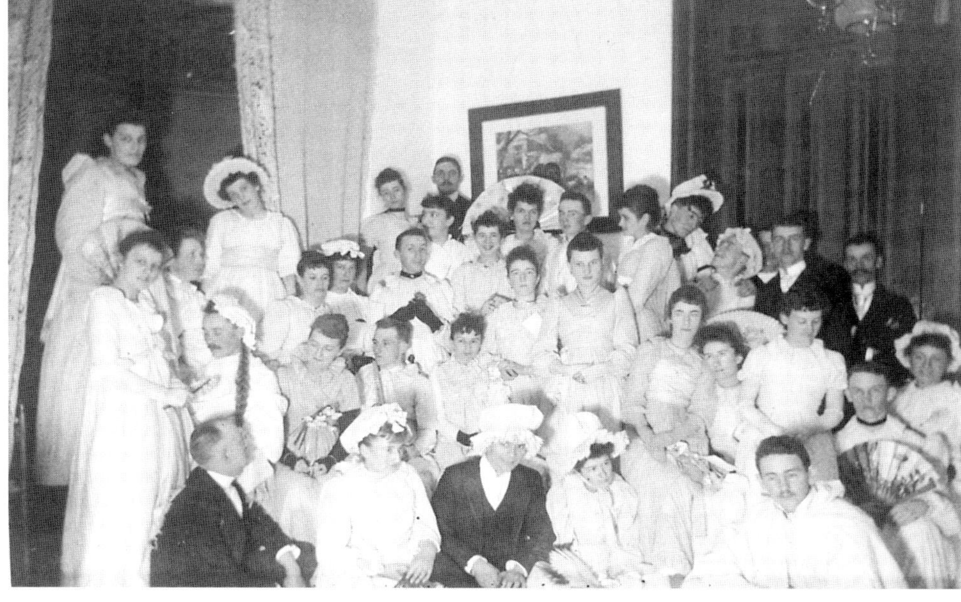

Mock Wedding
c. 1890, gelatin silver print
8½" x 5½"

Robert and Shirley Benz Collection

"Paul and Gertie principals—from this day they started going together and were later married—I was a bridesmaid."

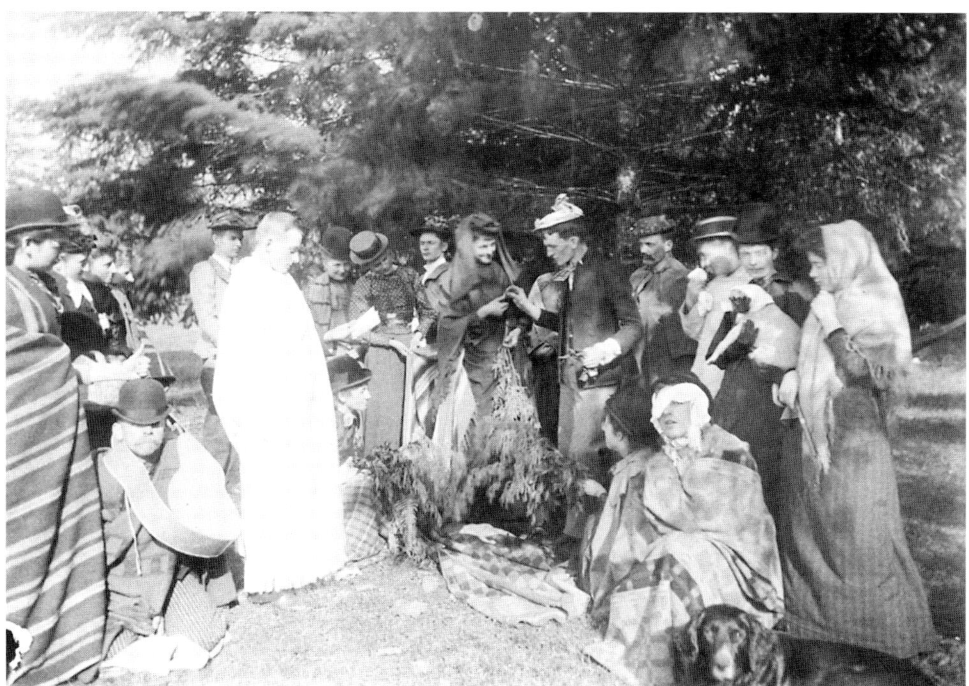

hometown could beat me at running." She remembered her childhood as "the wild, free, 'tomboy' life of a Western Oregon small-town girl," filled with sun, air, and exercise. Already showing her independent spirit and eye for the beauty surrounding her, she took long excursions alone in the Willamette Valley. She loved to feel the wind and rain on her cheeks or study the deep blue sky and fleecy clouds. The peaceful hills of forest green and ranges of snow-covered distant mountains layered against the sky left her inspired, as if she had "visited some far country and was still under its spell." At home, she spent hours drawing and "copying everything about her in nature," and envisioned her experiences painted on canvas. Her parents wisely saw and encouraged her talent. In the summer of her seventeenth year, Myra won a first place award for portraiture at the Oregon state fair. It was the first of 95 state fair awards she would win between 1886 and 1907.

Around the age of eighteen, Myra began private art lessons in Salem with the artist Clyde Cook. Hoping that culture would attract settlers, and knowing that art and education add strength to a community, the businessmen of Salem had sent Cook to study art in Europe so their children could receive up-to-date art instruction. Young Myra Albert benefited from their foresight. For a short time she attended Mills College in California, and Willamette University in Salem, but she set her sights on art school.

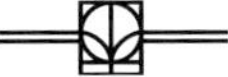

Meanwhile, in Ontario, Canada, Myra's future husband, Frederick Arthur Wiggins, was born on February 12, 1869, the same year as Myra's birth. He was the fifth of six siblings born there. Fred Wiggins' parents, of Scotch-Irish descent, had emigrated to Canada in the 1840s. In 1871, when Fred was two years old, his family made the trek to southeastern Kansas to homestead on the prairie near the town of Eureka. There, six more children were born and two daughters died in childhood.

The Wigginses' lives evolved around their strict work ethic, shaped by a Protestant austerity and the demands of the land and climate. Yet, Fred seemed to want more than prairie life and his family farm could offer. At age fourteen, he went to work in Thomas Holverson's general store, where he learned the rudiments of running a business. In 1886, as a seventeen year old, Fred was one of the first people in Eureka to ride the newly invented fifty-four inch high bicycle. When Holverson moved to Salem in 1888 and purchased a dry goods store, Fred came too, and continued in Holverson's employ. After a number of years, he opened "Wiggins Bazaar" in the same neighborhood on Commercial Street where he sold household and personal goods—shoes, notions, yarns, knit goods, mackintoshes, overalls, ribbons, laces, belts, hosiery, bicycles, etc. Fred loved the challenge of business and could sell anything.

About the time Fred first rode his bicycle, a sport and hobby club mania had surged across the country. Oregon provided the ideal environment for outdoor activities where hiking and mountaineering clubs became popular, as did clubs for a multitude of interests, from literature to music to women's suffrage. Some clubs combined interests like bicycling and photography. Newly created magazines provided readers with reports on yachting, canoeing, skating, football, cycling, bowling, rowing, and golf for men and women. Magazines like

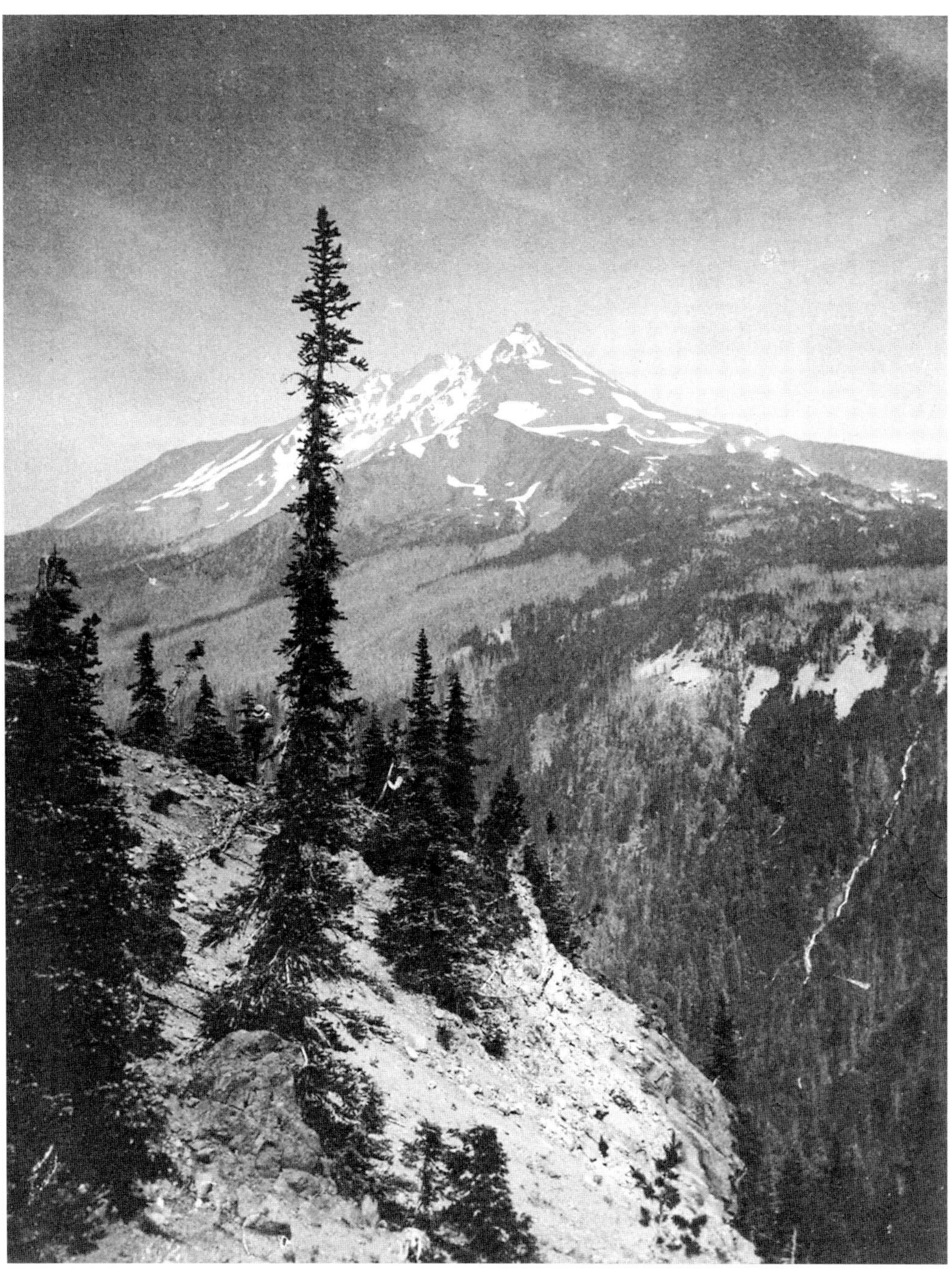

Outing capitalized on these hobbies by featuring, besides the sports news, a photography section detailing camera club news from around the country.

Shared interests probably brought Myra Albert and Fred Wiggins together around 1888. They were members of the same church and tennis club and enjoyed the new craze, bicycling. During their courtship they amused themselves with friends at parties, often in the mountains and at the beach. Photographs by Myra show groups of people in the mountains, sometimes in costumes, some with guitars, assuming humorous poses.

In a picture by Myra of a large group of young people, titled "Pink Greenaway Party," both men and women are dressed in feminine caps and dresses mimicking Mother Goose. The party must have been inspired by the popular Mother Goose books, illustrated by Kate Greenaway, and these Mother Goose revelers posed themselves carefully. Not only did Myra take the photograph, but she appeared in it as well, lighting a fuse attached to flashpowder and quickly positioning herself in the picture.

In August, 1888, Myra's family, along with a number of other families, camped on the beach at Slab Creek on the northern Oregon Coast. They took a "boating excursion" on the Nestucca River, went clamming in the bay, and inspected a "large salmon cannery." During a summer trip in 1889 to Little Nestucca Beach, over 100 people from Salem, including the Albert family, camped in 30 tents. One observer commented, "surf bathing is the great event of the day and is perfectly delightful. It is a long tedious road to this place, but all seem to be fully repaid for their trouble when they get here." He went on to say, the "Salem campers had another delightful concert in which literary and musical talent of a high order was displayed."

Myra had bought her first camera in 1889, but not because she wanted one. As she recalled, her brother Joseph had a sweetheart and wanted to take her picture, so being even then "somewhat a financier," he asked his sister to become part owner, knowing that their father would pay for her half of the camera. When it was finally her turn to use the large, wooden, glass-plate camera and tripod, she made her first images at the Oregon Coast.

Myra later wrote how,

> the country people came from miles around and inquired for the 'artist.' I realized the responsibility of my position and felt many secret misgivings as the fact often recurred to my mind that I had never even seen the inside of a plateholder . . . the dreaded day came when I was compelled to reload them. I obtained permission to use as a dark-room, the front room of the only house within miles around. I darkened the room as best I could and then placed a friend in front of each perpendicular crack in the wall, some of the most accommodating covering two cracks; but alas, I could not hang my friends from the ceiling! My despairing glance about the room fell upon a heavy wooden bedstead. This I draped to the floor with bedding and, crawling underneath with my precious plates, I there solved the mysteries of the hidden springs of a plateholder, with the aid of a smokey red lantern. Thereafter I performed the mystic rites in my tent.

This first outing with her camera yielded "more of experience than pictures," but provided her with enough incentive to continue experimenting, with varying results.

Not long after this photographic initiation, Myra traveled with her large camera by pack train into the forests around Mt. Jefferson. Led by the explorer "Old John Minto," she was accompanied by Minto's wife, daughter-in-law and niece, a botanist, and a geologist. Possibly, these women were the first white females to explore parts of this wilderness. To get there, with their horses and supplies, they rode the train east from Salem to the end of the line in the mountain foothills and proceeded into the wilderness by horseback. Myra strapped her large canvas camera box on one side of the saddle and sat on the other. The group trekked past rocky, precipitous cliffs, cooled themselves by tumbling mountain streams, and endured ever present mosquitoes.

While on the trail, winding their way through thick timber, a yellow jacket stung Myra's horse. The startled horse careened through the woods while Myra struggled to keep herself and her camera from crashing to the ground. At last, bruised and out of breath, she slid from the saddle, worried more about her camera and its thirteen glass plates than about herself. She found her equipment intact, and during the next few days, Myra photographed the snow-tipped crags of Mt. Jefferson.

After returning home, she was anxious to develop her plates. Not wanting to wait to turn her bathroom into a darkroom, she borrowed the darkroom of her friend, Helen Gatch. In their excitement, Myra and Helen forgot to rinse a tray Helen had used for a gold solution during printing. After developing Myra's plates in that tray, the plates were iridescent but still printable. While thinking about Helen Gatch and that event, Myra later revealed, "I taught her to take her first photographs and she taught me to develop my first plate. Later we lived

Mt. Jefferson, Oregon
c. 1890, gelatin silver print
6" x 8"
Portland Art Museum

side by side in Salem and entered many of the same contests, often each receiving prizes."

By the late 1880s, when Myra Albert and Helen Gatch learned to use their cameras and work in the darkroom, technological innovations had eased the difficulties inherent in photography. In the past, photographs were taken on glass plates that required coating with light sensitive emulsion, exposure, and immediate developing. Photographers had to either be next to a darkroom or transport one in a wagon. This problem was solved with the invention of the dry plate, so named because the light sensitive emulsion was applied to the plate and dried. Mass production of these plates enabled photographers to carry ready-to-use plates, take pictures as they wished, and develop them later at their convenience. Myra and Helen used dry plates for their pictures.

George Eastman realized the potential of this technology and in 1879 began to manufacture dry plates. In 1884, he produced Eastman Negative Paper and formed the Eastman Dry Plate and Film Company. When Eastman marketed the first Kodak camera in 1888, and coined the phrase, "You press the button; we do the rest," he helped pioneer the use of slogans in advertising. His innovative slogan capitalized on the recent popularity of push-button electrification. That year Eastman officially registered his invented word "Kodak" as a trademark, and in 1892 changed the company's name to Eastman Kodak.

Myra's knowledge of photography came from a combination of sources, including magazines, photography businesses, and her colleagues. By 1886, camera companies were targeting women as potential customers by advertising in newly established women's magazines like *The Ladies Home Journal*

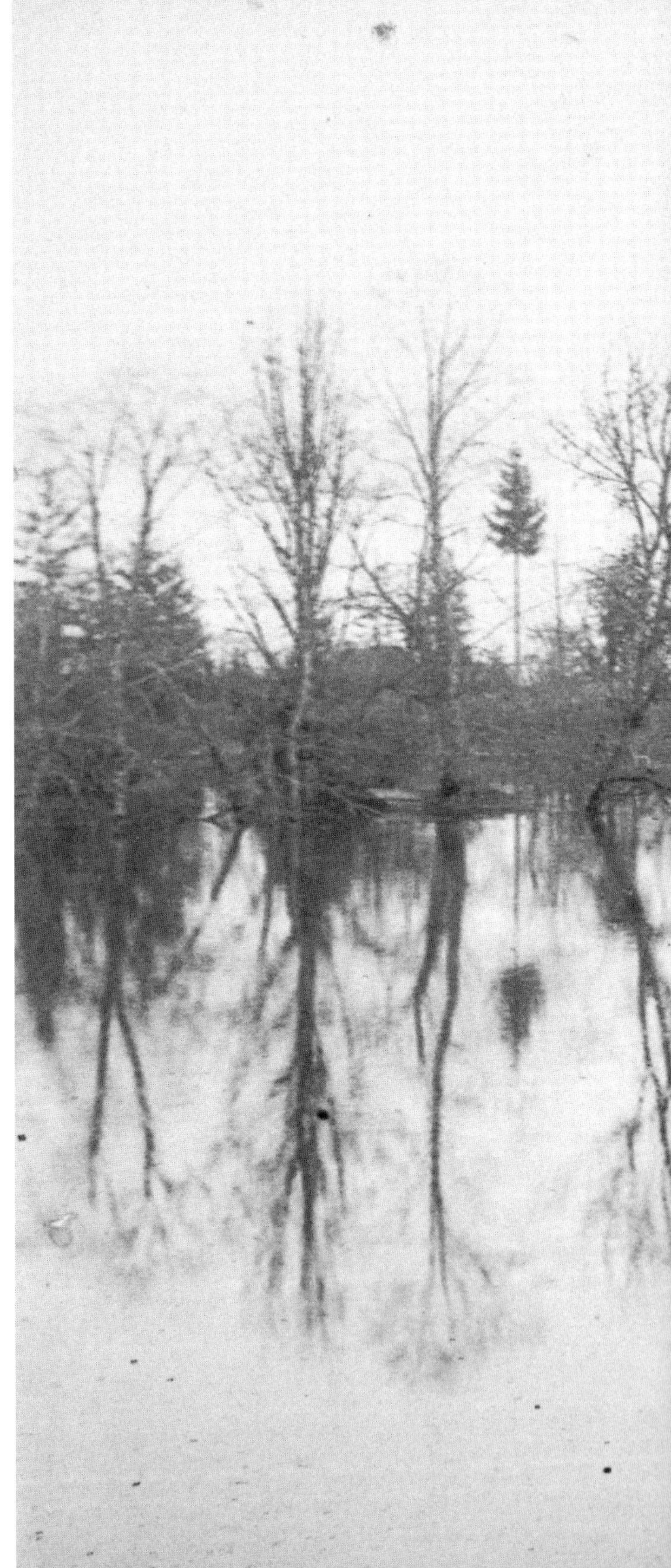

SALEM FLOOD
February 1890, gelatin silver print
6½" x 4"
Robert and Shirley Benz Collection

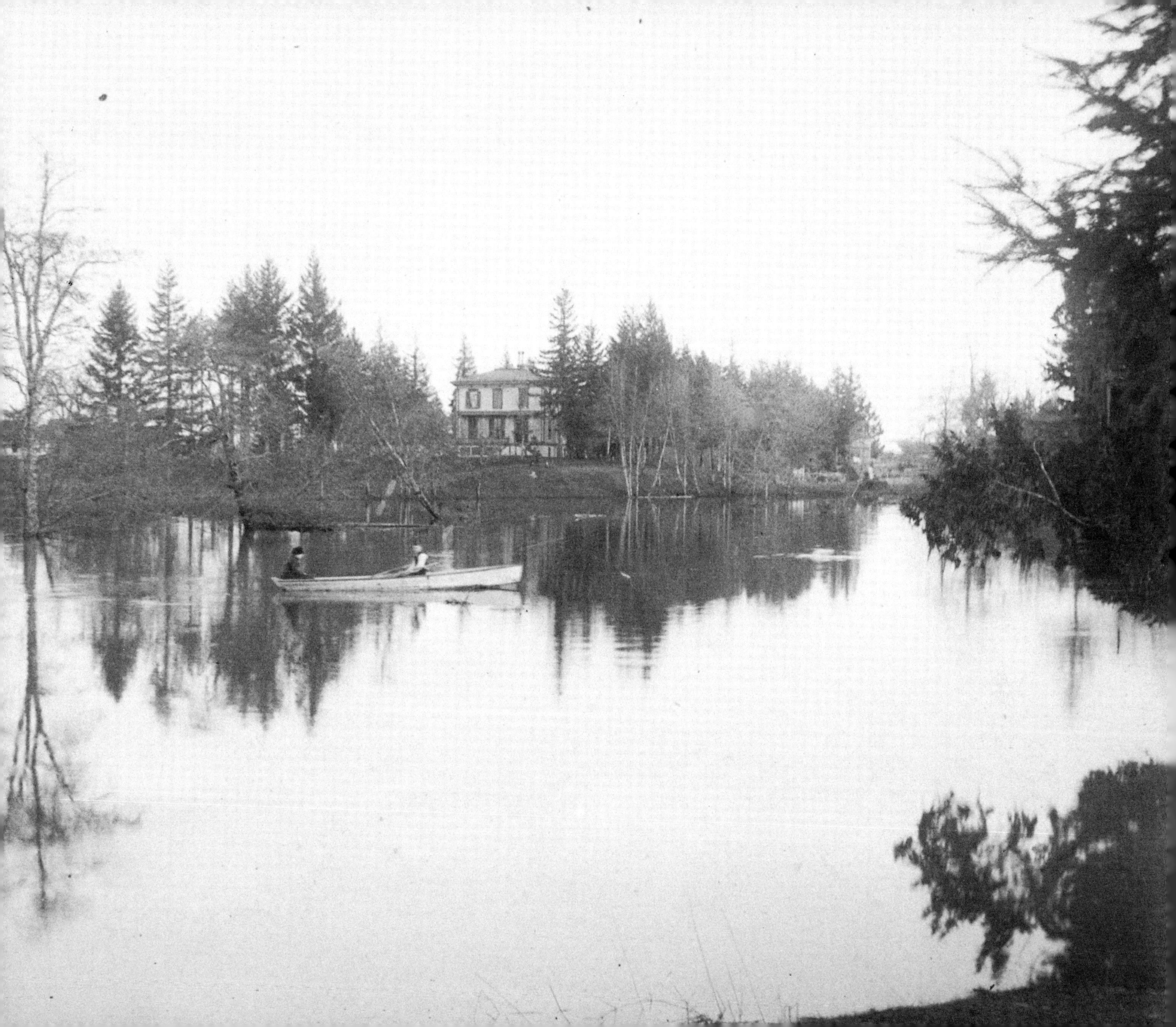

and *Cosmopolitan*. Magazines published articles that not only proposed ways these "new women" could be better mothers and wives, but also ways they could join the work force—and included instruction for starting a photography business. Women, the writers said, were well-suited for photography because it required only a small investment for equipment, very little training, and could be done at home. They asserted that women had the right temperament for putting people at ease, especially children, while taking their portraits.

At the same time, photography magazines like *Photo-Era* and *American Amateur Photographer* appeared and were closely studied by photographers from coast to coast. These magazines offered information on lenses, composition, cameras, and darkroom chemistry. They published travelogues and other articles about personal experiences with the camera that created a sense of the potential for adventure that photography offered. With her geographic isolation from larger communities of photographers, Myra benefited enormously from these journals, prompting her to write how she "endeavored to improve in the work by reading the Photographic Magazines which have been of great help to me." Magazine articles also encouraged photographers to work in darkrooms together so they could share their skills and have company at the same time. Wilena Knight, an artist and colleague of Myra's, unraveled the mysteries of photography alongside her.

Professional photography businesses also provided assistance to budding amateurs. In 1893, Mercantile Photographers of New York City responded by letter to Myra's questions about print developing: "Miss Albert, The formula for iron developer used with Bromide paper is as follows: a. ferrous sulphate, 1 oz., b. neutral oxalate of Potash, 6 oz., c. Bromide of Potash, 2 drops. Mix in order marked ... Hypo solution should be weak — say 1 to 2. I am under the impression that you have learned this manipulation from Miss Knight and will therefore not burden you with instructions."

Within two years of her plate-changing experience at the beach, Myra won a camera as first prize in the amateur division of a *West Shore Magazine* competition for her photograph "Camping Out." Nineteen of the forty-four amateur entries in the contest were Myra's, with many displayed at the Portland North Pacific Industrial Exposition in 1890.

During these early years, Myra photographed the Salem flood of 1890, with her family home in the distance safely perched above the waterline. She made other images reflecting the novelty of owning a camera, such as when she posed her friends' children, Gertrude Holverson, Ryth Gatch, and Kate Ladue, as two young women helping a child cross a foot bridge. In another instance, she framed children playing in a wagon by the Albert's barn. However, Myra's composition and subject matter were still that of the novice exploring her world.

In 1890, the year of Myra's first photographic triumphs, Margaret Bisland wrote:

"Women with their cameras surpass all traditions and stand as the equals of men in their newly found and now mostly ardently practiced art . . . When perhaps ten years ago, the novices first experimented with cameras as non-professionals, fully as many women as men learned to handle them . . . Our greatest painters have been men; have we not a right to expect that our most famous photographers will be women?"

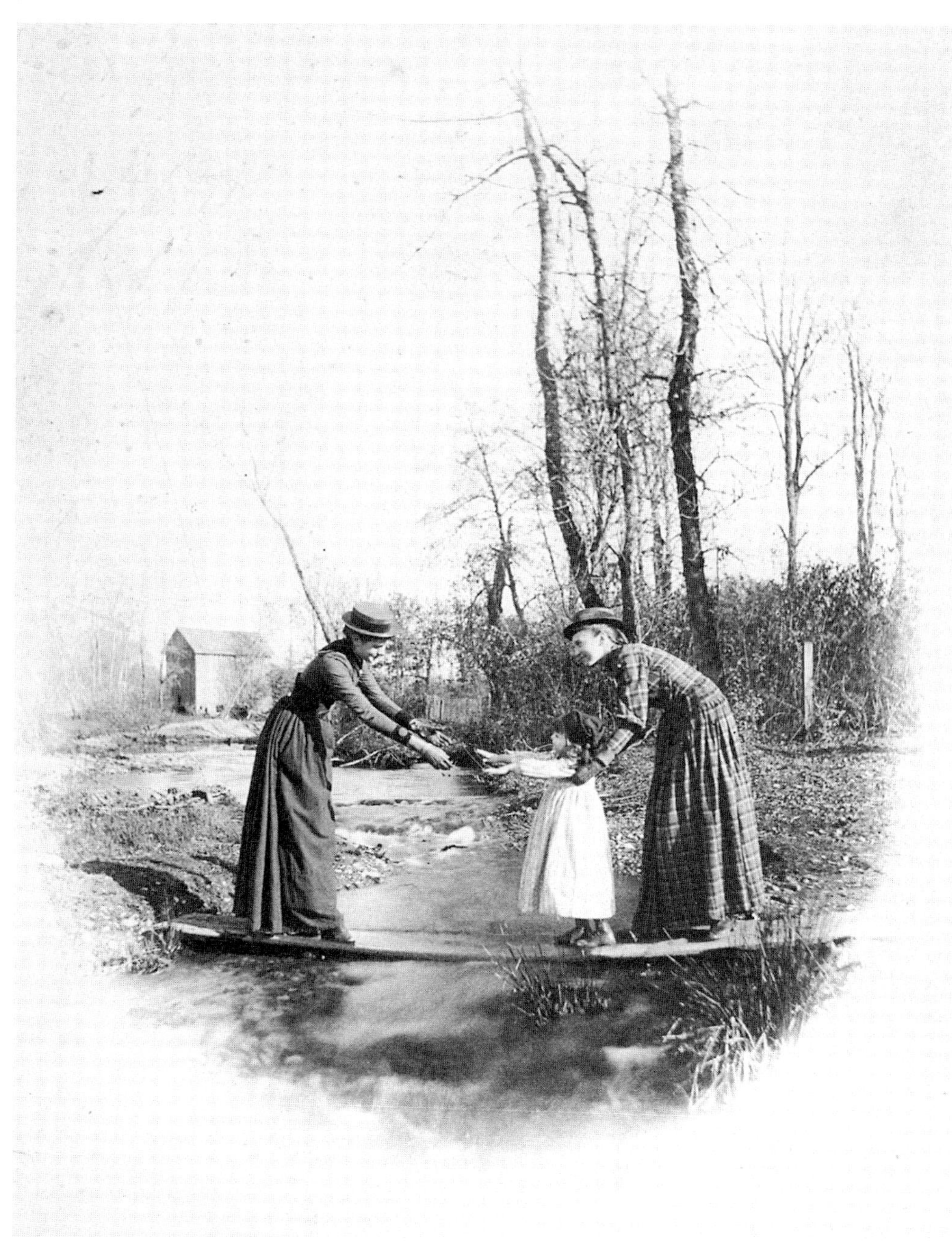

Untitled
Winter 1890-91, gelatin silver print
6½" x 8½"
Robert and Shirley Benz Collection

Gertrude Holverson, right; Kate Ladue, left; Ryth Gatch, center.

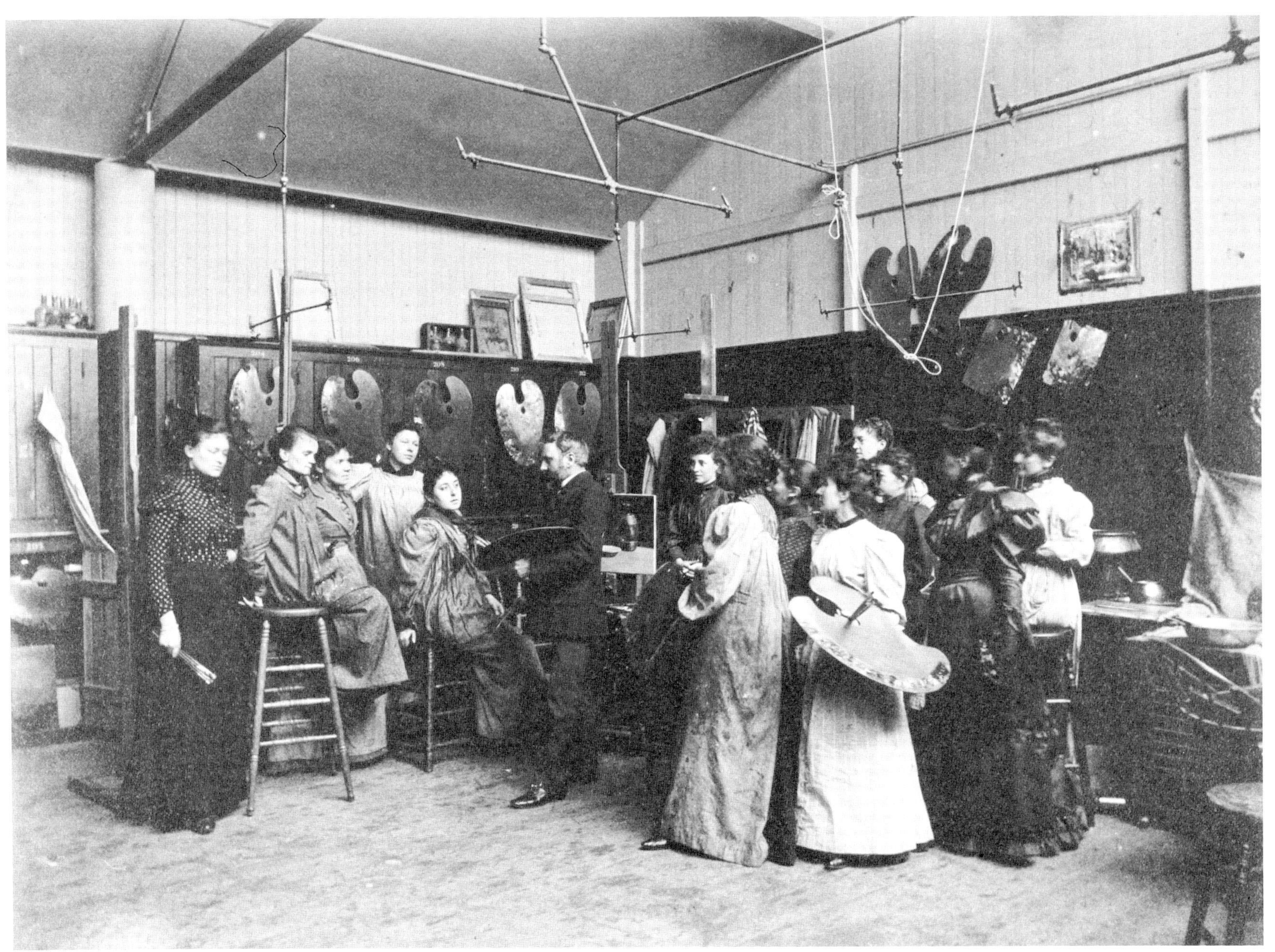

PART TWO

1891- 1896

At the turn of the nineteenth century, many women reveled in their modern social emancipation as they entered fields of work previously set aside for men. Colleges opened their doors to females and many women delayed marriage to pursue professions and create livelihoods outside the domestic sphere. By 1900, concerns raised about a lag in population growth sparked a debate in women's magazines between traditionalists espousing marriage and family, and those people encouraging women to seek careers. In the past, because men also dominated the art academies, serious art education had often eluded women. So, it was in the pioneer spirit that Myra Albert departed for New York City in 1891, to study at the Art Students League.

The League began in 1875 when a group of students left the National Academy of Design to form an independent art school. From its opening, the League supported the belief of equality between men and women as teachers and as students. It was here that Myra received the training that provided a foundation for her photography and painting career. When she began her studies, the League was housed over a livery stable on East Twenty-Third Street. Students came and went with no visible authority.

The Art Students League allowed students to select their instructors, and Myra chose William Merritt Chase, one of America's leading painters and teachers, as her mentor. For three years, she studied mainly under Chase, George DeForest Brush, Kenyon Cox, J.H. Twachtman, Willard Metcalf, and Frank Vincent DuMond. With other courses, she devoted one year to classes in still life and two years to portraiture, and sketched outside of class, bringing her work to Chase for criticism.

Myra took advantage of the city for training in other arts as well. While in New York, she studied voice at the Schwarenka Academy for one year and with Mrs. Theodore Toedt for two years. Myra recalled how she would put down her palette and run across a park to her vocal lesson. In 1893, she wrote her first poems, inspired by a "very dear girl friend."

Three years in New York City gave Myra a taste of independence unheard of for women in prior generations, while her father's wealth enabled her to carry on her lifestyle. She shared an apartment with Wilena Knight, her Salem friend who was studying

WILLIAM MERRITT CHASE'S ART CLASS, ART STUDENTS LEAGUE
c. 1892, gelatin silver print
8⅜" x 6¼"
Robert and Shirley Benz Collection

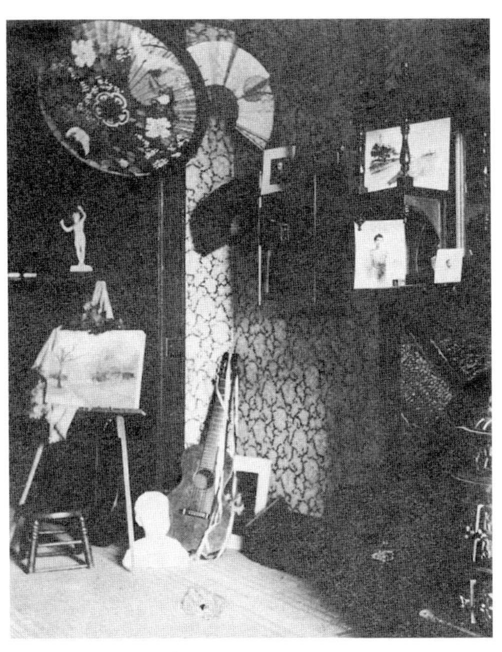

An Art Student's Flat, Lena's Corner
1891-92, gelatin silver print
3¾" x 4¾"
Robert and Shirley Benz Collection

with the painter Irving Wiles, and another colleague, Fan Freiot.

For entertainment during their first year together, the three girls combined their talents to create a "book." Using their sketches and poems, and pasting a series of photographs of themselves on stiff paper, they composed an amusing and sentimental story of the art student's life. Titled "Home Sweet Home with Variations in A Flat" and bound with ornamental string, the credits listed the photographs by Myra and pencil illustrations by Fan. The book opens with Wilena Knight's poem:

'Mid boarding house glories
Though long we may roam
Be it ever so humble
There is no place like home.
And there's nothing that falls
In the Art Student's path
Like a first floor front flat
With six rooms and a bath.

Opposite the poem, they pasted a photograph titled "An Art Student's Flat, Lena's Corner." Pictured in front of flowered wallpaper is an easel and painted canvas, a plaster bust, guitar, photos on a shelf, and a Japanese paper umbrella and fans hanging from the wall and ceiling. The "book" continues with poems, photos, and sketches, and concludes with a picture titled "When Company Comes," showing four smiling, spirited young women bunched in front of the fireplace.

Myra returned to Oregon to spend her summers on the beach and in the mountains. She photographed friends swimming in streams and lounging in campsites at Neskowin Beach on the Oregon coast, about sixty miles west of Salem. There they set up four or five large tents for family, friends, their chaperone Mrs. Dalrymple, and Ah Sin, John Albert's cook.

Myra continued her courtship with Fred Wiggins. They had announced their engagement in 1892. A letter from a girlfriend in Portland displayed mixed emotions about Myra's engagement:

> My Dear Myra, I was so glad to hear from you and also to hear I will see you soon even if it will be for a few moments, but I will be at the afternoon train to meet you and take good care of you till you leave in the evening . . . I am saving my congratulations to deliver them in person—I should have felt real anxious to see what you have to show me. Of course I have an idea what the "something" is but Myra it makes me sick to think of you ever getting married. I can't say exactly why either—I am not acquainted with the fortunate Mr. Wiggins but judging from what I am told he is a fine young man and he most assuredly is to be congratulated on winning the heart of the best and dearest girl in the world. Now Myra believe me to be in earnest when I truthfully say you are one of many and I would give or do anything to be like you. In my mind you are a model girl (and no joking) and a favorite of everyone who knows you.

After returning to New York City that fall, Myra became one of perhaps three female members of the New York Camera Club. She used the Club's darkroom facilities, and this is probably where Alfred Stieglitz's colleague, Joseph Keiley, taught her to brush develop prints with glycerine. Brushing a print with glycerine and developer created a "painterly" effect on platinum paper with no two prints

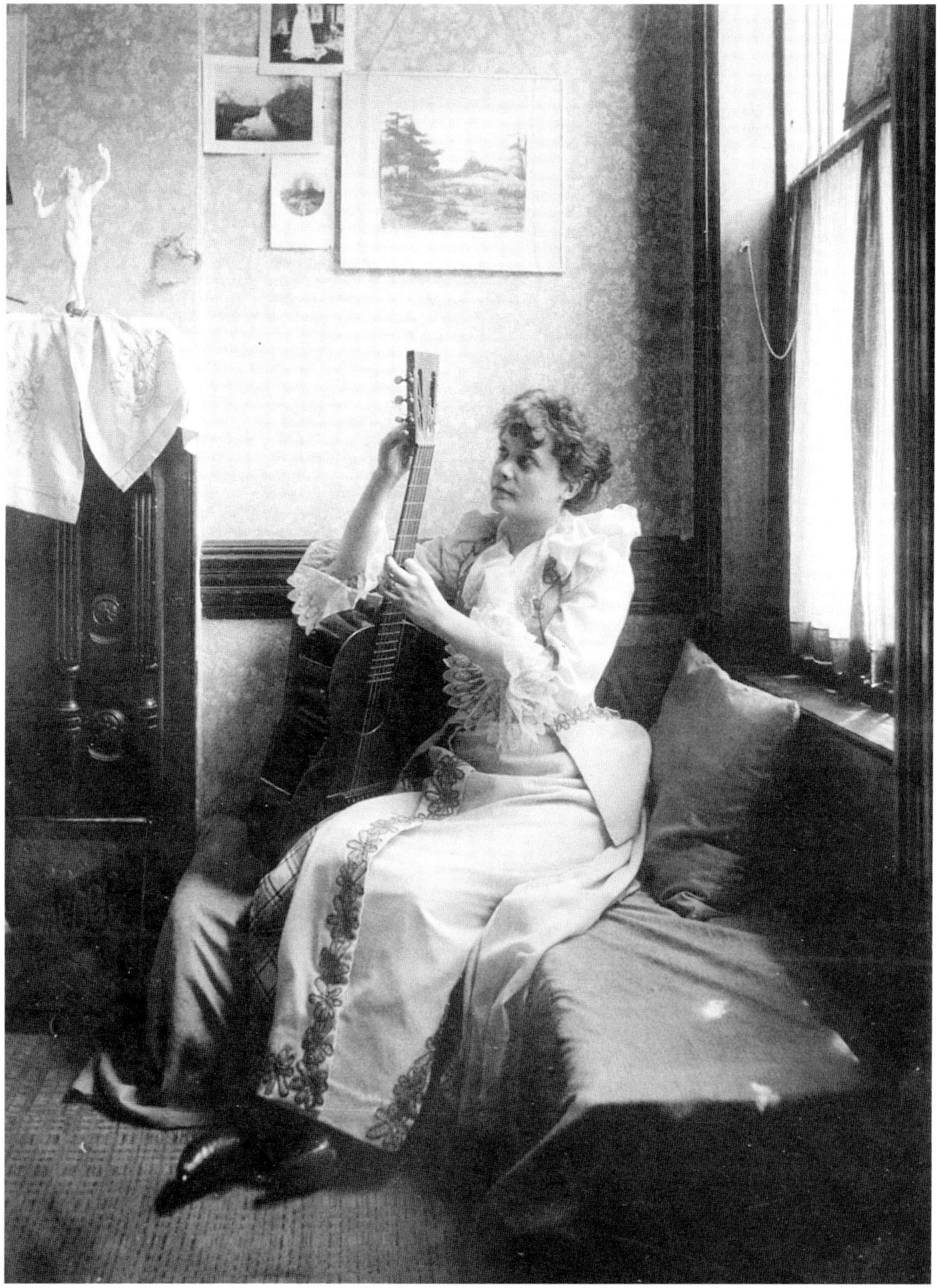

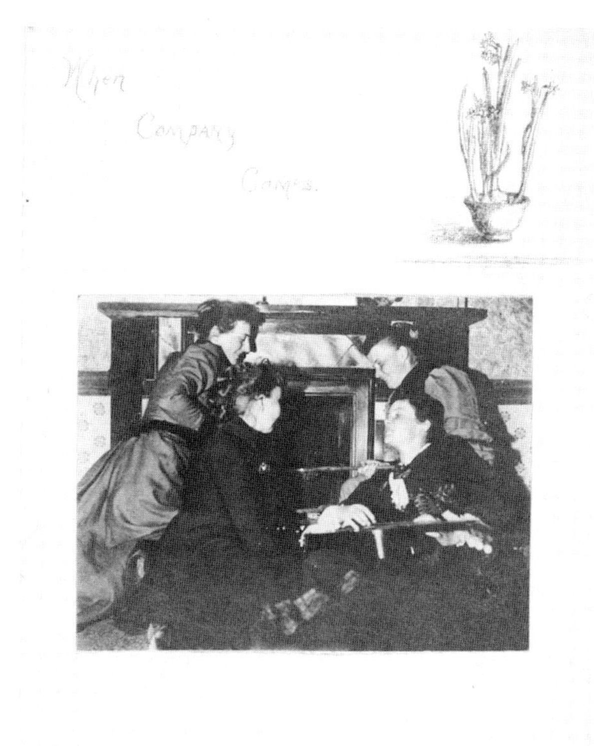

When Company Comes
1891-92, gelatin silver print
4¾" x 3¾"
Robert and Shirley Benz Collection
Myra Albert, upper left.

Lena Knight in Corner of Our Flat
c. 1892, gelatin silver print
6" x 8¼"
Robert and Shirley Benz Collection

exactly alike. She also experimented with cyanotype printing, commonly known as the blueprint process. Myra staged the pictures "Three Girls Flat," and "Boy Twins of New York," and printed them in this process.

During this time, pictorial photographers like Stieglitz and Keiley often sought a naturalistic, soft-focus style. Some pictorialists altered their negatives or manipulated photographic papers and developing processes to achieve artistic effects. In their efforts to attain individuality of expression, pictorialists often experimented with various printing techniques and materials.

While at the Art Students League, Myra photographed Chase's painting class and Augustus Saint-Gauden's sculpture class on the six and one-half inch by eight and one-half inch glass plates of her camera. Only women are shown in Chase's class, because the men left before she took the picture. More than half a century later, these photographs illustrated the story of the League in a catalogue celebrating the Art Students League's seventy-fifth jubilee year.

While Myra thrived in New York City, George Eastman enjoyed the fruits of his advertising campaigns. The recent creation of the Kodak Girl no doubt spurred many women to buy Kodak cameras. The Kodak Girl appeared in Eastman's ads as a young woman, with her striped shirtwaist dress flapping in the wind, gazing beyond the Kodak camera in her hands. Rather than a passive onlooker, The Kodak Girl was an active and curious participant. "The 'Kodak' girl is said to be a terror at Chatauqua," stated the *Photographic Times* in 1891. "She is especially numerous, and her camera is poked and pointed at everything. Lovers have a hard time getting out of her range. It matters little whether the subject be religious or romantic, or the spot be sacred or very ordinary, the 'Kodak' girl will be found around, adjusting her lens to a proper focus and 'taking in' the sights." Myra fit the description of the independent spirit taking pictures, but she was already aware of being more than a mere "snapshooter." She carefully planned and composed her pictures with an eye toward fulfilling the potential of modern photography and her future as an artist.

In mid-1893, when Myra crossed the country to and from New York City, she stopped in the Midwest to visit the World's Columbian Exposition in Chicago. To celebrate American progress in manufacturing, agriculture, machinery, mining, and culture, the fair's grand courtway guided visitors to beaux-arts buildings and displays demonstrating modern American inventiveness. In the Electricity Building a model home "suggested the

SWIMMING POOL, MEHANIA
"about 1891," gelatin silver print
6¼" x 4"
Robert and Shirley Benz Collection

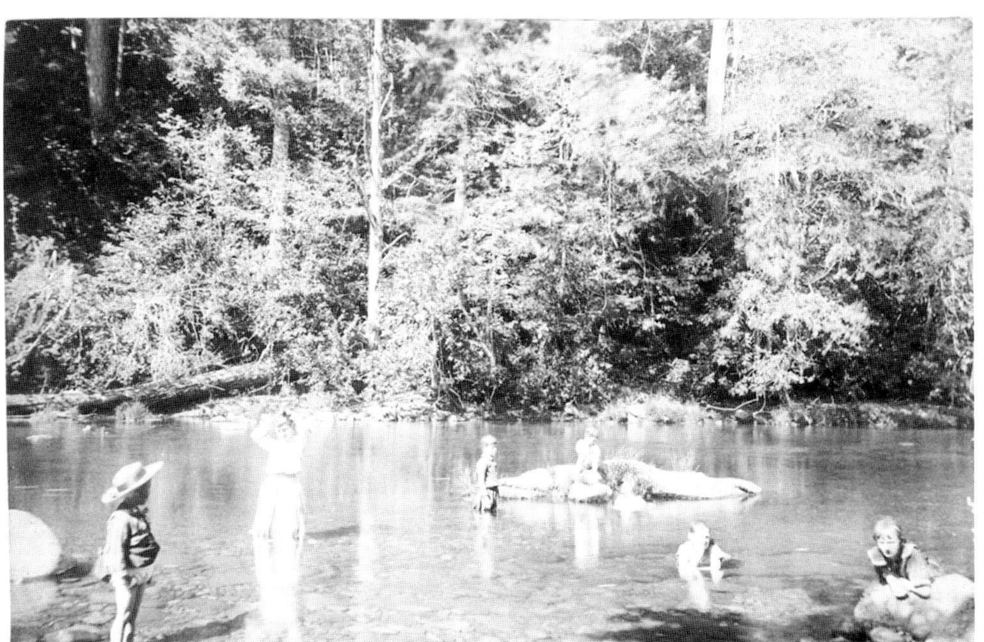

domestic future: electric stoves, hot plates, washing machines, carpet sweepers, plus electric doorbells, fire alarms and innumerable lighting fixtures."

For fifty cents, visitors could buy two turns on the 264-feet Ferris wheel, built by George Ferris. With thirty-six cars, each larger than a Pullman coach and accommodating sixty people, the Ferris wheel rotated 2,160 people in the air. In the midst of these wonders, the Exposition introduced "Americans to Cream of Wheat cereal, Aunt Jemima pancake mix, Juicy Fruit gum, Shredded wheat, and Pabst Blue Ribbon, the fair's award-winning beer." Fair-goers were charged two dollars to carry their cameras into the fair, but this entitled them to use the film-changing and developing darkrooms set up on the grounds by Kodak.

The Fine Arts Palace held over two thousand American and foreign works of art including paintings by Millet, Degas, Monet, and Whistler. For Myra, in the midst of developing her own artistic style, such a collection must have triggered a multitude of ideas.

While at art school, Myra joined the Society of Amateur Photographers of New York. In 1893, several of her photographs from her trip to Mt. Jefferson hung in the First Annual Members Exhibition of the Society of Amateur Photographers of New York organized by Alfred Stieglitz. Stieglitz was the editor of the Society's magazine, *American Amateur Photographer*, and already well known in the photographic world. The exhibit opened March 14 in the Society's rooms at 113 W. 38th Street. The review of the exhibit in *American Amateur Photographer* noted that works "by Miss Myra Albert, were very clear photographs of Mt. Jefferson, on aristotype paper of a reddish color. We think these same pictures in platinum would have appeared to better advantage." A lukewarm review from her first Eastern exhibit did not discourage Myra.

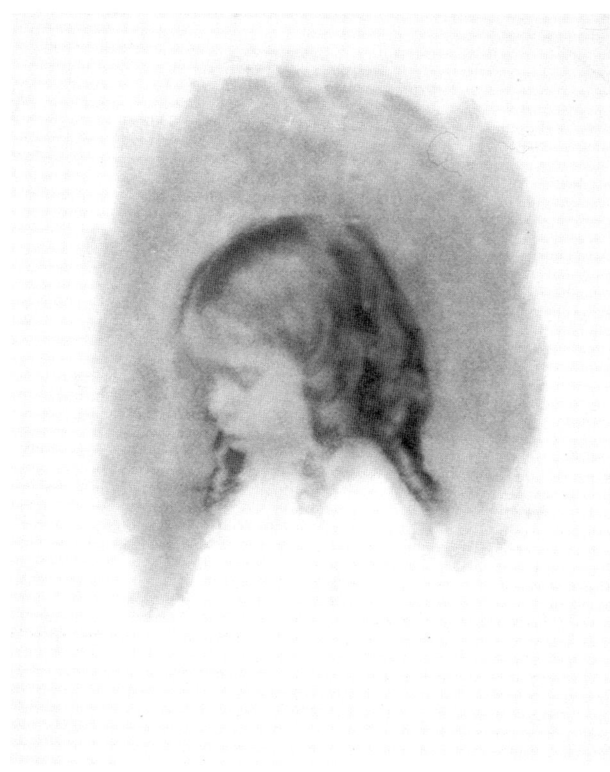

UNTITLED
c. 1892, brush developed with glycerine on platinum paper
4" x 5⅜"
Portland Art Museum

Over forty members of the Society had submitted work that was viewed by nearly two thousand visitors. The exhibit was later shipped to Philadelphia for a Joint Exhibition with the Philadelphia Camera Club at the Pennsylvania Academy of Fine Arts. There, the exhibit was described in the Society's magazine as "the finest exhibition of photographs ever held in the United States. This exhibition has also proven without a doubt that real works of art can be turned out by means of the camera and plates, and that the days of sneering at our attempts are over." The author, Alfred Stieglitz, then cautioned, "Of course, there are but few

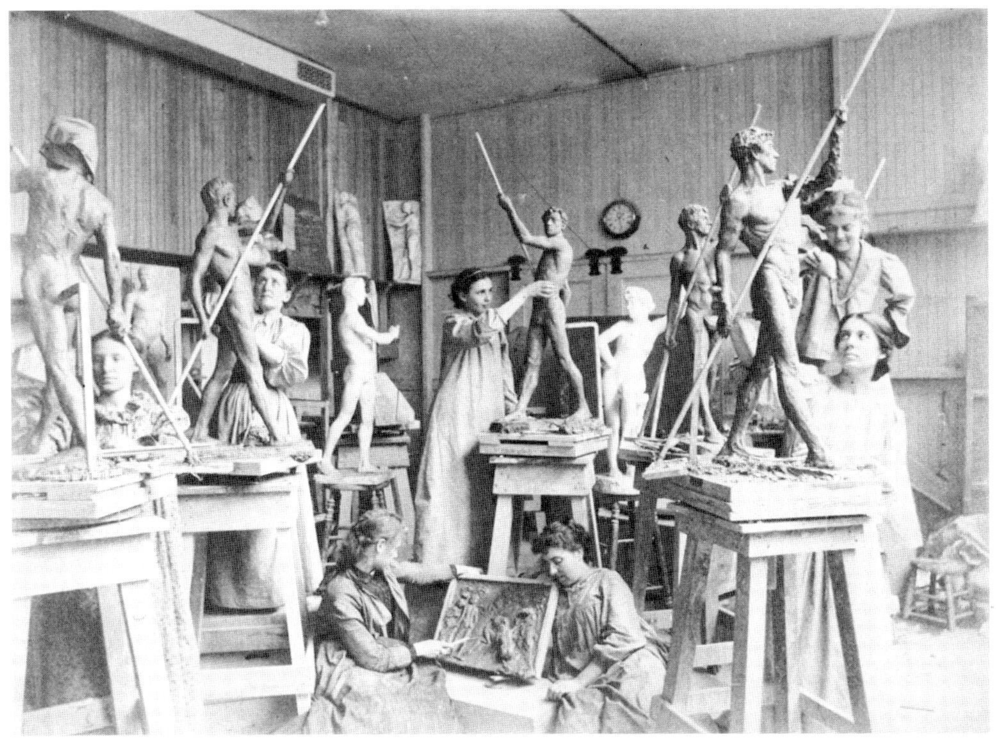

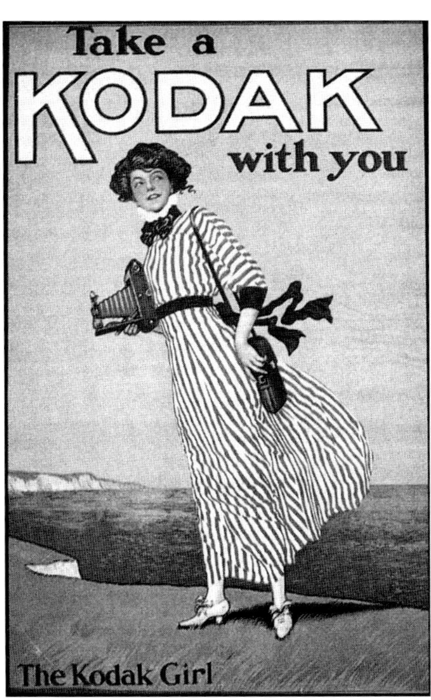

Augustus Saint-Gauden's Sculpture Class, Art Students League
c. 1892, gelatin silver print
8⅜" x 6¼"
Robert and Shirley Benz Collection

Kodak Girl Advertisement
Oregon Historical Society Library

pictures shown which were of real art value; still there were some and that is one tremendous step forward."

That step forward was imbued with controversy. Stieglitz would settle for nothing less than the acceptance of photography alongside painting as an art equally capable of emotional expression. When critics claimed photography too scientific and mechanical to be art, pictorial photographers responded by creating work dependent on composition, massing of light and shade, correct tonal rendition, and textures. The challenge, as Stieglitz saw it, was to convince the art establishment to accept photography as an art, and in this era, art photography meant pictorial photography created by amateurs.

In her photographic heyday and thereafter, Myra always emphasized her status as an amateur, as opposed to being identified as a professional, photographer. The latter represented the standardization of photography—that is, the look-a-like portraits mass-produced by studios. Amateur status implied originality, variation, and creativity, and allowed for experimentation and diversity. Magazines, newspapers, commercially sponsored competitions, and juried salons and exhibitions offered the public opportunities to view amateur pictorial photographs, but American art salons and galleries refused to include photographs alongside paintings.

Within this controversy, Myra saw opportunity when she submitted her work to *The Photo-American* in 1894, and proved her prowess as photographer, writer, poet, and adventurous spirit. "We know they [women] are willing to stain their fingers with pyro [developer], to ruin their complexions in the sunshine, and uncurl their hair in dampness," wrote editor W.F. Hapgood, "but to prove these sacrifices worthwhile, we propose to give readers . . . a series of illustrated papers kindly contributed by amateurs of the fair sex, who have already won their laurels in prize competitions. The first one to tell us how the world looks to her is Miss Myra Albert, whose views are taken across the whole width of our continent, and whose work has become well-known for its excellence, both artistic and technical."

Myra's article, titled, "Amateur Photography through Women's Eyes," nostalgically described her trip to Mt. Jefferson: "I recall a . . . delightful summer trip to Mt. Jefferson, when mounted on a sure footed Cayuse, with my camera strapped to the saddle, our jolly party kept the trail along the snow line . . . to where before

'the foot of woman never trod,
Nor feet of camera ever prod.'

My well trained horse one moment sinking into the yielding snow, the next, crushing beneath his feet the most delicate of flowers."

Myra identified her equipment—Darlot and Gundlach Perigraphic lenses, six and one-half inch by eight and one-half inch glass plates, "and about as large a camera as a lady can manage." She asserted that "the composition of a picture claims my first attention, for what is more disturbing than an unpleasant one?" Four of her photographs illustrated the article—"Babes in the Park" (taken in Central Park, New York City), "Autumn," and two views of Mt. Jefferson. In "Mt. Jefferson from Grizzly Tarn, Oregon," a man with his dog gazes at Mt. Jefferson in the distance, surrounded by "lofty spruce and pines bereft by fire." In "Mt. Jefferson, Oregon," she includes two men as tiny figures perched on a ledge with Mt. Jefferson rising beyond the ridges. A waterfall cascades diagonally from the right of the picture.

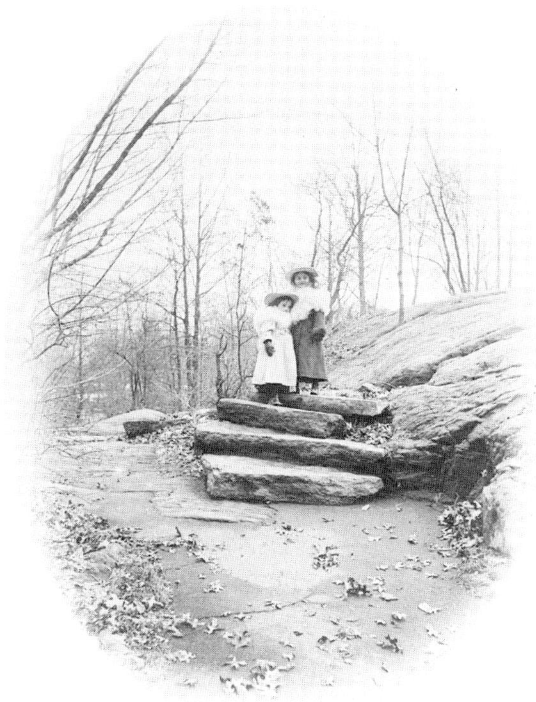

Babes in the Park
c. 1892, gelatin silver print
6½" x 8½"
Portland Art Museum

From the start of her career, Myra knew the value of self-promotion. Her work needed to be seen. The *New York Herald* and *Camera Mosaics*, a weekly photography journal, also published her work in 1894. The *New York Herald* included, on a full page spread of twenty photographs, three small reproductions—"Babes in the Park," "Mt. Jefferson," and "The North Fork of the Santiam, Oregon" that showed her brother Harry as a small figure fishing the river rapids, dwarfed by majestic mountains. While the New York paper featured her photographs in both urban and wilderness contexts, *Camera Mosaics* portrayed, in a large eight by ten inch format, her pictures of the "untamed" Mt. Jefferson wilderness. These photographs set Myra apart from most Eastern photographers who did

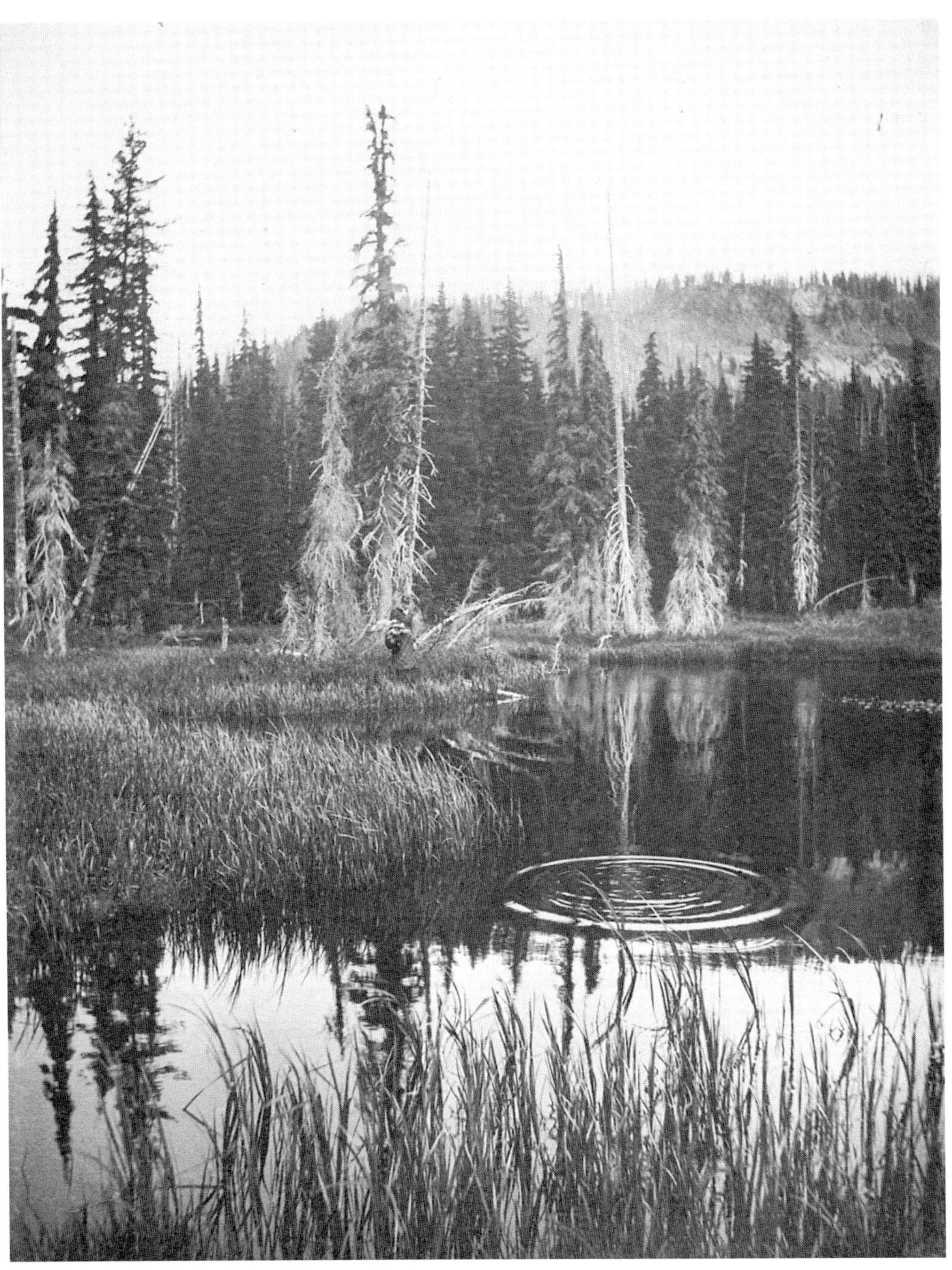

not have such subject matter at hand. Myra's enthusiasm for adventure merged with her artistic bent to create a unique spot for herself among late nineteenth-century photographic artists.

Despite her friend's pleas to reconsider her plans, Myra Albert married Frederick Wiggins in the First Presbyterian Church in Salem, on November 24, 1894. Following the wedding, friends and family attended a reception at John and Mary Albert's Victorian home on Winter and Oak streets. After the reception, she grouped the wedding party of twelve people and set up her camera for a flash powder photograph. She placed the powder in the pan, lit a paper fuse, and ran to take her place by her husband. In the finished image, Fred's eyes were closed so she made tiny pin pricks in the negative to "open them up." Although Myra posed with her head bowed as a demure bride, only a woman sure of her talent would attempt to immortalize herself at that moment.

While Myra Wiggins painted and photographed, Fred Wiggins continued to clerk at the Holverson & Co. Dry Goods store at 301 Commercial Street. Joseph and Harry Albert worked for their father at the Capital National Bank, and Blanche Albert married George Rodgers. Claude Gatch, husband of Myra's friend, Helen, served as mayor of Salem. It was still a small enough town that position and achievements by individuals were noticed and what people did mattered.

Myra Wiggins celebrated her accomplishments, but on May 29, 1896, she also experienced one of life's great transitions when she gave birth to her only child, Mildred. Mildred was born in a hospital because Myra and Fred "wanted the best" for their baby, who later, for reasons that will become apparent, became known as "Dutchy" Mildred.

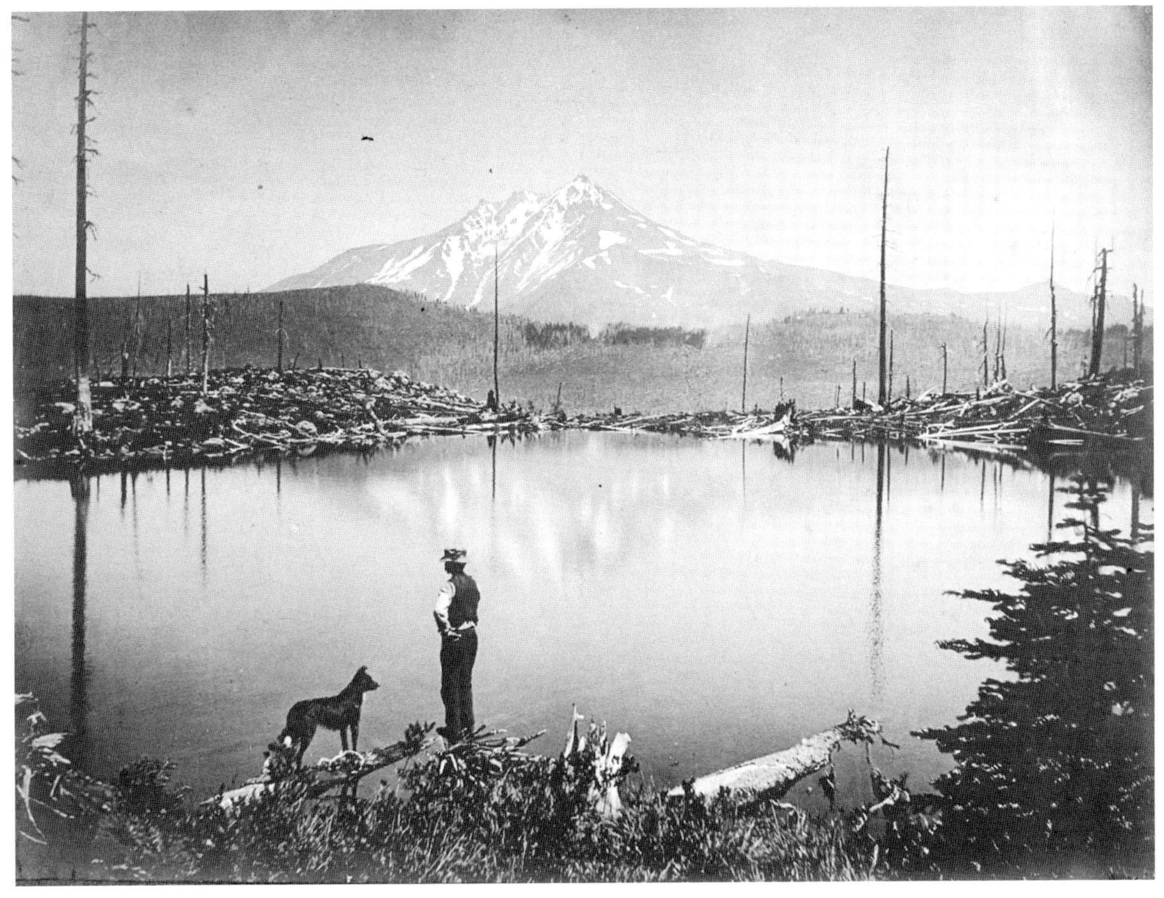

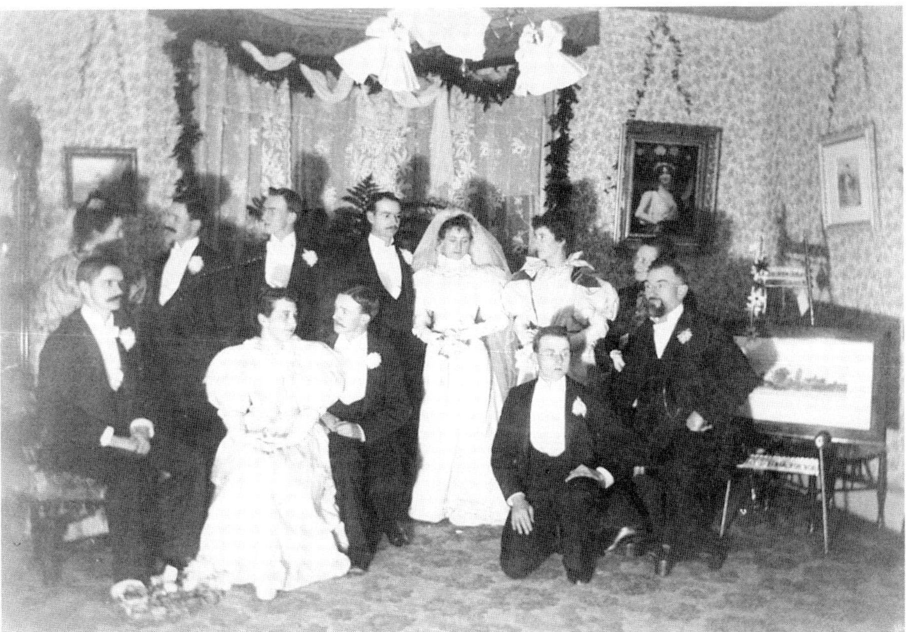

Mirror Tarn, Oregon
c. 1891
8⅜" x 10⅜"
Portland Art Museum

Mt. Jefferson from Grizzly Tarn, Oregon
c. 1891, gelatin silver print
8⅜" x 6¼"
Portland Art Museum

Wedding Party of Myra Albert and Fred Wiggins
1894, gelatin silver print
8" x 5½"
Robert and Shirley Benz Collection

Standing, left to right: unidentified woman, Dr. Frank Gifford, Harry Singleton, Fred Wiggins, Myra Albert Wiggins, Jesse Dalrymple, Mary Albert. Seated, left to right: unidentified man, Blanche Albert, unidentified man, Joseph Albert (kneeling), John Albert.

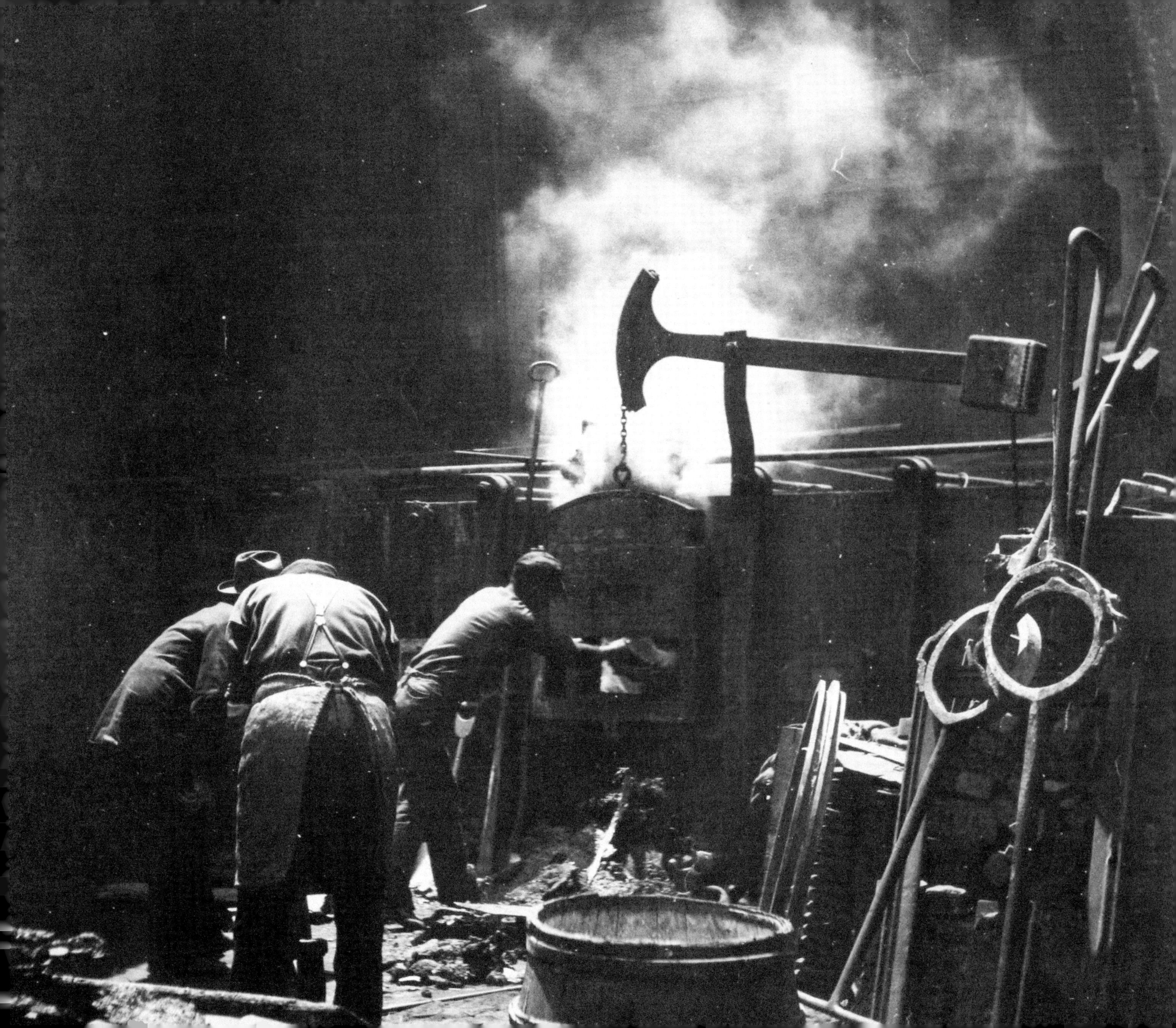

Part Three
1897- 1899

In the early 1890s, technical advances in the halftone method of reproducing photographs enabled magazines and newspapers to introduce fine photographs to a wide audience. Many publications held competitions, whereby photographers vied for cash prizes and the winners received free publicity. Manufacturers of photographic equipment and supplies recognized the opportunity to promote their products by sponsoring these contests, and Eastman Kodak and Bausch & Lomb offered two of the most lucrative competitions. Myra responded with enthusiasm to this format because it provided her a chance to compete in photographic contests despite her residing in far-off Oregon.

In July, 1897, the Camera Club of New York published the first issue of *Camera Notes*. Created and edited by Alfred Stieglitz, *Camera Notes* contained the finest work in pictorial photography, commentaries about current trends in photography, and critical reviews of exhibitions. By including articles addressing creative and technical aspects of photography, book reviews, Camera Club news, and reports from abroad, the magazine became an important force in shaping the course of photography. Although photographers contributed most of the articles, Stieglitz also published essays by critics such as Sadakichi Hartmann and Charles Caffin, who expressed their opinions on turn-of-the-century aesthetic concepts and ideas. Stieglitz used *Camera Notes* to promote his personal agenda as well. Advertising revenues helped to cover publishing expenses, and, in the first issue of *Camera Notes*, the Kodak Company announced its first Eastman Prize Competition.

Always thinking ahead, Wiggins had the competition in mind when she went to San Francisco that summer. While there, she used her new Number 5 Kodak camera to create "The Forge," and submitted the image to the Eastman contest where it earned a $25 prize. Why she chose to photograph inside a foundry is not known. None of her work, either before or after, relates to it in content or theme. It does, however, illustrate her style of making photographs by quietly disengaging herself from her subjects, so they would remain relaxed and self-absorbed. Wiggins caught the smoke and mist above the forms of the people and machinery, creating an image George Eastman liked so much that he hung it in his office.

The Forge
1897, 6⅝" x 4¾"
gelatin silver print
Portland Art Museum

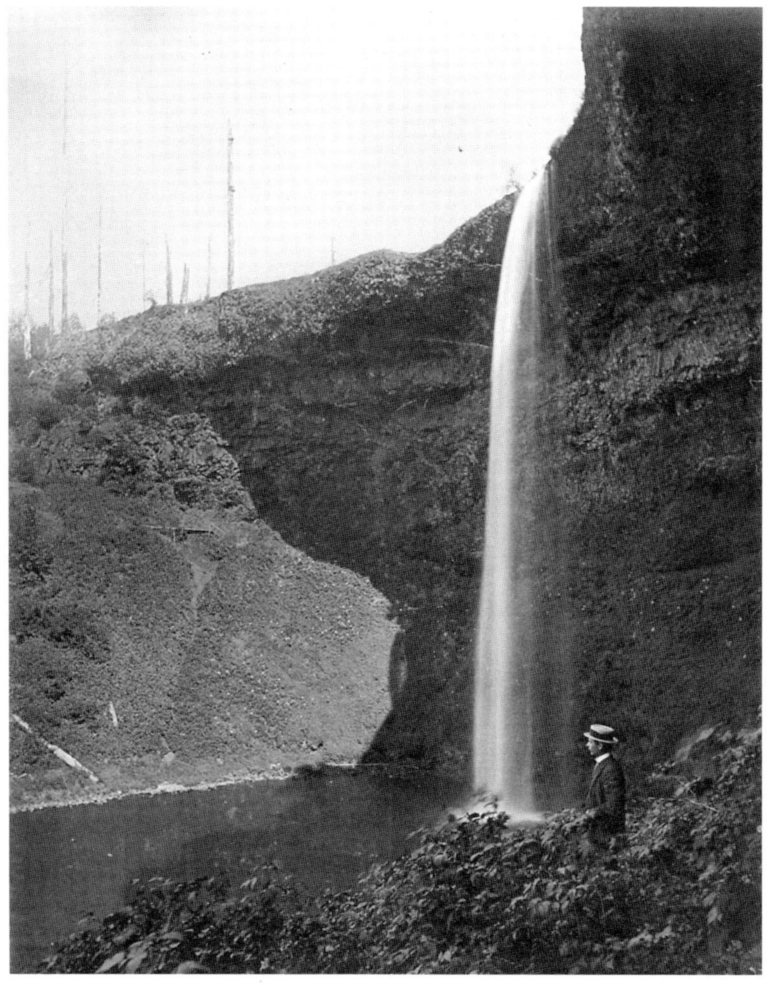

Silver Creek Falls
1894, gelatin silver print
6" x 7¾"
Robert and Shirley Benz Collection
Fred Wiggins in foreground.

Fifty thousand people viewed the Eastman exhibit in London in October, 1897, and in New York's National Academy of Design in January, 1898. The New York *Mail and Express* recognized "The Forge" as an impressive picture "in which light and shade are well balanced." *Godey's Magazine* reproduced the photograph, declaring, "The most striking of the photographs shown at this exhibit was probably 'The Forge.' It was the work of an Oregon woman, Mrs. Myra Wiggins. In its enlarged form, it took on a much greater power. Its dense gloom, with the bright flare of steam, and the absorption of the men bending to their work, make up an ensemble of remarkable force." The Eastman exhibition included work by some of the best photographers in the country, including Alfred Stieglitz and Washington, D.C. photographer Frances Benjamin Johnston. For the first time, Wiggins' work hung alongside photographs by people she had admired from afar, while her name received the praise and recognition she sought. These photographers set an example of high technical and artistic quality that viewers could examine and emulate.

Subsequently, *Camera Notes* recognized the potential for corporate profit-making from this contest and its impact on photography by suggesting that "the Eastman Company will sell many Kodaks and much film as the indirect, or if you please, the direct result of the exhibition . . . furnishing an example which will have an influence for good on every art exhibition that may hereafter be held in London or New York . . . pictorial arts have been elevated and in these two Kodak exhibitions has photography been glorified."

While this competition made good business sense for the Kodak company, it served as a starting point for Wiggins' enterprising plans. By now, she had learned how to connect with the people who mattered, and how to use the system to overcome her geographic and financial obstacles. She realized that magazines, newspapers, and the burgeoning corporate world could promote her work and that their cash prizes could help pay her expenses.

Wiggins' successes did not go unnoticed in Salem. Her picture of Mt. Jefferson had recently earned a first prize camera in a *Recreation Magazine* contest. A Salem newspaper recognized Myra Wiggins' and Helen Gatch's accomplishments in 1897 by announcing, "Mrs. Myra Albert Wiggins, daughter of Banker Albert, has . . . won the first prize for amateur photography awarded by an Eastern art magazine—and she won over 607 competitors who entered 1214 specimens against her. Mrs. Claude Gatch, wife of the popular Odd Fellow grand lodge officer and Salem bank cashier, was also recently awarded first prizes in competition with American photographers from every state in the Union." Despite their accomplishments, Wiggins and Gatch were still identified in print with their male associates—in this instance, Wiggins with her father, rather than her husband, as was the case with Helen Gatch.

In the mid 1890s, as Myra launched her art and photography career, her artistic vision merged in harmony with the changing interests of the country. As cities grew, masses of people intent on escaping to the out-of-doors took to bicycling, mountaineering, gardening, visiting the countryside, and, wherever they went, photography. Out of this back-to-nature zeal emerged the Arts and Crafts movement that served as a catalyst to a new lifestyle embracing simplicity, beauty, and closeness to the natural world. The Arts and Craft movement launched a backlash to the opulence of the Victorian Age with its demand for material goods, fussy interiors, and strict societal expectations of both men and women. Instead, self-reliance, independence, and self-expression became the hallmark of individuals. This way of life produced a unique style of artistic expression that followed a new set of rules. The Arts and Crafts movement united artistry and technical achievement, and beauty and utility, in all aspects of material life from furniture, pottery, and weaving, to painting and photography, and even to a new style of house called the bungalow.

Arts and Crafts photographers embraced or appreciated the picturesque beauty of country life and they idealized peasants for their simplicity and attachment to the rhythms of nature. For these photographers, the "canons of art"—the arrangement of lines, light, balance, contrast, massing, and spacing—were as crucial to creating pictorial photographs as they were to painting.

According to the movement, each aspect of a work of art had to be integrated into a unified whole. Personalized monograms replaced flamboyant signatures on photographs, and *The Craftsman* magazine even provided detailed instructions for designing monograms. Wiggins created her monogram based on the form of a cartouche. A vertical rectangle contained her initials, with the A enclosed

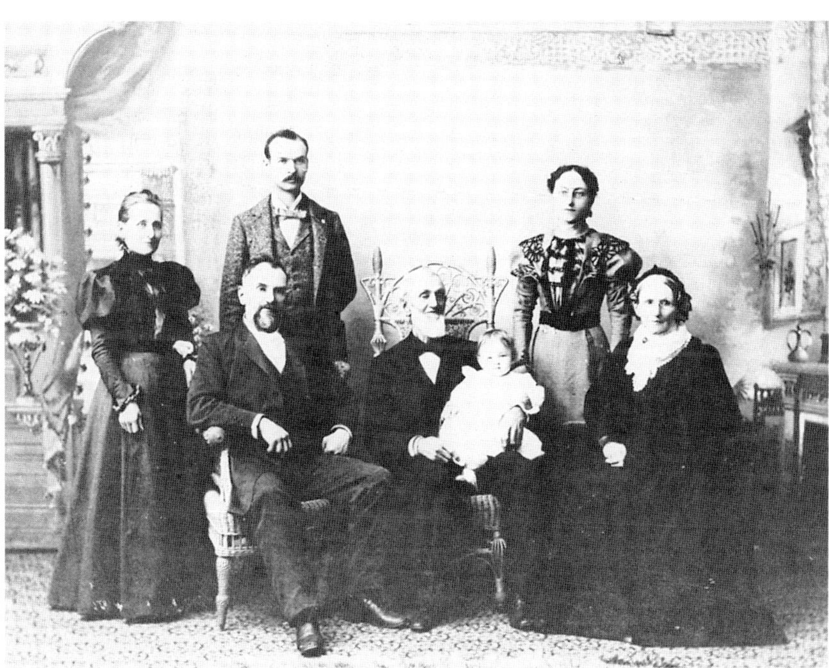

ALBERT FAMILY PORTRAIT
1896, photographer unknown, gelatin silver print
9½" x 7½"
Robert and Shirley Benz Collection
Standing, left to right: Mary Holman Albert, Fred Wiggins, Myra Albert Wiggins. Seated, left to right: John Albert, Ebin Albert holding Mildred Wiggins, Jane Gilchrist Albert.

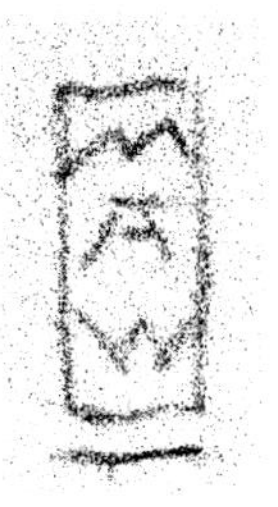

Myra Albert Wiggins' Monogram

Indian Basket Maker
1898, platinum print
3¼" x 2¼"
Portland Art Museum

Unloading the Catch
1898, gelatin silver print
7¼" x 5¾"
Portland Art Museum

by the M and the W. In an article in *Camera Work.* pictorialists were encouraged "to study the Japanese sense of space as a guide in creating and applying their monograms."

Japanese art, noted for its clean lines and simplicity, influenced the "craftsman" style as a means of bringing nature and day-to-day life closer together. Many photographers, including Wiggins, printed on Japanese tissue, producing a delicate image both in texture and tone. Moreover, the movement's admiration for Native American culture and its closeness to the outdoors resulted in national efforts to preserve the art of Native Americans and emulate their basketry, pottery, and rugs.

Myra fit into this movement with ease. Her love of nature and beauty had long been integrated with her independent Western pioneer lifestyle, while her travels into the mountains had proved her physical strength and self-reliance. Her wilderness

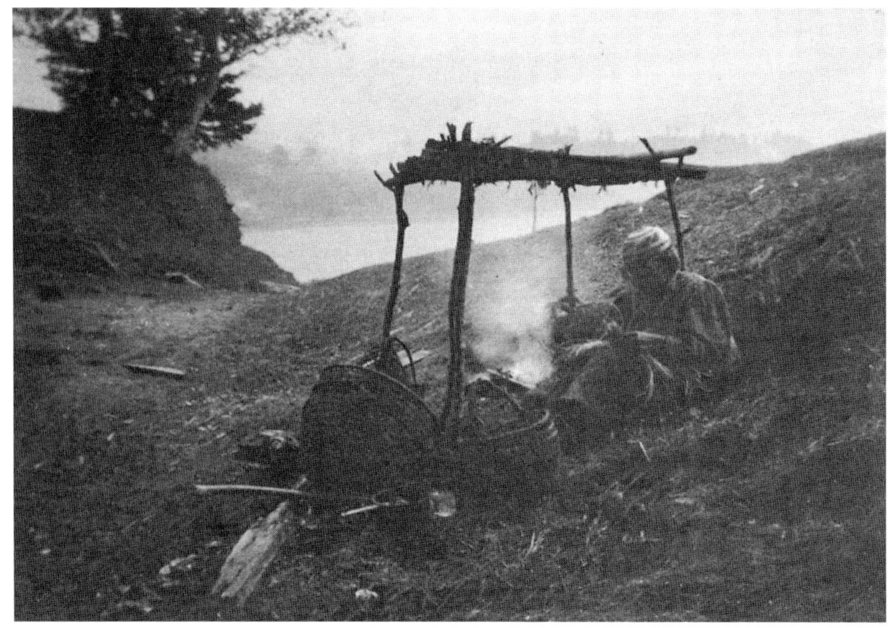

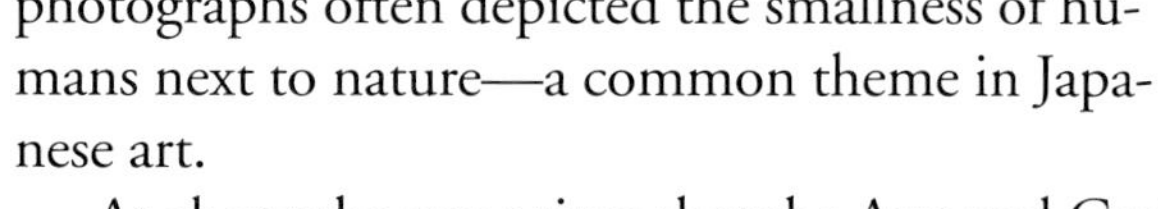

photographs often depicted the smallness of humans next to nature—a common theme in Japanese art.

At about the same time that the Arts and Crafts movement surfaced, Wiggins photographed "Indian Basket Maker" and "Unloading the Catch," depicting solitary Native American women working outdoors close to nature. These images represent simplicity and respect for hard work, embraced within artistic expression. In "Unloading the Catch," a Native American woman is bent beside her canoe with a steep rocky cliff in the background, all of which is reflected on the wet beach. Everything about the scene is enmeshed in nature and native art, from the woman's handmade clothes and basket to the well-crafted canoe. Wiggins expressed the same ideals in "Indian Basket Maker" where Native American utility, craftsmanship, and the natural environment were fused within a simple composition.

In the fall of 1898, "Unloading the Catch" earned a Ladies Competition first prize silver medal in the American Institute Salon, at the National Academy of Design. Europeans had for many years exhibited paintings in salons, where a rigorous jurying process approved only the best work. To maintain high standards, photography salons emulated this tradition. Four hundred and eighty-four photographs, framed in heavy, dark wood, crowded the gallery walls from chair rail to ceiling. Next to "Unloading the Catch," hung two more Wiggins photographs, "Sheep" and "A Promise of Rain," that sentimentalized rural life.

The exhibition catalogue described the salon as "the largest number of professional and amateur prints ever exhibited in the U.S.," including works by such artists as Frances Benjamin Johnston,

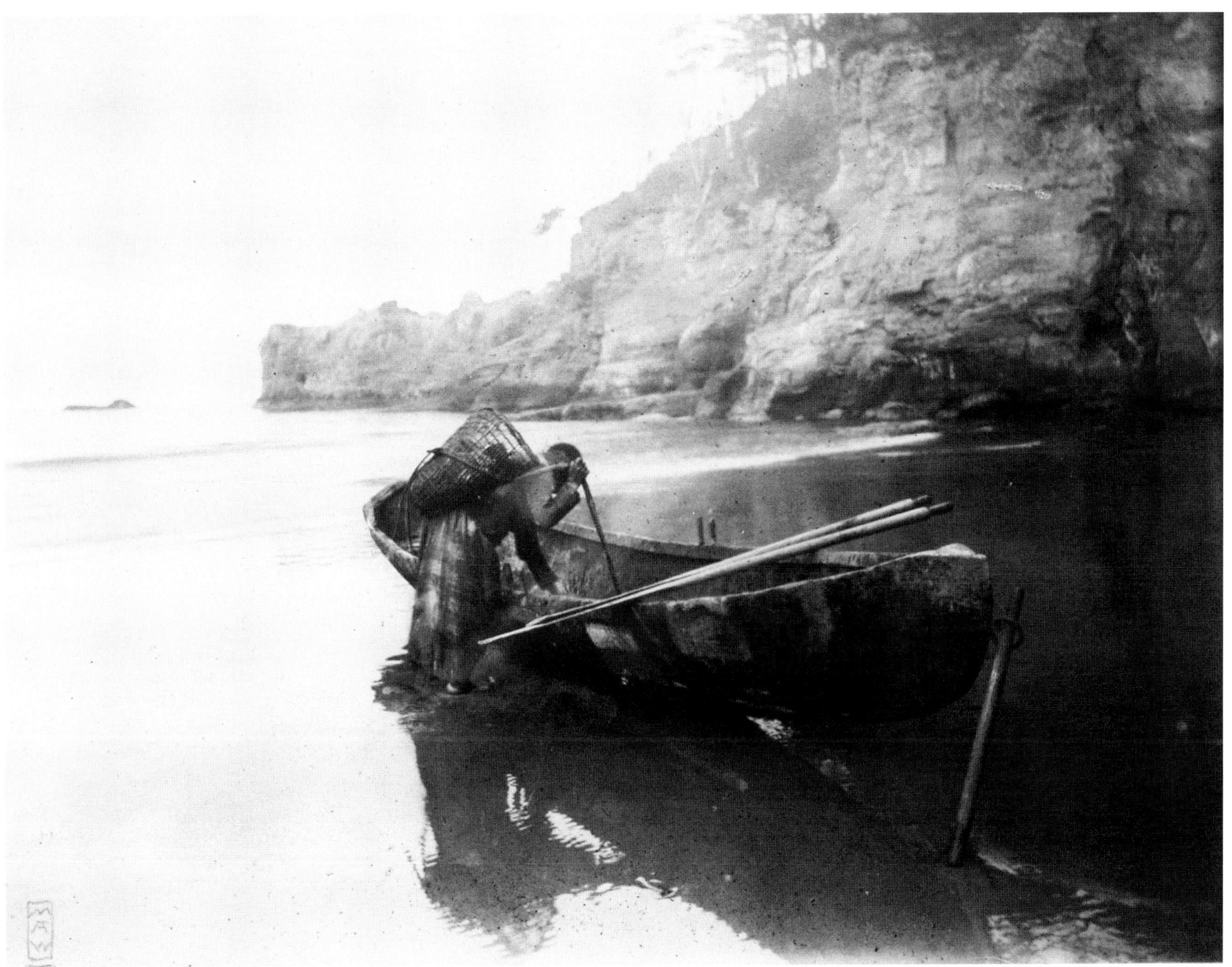

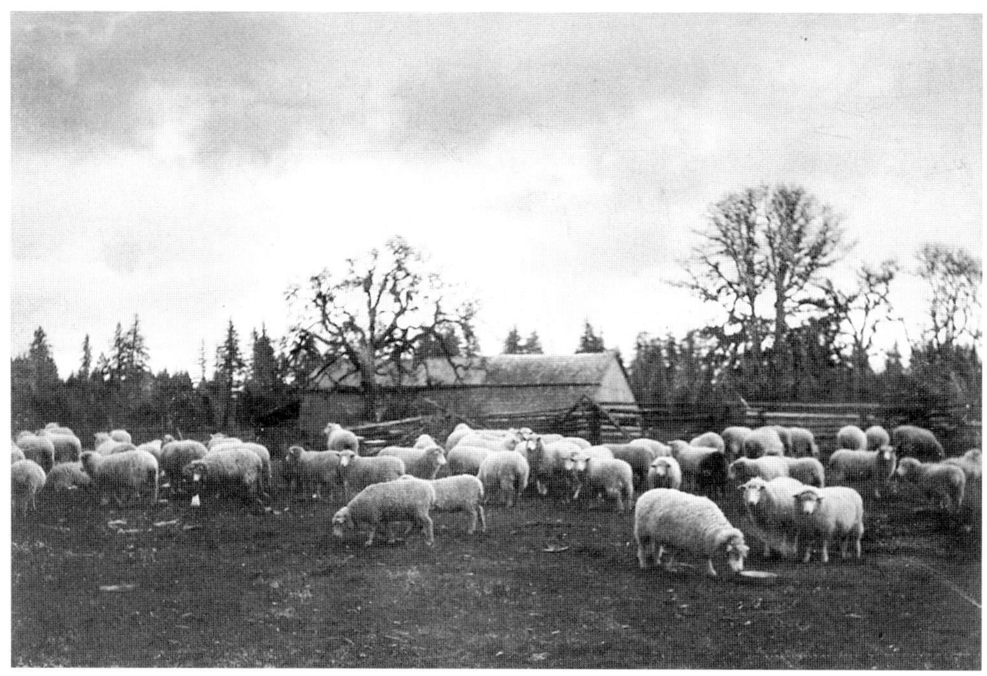

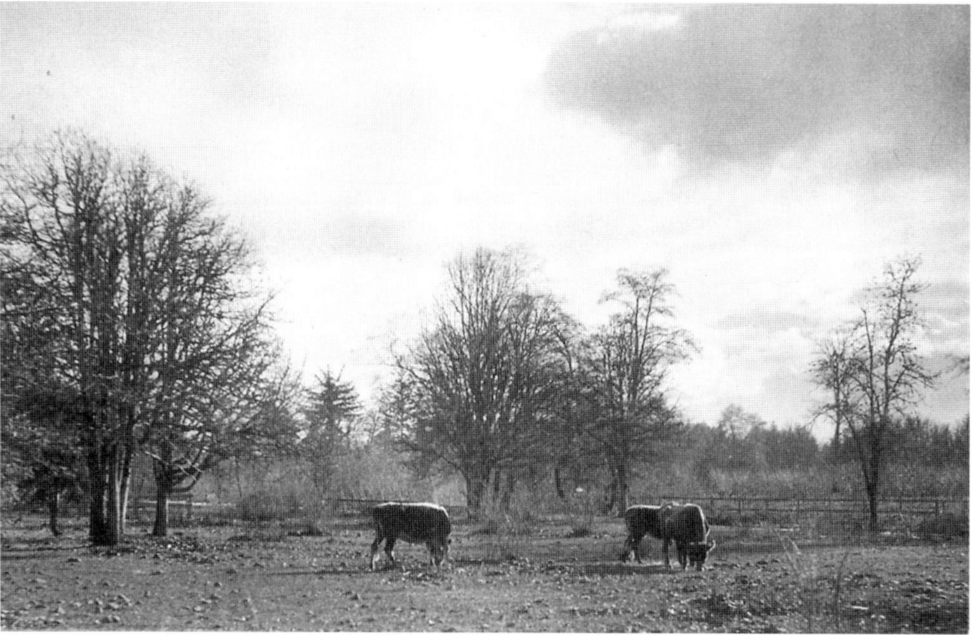

Zaida Ben-Yusef, Emma Farnsworth, and Alfred Stieglitz. Photographs by Ben-Yusef of New York City and Farnsworth of Albany, New York, often appeared with Wiggins' work in competitions and salons. Ben-Yusef attracted a prosperous clientele of celebrities to her studio in New York City, while Farnsworth earned a name for herself by producing award-winning work. Early women photographers such as Wiggins, Farnsworth, Ben-Yusef, Johnston, and Gertrude Käsebier helped set the standards of excellence in pictorial photography.

Wiggins wasted no time basking in her success. In 1898, she produced her first Dutch pictures, later claiming that, to the best of her knowledge, she had originated the "American-Dutch genre studies" in photography. Her inspiration came from the Old Masters' paintings of Dutch domestic scenes, and from some old Dutch garments, over one hundred years old, handed down in the family of her aunt who was from Holland. The clothes consisted of a brown silk dress, handkerchiefs, and several caps. The dress, or a copy of it that she made later, was worn by all of Myra's women models; she also made a similar child's outfit. She transformed her dining room into a Dutch house's interior by stretching burlap over the walls and parts of the tall windows. She pasted strips of black paper on a window to make the opening look like old-fashioned small window panes, and laid rough boards on the floor. She nailed legs to a rough table top, and laboriously sawed and hammered together a cradle. The room stayed "Dutch" for several months while Wiggins completed her photographs.

The Dutch peasantry embraced a sturdy, simple lifestyle idealized by the Arts and Crafts movement. The Dutch worked outdoors, dependent on the sea and land, dressed plainly, and even wore hand-carved wooden shoes. Their homes were unpretentious, utilitarian, and earthy. Now, Myra used her daughter, Mildred, and housekeeper Alma Schmidt to create a personal interpretation of Dutch domestic life in her home in Salem.

Perhaps the best known of Wiggins' Dutch photographs was "Hunger ist der Beste Koch" (Hunger is the Best Cook), where two-and-a-half year old Mildred Wiggins, wearing a Dutch dress and cap with wooden shoes dangling from her feet, sat at a table by a paned window, eating a simple meal. Besides appearing in exhibitions and magazines, this photograph gained distinction when the Maltex Cereal Company appropriated it for an advertising campaign. Mildred Wiggins, as the little Dutch girl, appeared across the country on billboards, in advertisements in women's magazines, in brochures, and on the product's cereal box itself.

Unfortunately for Wiggins, a newspaper had illegally sold the picture to the Malt Breakfast Food Company of Burlington, Vermont. She recalled, "as a result it was printed in colors in heroic size and was displayed on billboards from New York City to Portland and Seattle. While crossing the continent, I looked out the train window at almost every stop and saw my little girl in striped yellow and black stockings decorating a billboard. When the food company learned that I was the real owner of the negative they sent me one hundred dollars but there is no way of finding out what they paid the dishonest newspaper and I was not wealthy enough to sue the then largest illustrated newspaper in the country."

In 1899, "Hunger ist der Beste Koch," with "Looking Seaward," a photograph depicting a couple of men fishing on a distant rock at the ocean's edge, hung in the second Philadelphia Salon. This salon was organized by the Photographic Society of Philadelphia and Pennsylvania Academy of Fine Arts. Previously, salon juries had included painters, much to the ire of Alfred Stieglitz who publicly denounced the practice. The jurors, photographers Frances Benjamin Johnston, F. Holland Day, Clarence White, Henry Troth, and Gertrude Käsebier, selected work by both recognized and unknown photographers. Eduard Steichen's (as he then spelled his name) softly focused photographs appeared in this salon, and Gertrude Käsebier's studies of women and children gained a following here as well. For Myra, this exhibition signified a personal triumph and reward for her great efforts. Her geographic isolation did not inhibit her artistic spirit, but instead she turned it to her advantage. The mountains and rural lifestyle of the West provided an accessible context for Wiggins' work that expressed her personal ideas—ideas that meshed with the popular Arts and Craft trend.

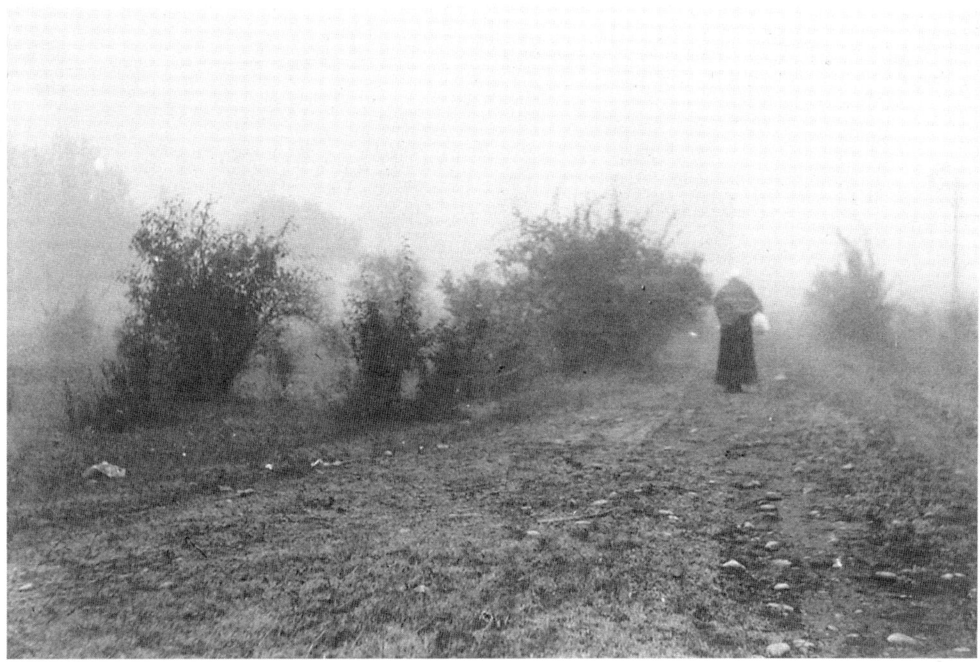

Sheep
c. 1898, gelatin silver print
8" x 6"
Portland Art Museum

A Promise of Rain
1898, gelatin silver print
6½" x 4½"
Portland Art Museum

The Gathering Mist
1899, gelatin silver print
6⅞" x 4⅝"
Portland Art Museum

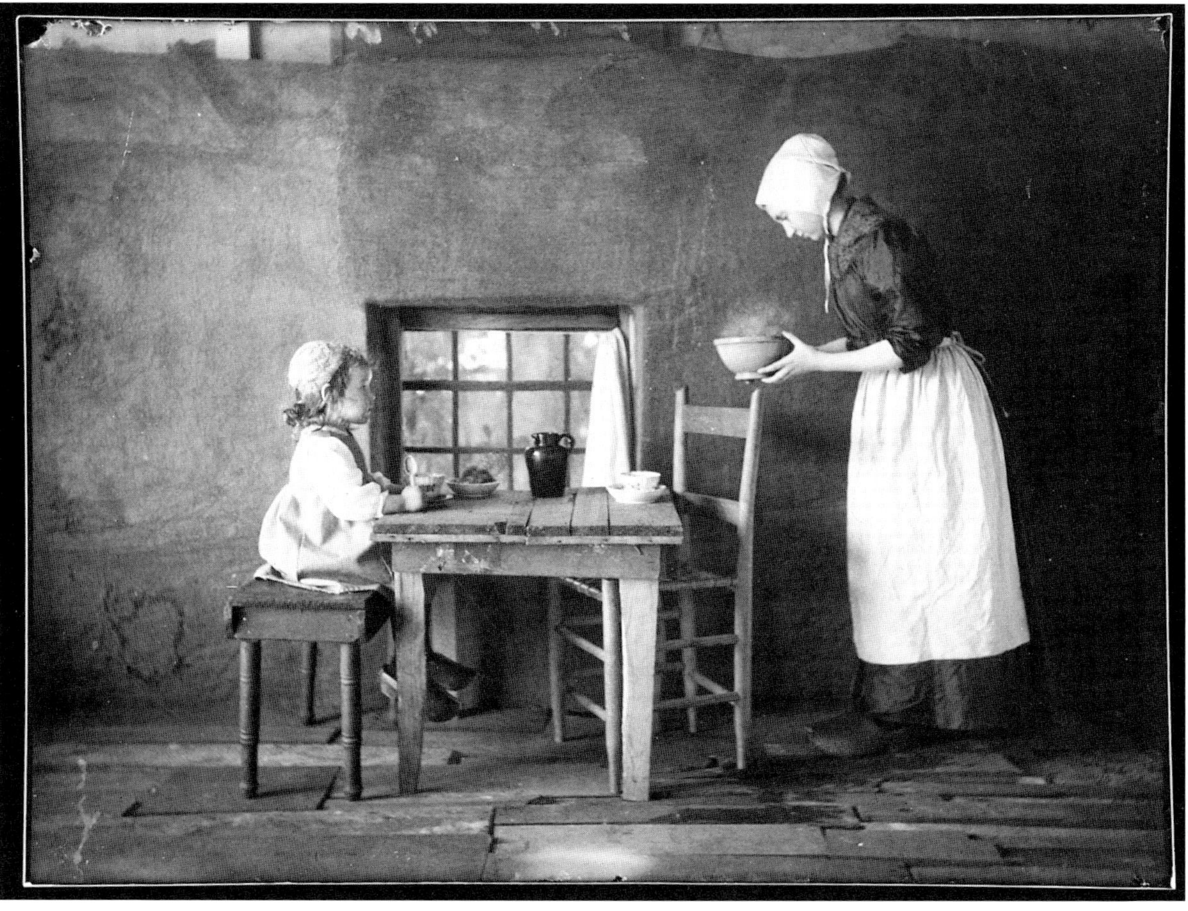

Great Expectations,
later titled Hunger is the Best Sauce
1898, gelatin silver print
Portland Art Museum

This uncropped print indicates how Wiggins hung burlap to create her Dutch tableau.

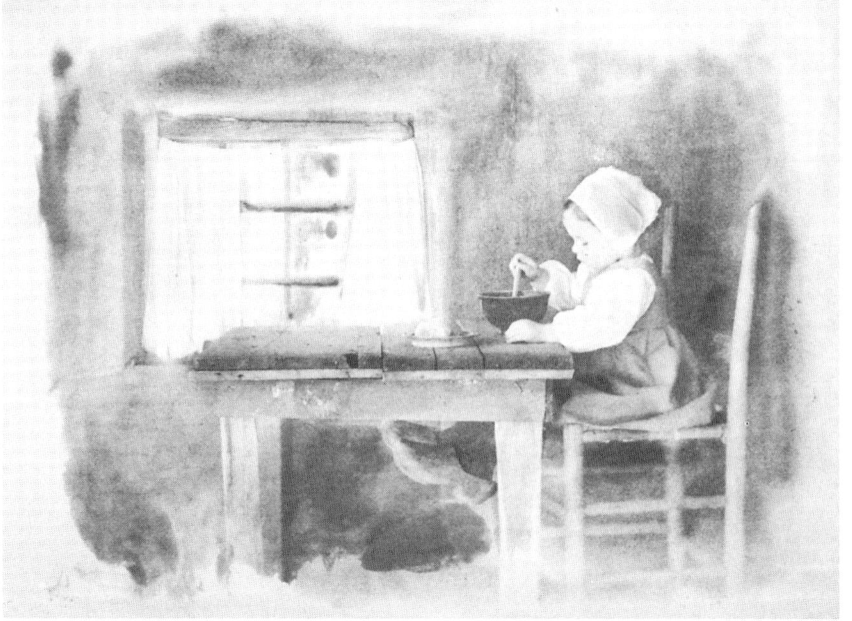

Variation on Hunger ist der Beste Koch
c. 1898, brush developed with glycerine on platinum paper
7" x 5"
Portland Art Museum

Stieglitz used "Hunger ist der Beste Koch" in *Camera Notes* to illustrate the list of exhibitors in the Camera Club Members' Exhibition held that spring. Use of her photograph in the journal signalled Myra's approval by Stieglitz, who exercised strict control over the magazine. He published only the best photographs. With *Camera Notes* under his close, critical supervision, most Camera Club members could not hope to have their photos appear in the magazine.

Consequently, requests from magazine editors asking for samples of Wiggins' work arrived in Salem. *Photo-Miniature* published "Unloading the Catch" in its "Photography Outdoors" edition, and *Photo-Era* featured "Hunger ist der Beste Koch" in an article about the Philadelphia Salon, while describing some of the 350 pictures by 119 exhibitors. The latter photograph also appeared in the *London Graphic* as the winner of a monetary prize. Wiggins used "Hunger ist der Beste Koch" as the inspiration for other work. In 1899, she painted "Morning Blessing," an enlarged profile of the sweet Dutch girl. Another version of "Hunger ist der Beste Koch," titled "Great Expectations," portrayed Wiggins' housekeeper, Alma, wearing the Dutch dress and cap while serving Mildred a steaming bowl of food.

Alma posed for "The Lacemaker," a sentimental study of a Dutch peasant engaged in a creative, domestic activity. The rectangles of the window, table, and apron create a triangular composition, with the skirt folds bringing the viewer's eye to her hand-carved wooden shoes. Alma's prayer-like bowed head leans intently toward her craft, balancing the curve of her skirt, while a bent table leg indicates the informality of peasant life and lack of Victorian pretensions. The contrast of light and dark, the homemade furniture, clothing, and curtains, along with the act of making lace, contribute to the sentimentality of the scene.

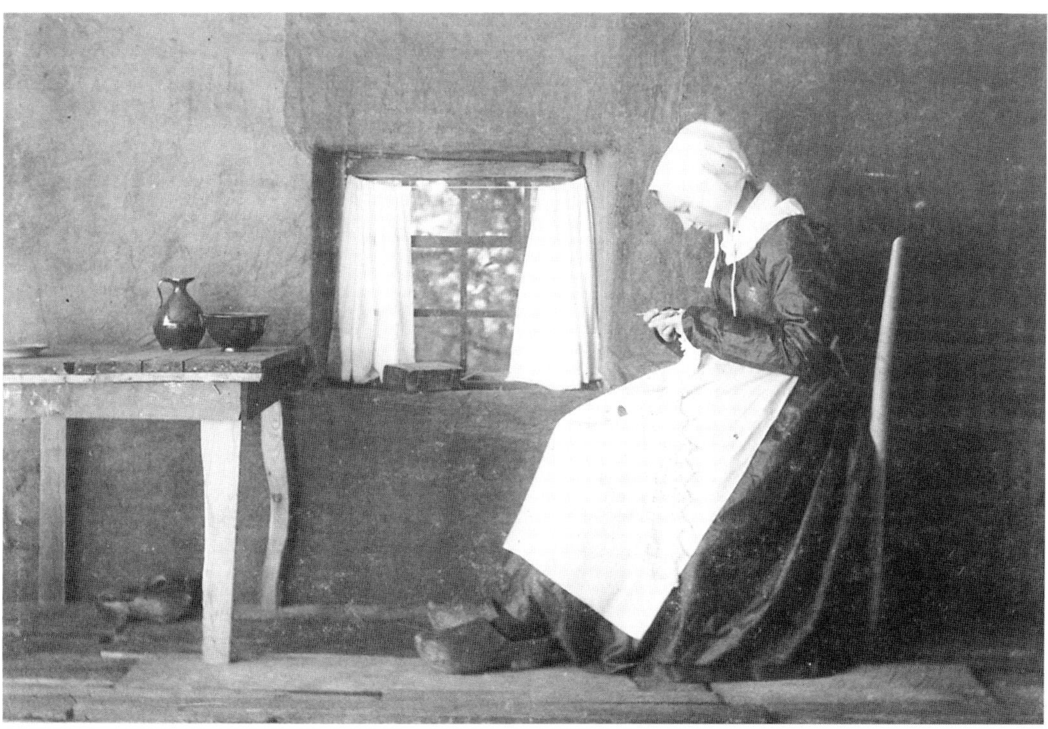

THE LACEMAKER
1899, gelatin silver print
8" x 6"
Portland Art Museum

Out of ten thousand photographs, "The Lacemaker" won second prize in the Women's Class section of the Boston-based *Youth's Companion* magazine competition in 1899. Edgar Felloes of Portland, Oregon, earned the Grand Award, and Helen Gatch received an honorable mention. Stieglitz, Käsebier, Johnston, and Farnsworth received prizes and their photographs appeared in the magazine alongside Wiggins' work. The exhibition brochure boasted, "Much of the figure work is worthy of the highest praise, showing that the artistic nature can best express itself to excellent purpose through the medium of the camera."

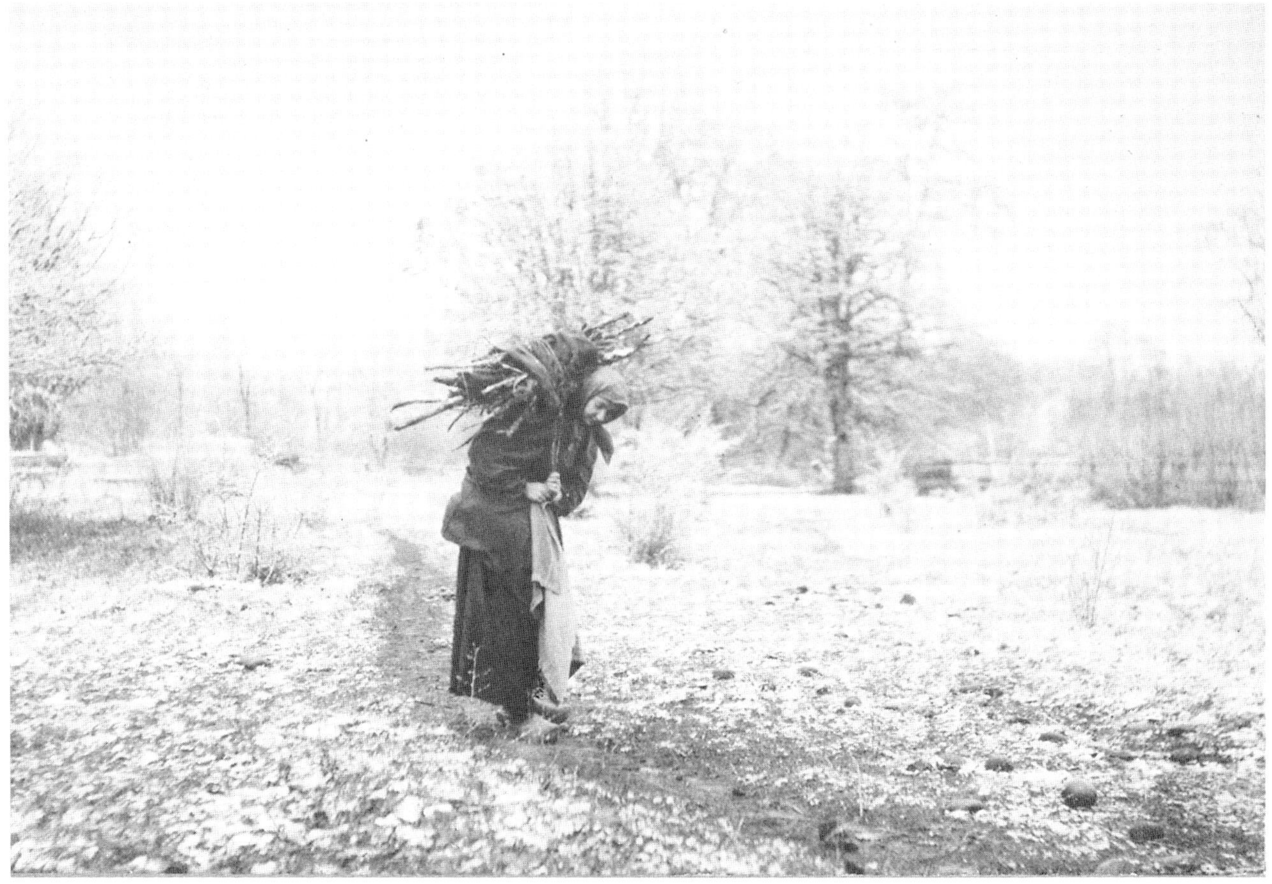

THE FIRST SNOW
1899, gelatin silver print
6⅛" x 3⅛"
Portland Art Museum

That year, besides her Dutch pictures, Wiggins photographed "The Gathering Mist," a $50 prize winner for landscapes in the Heinn Specialty Company competition in Milwaukee, Wisconsin. Her photograph "The First Snow," depicting a lone woman in the countryside weighted under a bundle of sticks, hung in the American Institute in New York. Both photographs are vested with simplicity and portray a vague narrative free of details, but suggest a soft atmosphere and mood of time and place.

Wiggins' talent for creating original subject matter brought her success and a national reputation. Wiggins' work also earned her a sizable income when women were just beginning to enter the work force, usually as single women waiting for marriage. But she was restless, always looking for the next frontier.

On August 3, 1899, Myra and Fred traveled to Alaska where the discovery of gold had kindled intense public interest. Articles in *National Geographic* described the climate and geography, as well as the endless possibilities for economic exploitation, and John Muir wrote eloquently about the Alaskan wilderness. The gold rush greatly stimulated business activity in the Pacific Northwest, as

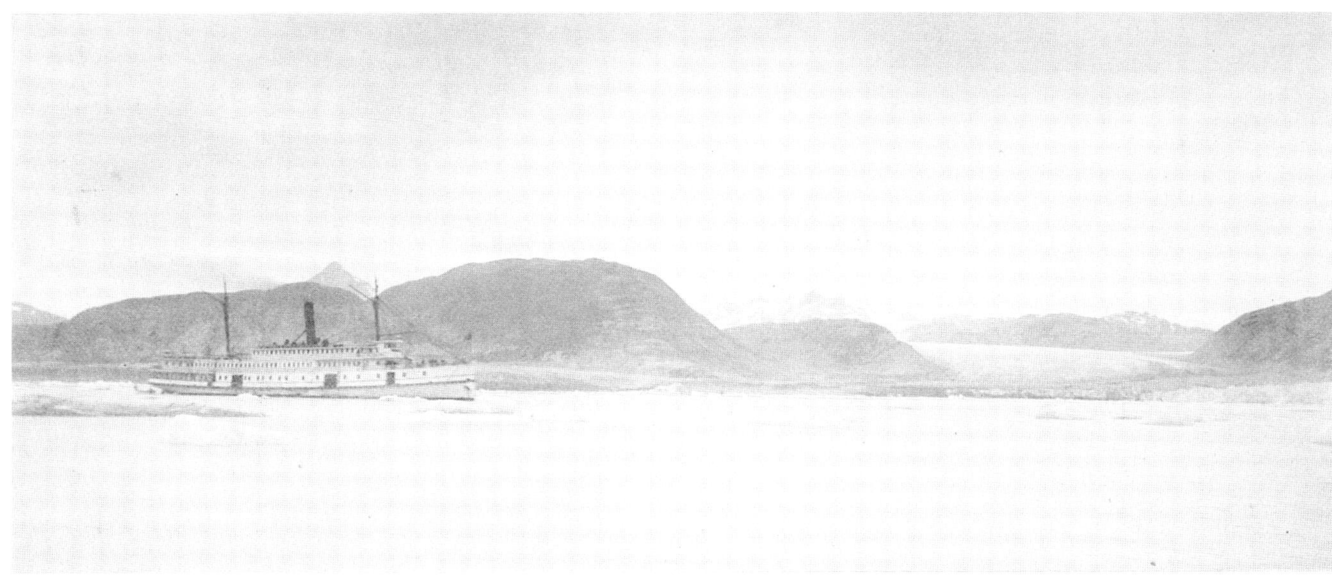

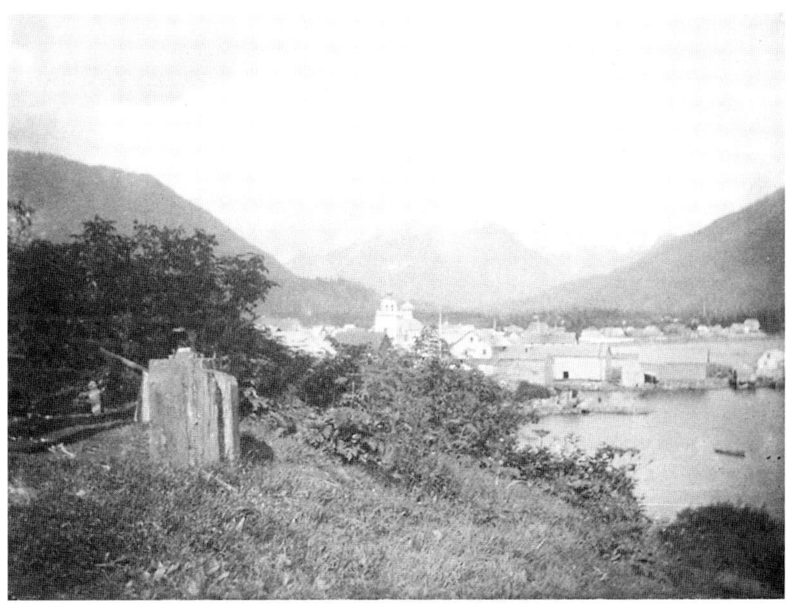

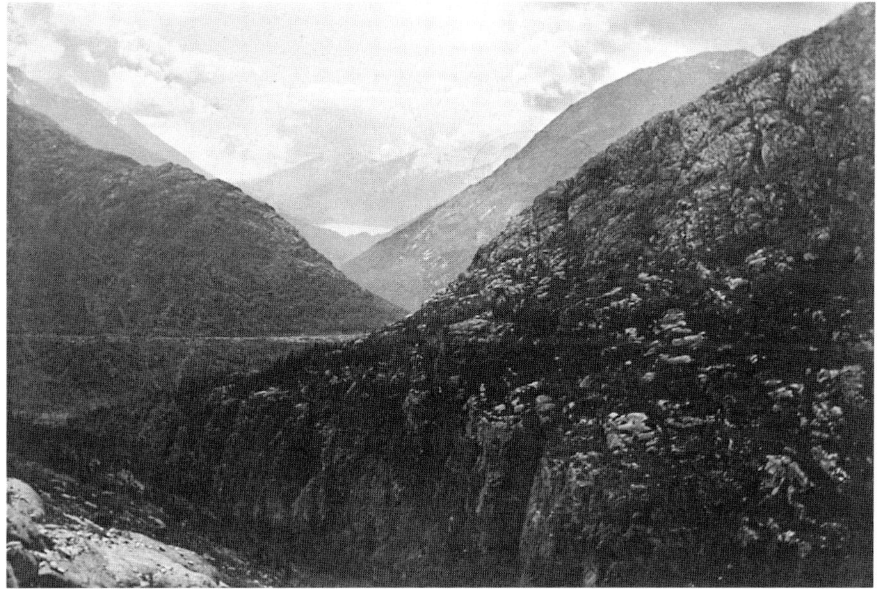

The "City of Seattle" in Glacier Bay with the Muir Glacier in the distance
1899, gelatin silver print
7⅜" x 3⅛"
Portland Art Museum

Sitka, Alaska
1899, gelatin silver print
4⅛" x 3⅛"
Robert and Shirley Benz Collection

White Pass
(Lynn Canal in Distance)
1899, gelatin silver print
7" x 5⅝"
Robert and Shirley Benz Collection

Seattle expanded rapidly from a small town into a large city. Steamships sailed between Skagway, Alaska, and Portland and Seattle, where front-page newspaper advertisements by the Alaska Steamship Company promoted "complete Alaska outfits" for women, including furs.

Travelers observed "the most picturesque inland sea in the world, hemmed in on both sides by wooded islands, with tall, snowcapped mountains standing back from the coast, presenting a panorama that is equaled in few salt-water trips in the world." Wiggins' photographs depict a rugged landscape she described as "very picturesque" with "very little open seas" and "very little seasickness." In the remoteness of one picture sits a steamer, "'The City of Seattle' in Glacier Bay with the Muir Glacier in the distance." In another, the town of "Sitka, Alaska" is shown wedged between the mountains and water, emphasizing the contrast of the natural world with human intervention. This theme continues with the image "White Pass (Lynn Canal in Distance)," about which she commented, "The road from Skagway to summit 21 miles, said to have cost three million dollars. Fine engineering."

LOOKING SEAWARD
c. 1898, gelatin silver print
8" x 6"
Robert and Shirley Benz Collection

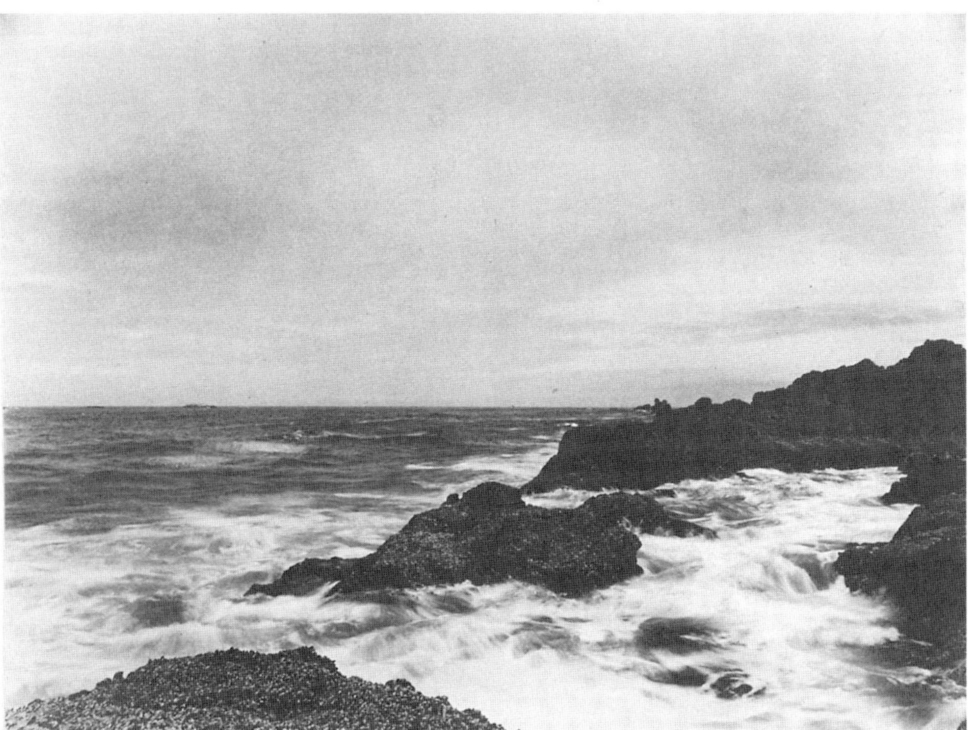

Alaska represented adventure to Wiggins. However, a woman leaving behind a three-year-old child to travel must have raised eyebrows in late nineteenth-century Salem, but, with a housekeeper, grandparents, and aunts and uncles in Salem, Mildred was not abandoned or neglected. To Mildred, this lifestyle "was just the way things were." The Wigginses returned from Alaska on August 17, and only three days later, Myra and Mildred left Salem for the beach at Newport, Oregon.

Sometime during this year, Wiggins and her Salem colleague, Wilena Knight, organized a studio exhibition of their work. Their self-published catalogue listed seventeen oil paintings, six pencil sketches, and fifteen photographs by Wiggins. A cyanotype photograph titled "Myra and Lena's Studio Exhibition," showed a wall of paintings hung salon style, a palette and potted fern sitting on the floor to one side, and a gas lamp hanging from the ceiling. Wiggins would soon note, however, that "Lena Knight was married and moved away and I carried on alone." At a time when photographers with art school training, such as Frances Benjamin Johnston and Gertrude Käsebier, were choosing between painting and photography, Wiggins managed to sustain both artistic disciplines.

Assisted by housekeeper Alma Schmidt, and surrounded by family and friends, Wiggins remained immersed in her work. "How do you ever manage to do so much, Myra?" wrote her former roommate, Fan (Frances Freiot Gilbert), from her Albany, New York, home. "It seems as if the days must be longer out in Oregon for any mortal to accomplish as much as you do." Relief from cooking, cleaning, and the various responsibilities that Alma oversaw helped, and, like many women photographers of the time, Wiggins utilized her environment in her work.

Even her bathroom became a temporary darkroom, as she later noted: "in all my work in photography for over thirty years, I have never possessed a real darkroom, so you will realize what a long suffering family I have. Many a time the bathroom has remained darkened for nearly a week at a time, and any member of the family took a bath at the risk of being developed with pyro or fixed with hypo." Wiggins further recalled, "after I married, my husband was more understanding, although he hated darkrooms. I must also give my family credit for much patient posing. Why my husband even grew a beard for me once, so that I might get a 'Vandyke-like' study of him, but he looked more like a criminal instead, so I gave him up as a model . . . There is scarcely one of my prints but brings to mind memories of great effort and even tears."

Wiggins rarely went to bed before four or five o'clock in the morning. At night, when she had her world to herself, she caught up on work, painted, or wrote poetry. During this time, she sometimes read the newspaper while standing to stay awake, but twice she fell and broke her nose when overcome by sleep. On one occasion, she was scheduled to speak to a women's organization the next day. She went to a doctor, who fixed and bandaged her nose, and she arrived at the meeting to give the talk as planned. Wiggins' niece recalled having voice lessons from her beginning at eleven o'clock in the evening. Myra remembered how Fred, during the first years of their marriage, deplored her habit of staying up late. As an "obedient bride," she demurred, but, when all was quiet, she wrote poetry by the glow of a flashlight, leading her to reflect, "I sincerely wish that the muse would work at a more convenient and conventional hour!"

Myra Wiggins' ambitions and ideas intersected at high speed as she ran from painting, to poetry, to photography, to singing. Time, she believed, was more valuable than money.

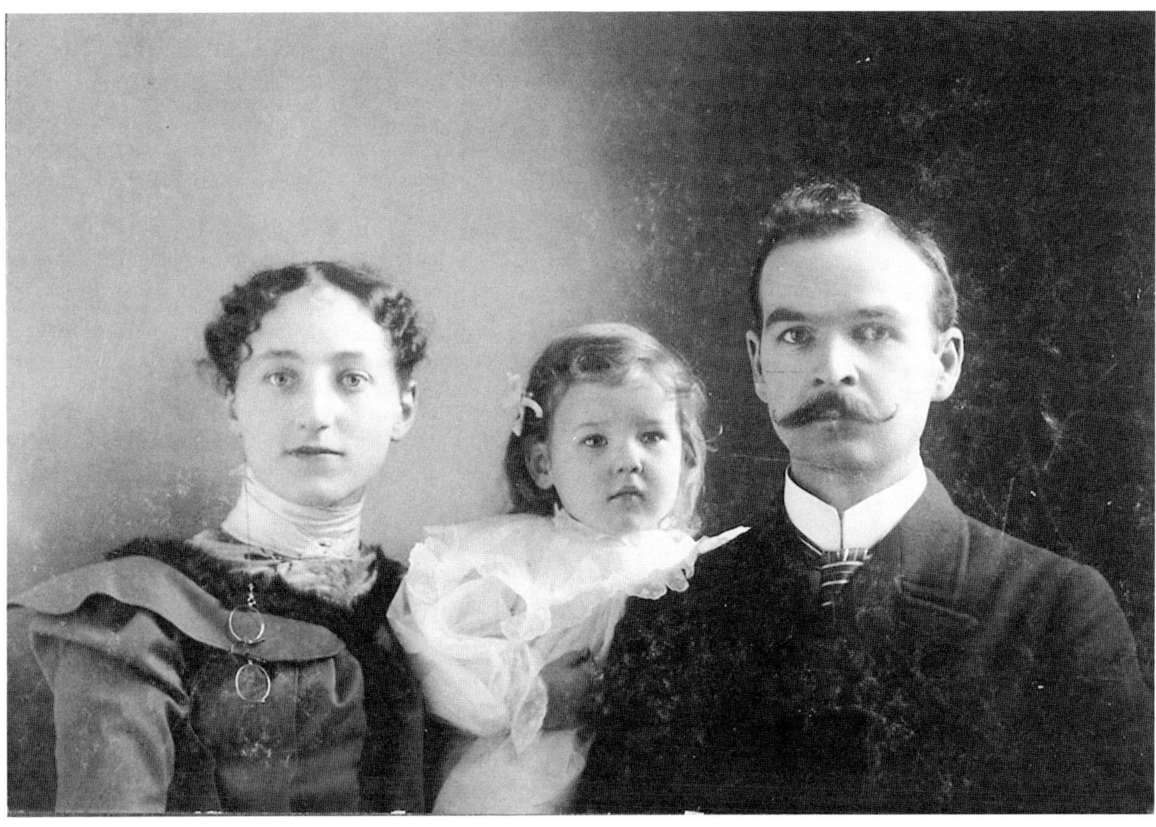

WIGGINS FAMILY PORTRAIT
1899, gelatin silver print
5½" x 4⅞"
Portland Art Museum
Pickerill Co., 243 Commercial St., Salem, Oregon

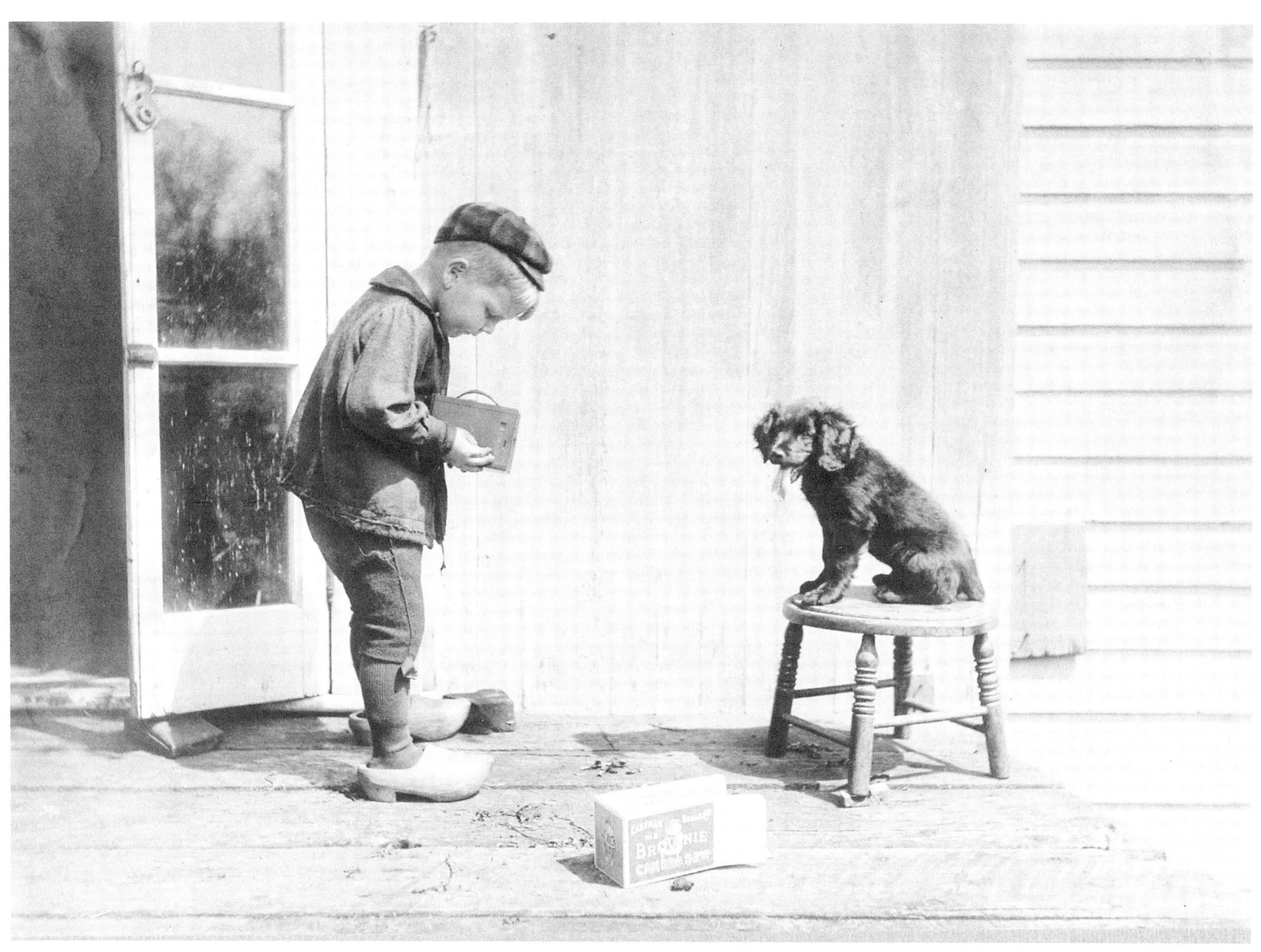

Part Four
1900

In 1899, Kodak published a new catalogue of products for the next century, titled *The Witchery of Kodakery.* This "catch phrase . . . already gone around the world" reflected the novelty and special magic of photography. Kodak's new line of hand-held cameras made picture-taking a common, everyday experience, and the manufacture of over 100,000 cameras triggered a fad that showed no sign of disappearing. To equate "Kodak" with photography, the Eastman Kodak Company defined enthusiastic snapshooters as "kodakers" who went "kodaking." Sometimes, however, the aggressiveness of kodakers ruffled people who were caught unprepared by the ubiquitous camera. *The Ladies Home Journal* commented about the "etiquette of the kodaker" not keeping "pace with the development of the kodak." The *Journal* suggested appropriate "Kodak Manners" to the "girls and young women" who "have an idea that everything and everybody may be considered fair game for their cameras."

To offset the idea that cameras were only for shooting family snapshots, George Eastman furnished camera equipment and darkroom supplies to well-known photographers, and acquired their photographs to promote his products, while also occasionally commissioning them to create pictures for advertising. Eastman, for example, used Myra's pictures to demonstrate his company's merchandise. She staged a scene of a child aiming a Kodak Brownie at a patiently seated dog to show that even children could use a camera. In another image, two young women held a developed roll of film to the window light, with a film developing tank and reel on a table beside them. The subject matter and composition implied that women could develop film, that it could be done as a social activity with friends, and that it was a clean and simple task.

About this time, as the old century turned to the new, two significant events occurred in Fred and Myra Wiggins' lives. In January 1900, Fred announced the closure of Wiggins Bazaar and his plans to open a new business selling bicycles, sewing machines, and organs. Myra, meanwhile, on the basis of twelve of her negatives, won the Ray Camera Company's Grand Award—a free trip from New York to Paris.

The Paris Exposition opened in 1900 welcoming in the twentieth century with 83,000 displays depicting modern-day achievements. Visitors like

Advertising Photograph for Eastman Kodak Company
c. 1900, gelatin silver print
7⅞" x 5⅞"
Robert and Shirley Benz Collection

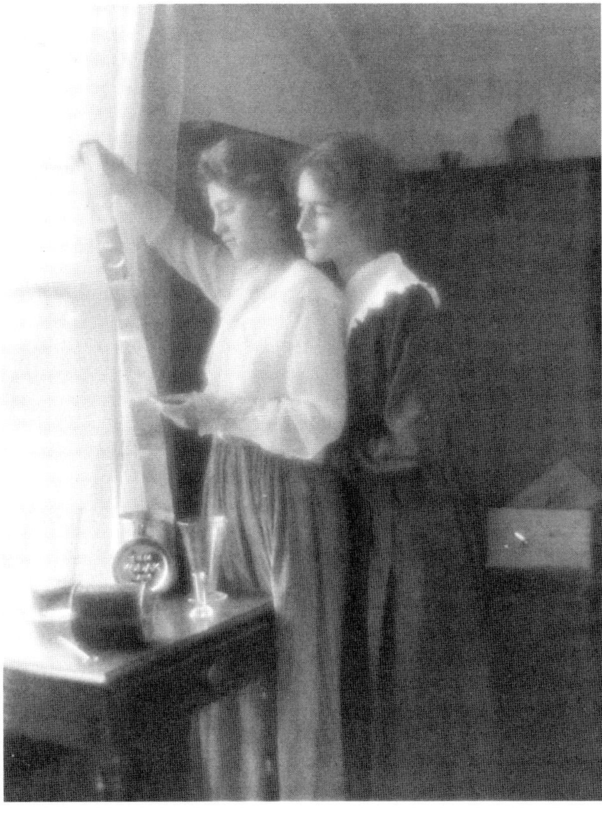

Advertising Photograph for Eastman Kodak Company
c. 1900, gelatin silver print
6⅛" x 8"
Portland Art Museum

Myra Wiggins and others from around the world could easily spend an entire day at the Petit Palais viewing its 5,000 works of art, or glean the history of French art up to the present time at the Grand Palais. Ten-thousand light bulbs illuminated one exhibition palace, heralding the development of electricity. People were introduced to the first moving sidewalk, called "the street of the future," and thousands of tourists carried cameras with them to snap a personal record of the exhibition.

The exposition set strictly defined rules for photographers, as explained by the Eastman Kodak Company: "Kodaks will be admitted to the exposition free of charge to be used through the day; tripod cameras only until 1:00 PM and will cost 25 cents per day per apparatus. Season tickets will be issued for tripod cameras on which must appear a photograph of the person receiving them . . . cost 1000 francs. Moral—Take a Kodak With You."

On her way to New York City in April, en route to Europe and the exposition, Wiggins stopped in Albany, New York, to visit her former roommate, Fan. While there, Wiggins received a letter from Frances Benjamin Johnston inviting her to participate in an exhibition of women photographers Johnston was organizing for the Paris Exposition. The United States Commission had named Johnston a delegate to the International Photographic Congress in Paris, July 23-28, and had asked her to speak on the subject of women photographers in America and organize an exhibit of their work. "The Commission recognizes this work as unique," wrote Johnston, "and it is their desire that the wonderful achievements of American women in Photography should be adequately and worthily represented at this Congress." From Wiggins and thirty-four other women photographers, Johnston solicited biographical statements and up to ten mounted prints "of what you consider your highest and best product, showing as much diversity as possible and perhaps covering different periods of your progress."

Wiggins requested her negatives to be sent from Salem, and, on June 23, she submitted eight photographs taken in Oregon, California, New York, and Alaska over a period of ten years. She apologized for the mounting and printing of some of the prints, having "only received my negatives six days ago." She included a brief description of her photographic background and mentioned her use of silver solio, aristo-platino, bromide, and platinum papers.

"Any of the photos may be published," Wiggins concluded, "but if 'Hunger ist der Beste Koch' be reproduced in this country, permission should be obtained of the Maltex Cereal Co. of Burlington, Vermont who are using it as an advertisement."

Meanwhile, Johnston mailed a roster of photographers to Alfred Stieglitz who heartily responded, "The list of women photographers you sent me is complete, and I can think of no one that you may have overlooked. I'd certainly ask them all. The women in this country are certainly doing great photographic work and deserve much commendation for their efforts." In six weeks, Johnston gathered a collection of 142 photographs by 28 women. They had sent mainly portraits, genre scenes, and costumed figure studies with a few landscape, flower, and documentary works. Besides four of Myra's photographs, the collection included work by Emma Farnsworth, Zaida Ben-Yusef, Gertrude Käsebier, and Catharine Weed Ward, an American photographer and writer living in England.

On July 6, 1900, the Washington, D.C., *Evening Star* praised Johnston's efforts: "To startle the old world with a revelation of what the women of this country have accomplished in triumph over the remainder of the world, Miss Frances Benjamin Johnston of this city, one of the most widely known of women photographers, has succeeded in securing a collection of pictures of incomparable beauty from her feminine colleagues, which she is taking to Paris, to be exhibited at the international photographic congress in the French capital as a feature of the great exposition now in progress." Later, in Paris, Johnston would address the members of the congress, who "expressed their great admiration" for the "remarkable works" on display.

While Johnston continued her hasty preparations for the exposition, Wiggins spent a month in New York City attending classes at the Chase School of Art and taking vocal lessons, probably from her former teacher, Madame Toedt. She also visited Gertrude Käsebier's studio. Käsebier, by this time, was a reputable photographer known for her pictorial style of portraiture and mother-child photographs. "I finally mustered courage enough to go the day before we sailed," wrote Wiggins, "and I had a delightful time. She was perfectly lovely to me, and I looked through large portfolios of her photos. She is an artist if there ever was one." Completing her photographic business, art and vocal classes, and visits to friends, Myra and her father, John Albert, who had joined her in New York, sailed for London on June 27. Before Myra left, George Eastman presented her with an expensive hand-held Kodak camera to use on the trip.

"We have been in sight of the beautiful land since early morning—Merrie Old England—we have just passed Eddystone lighthouse . . . It seems good to see the land again and everyone is happy," wrote Wiggins, on Wednesday, July 4, 1900, from the U.S.M.S. *St. Paul.* Several days later, after sightseeing, she added, "The whole of London and everything in it is picturesque. I was really surprised."

Five days later, at the Exhibition Hotel in Paris, she commented: "Paris does not impress me as London did, perhaps because I saw London first. The main objection to Paris is the wind and dust—it is like San Francisco, especially out here on the grounds." But, the French capital still maintained some intrigue, as she wrote, "I hope to get some good pictures in Paris. Their queer little inside

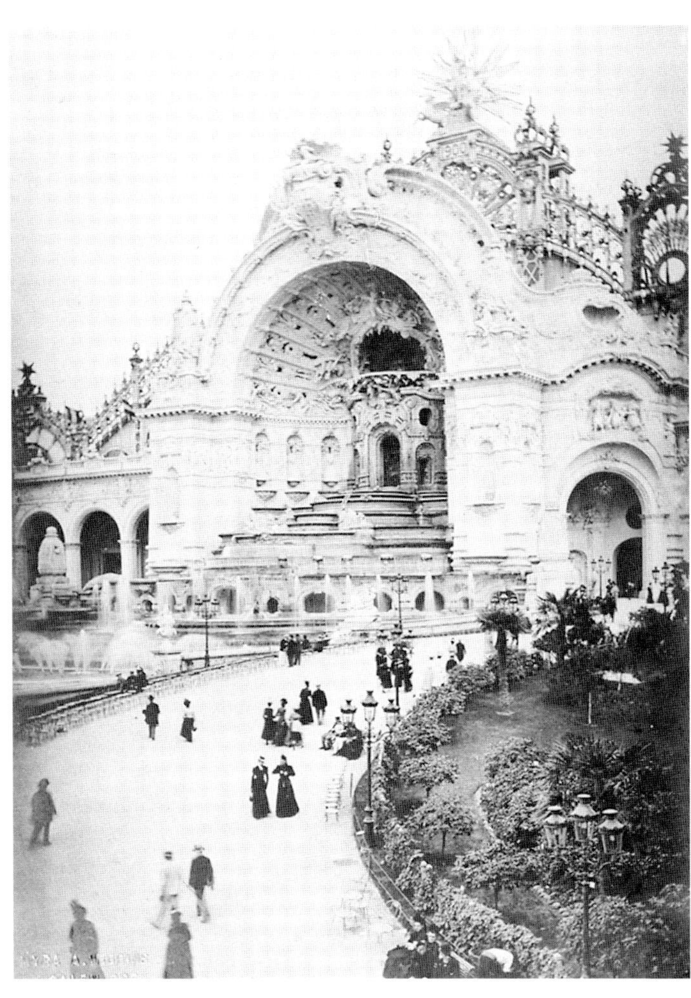

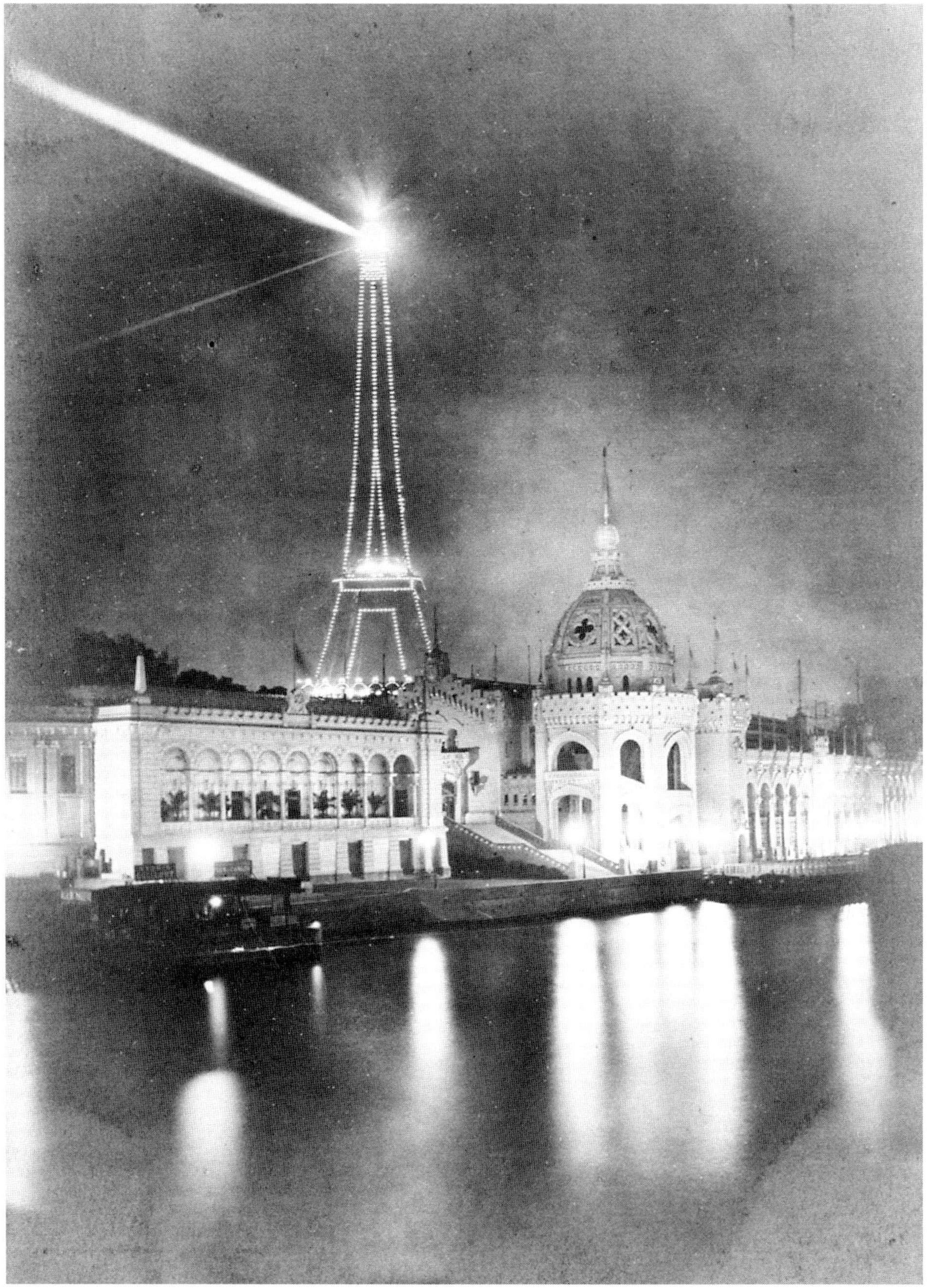

Head of the Grand Court
1900, gelatin silver print
4¾" x 6⅝"
Portland Art Museum

Paris Exposition at Night
1900, gelatin silver print
4⅞" x 6¾"
Portland Art Museum

courts in the poorer quarters are what interest me. You will find anything from a cow to a drinking fountain in them—and the people are so interesting . . . They rarely wear hats, boys and girls wear black aprons with long sleeves and leather belts. The boys sometimes wear a Tam O'Shanter cap, and they carry their books in black book bags."

As arranged by Cook's Tours, Myra Wiggins and John Albert visited Notre Dame, Napoleon's Tomb, and Versailles. "Thousands of people are out there [at Versailles] everyday," she wrote. "There were about twelve carriage loads of Cook's people—thirty-six in our carriage, six horses. Our first class dining room seats over one thousand persons at once, and there is a second and third class room just as large, I think. We have a six-course dinner every night, and a fine breakfast, and we furnish our own luncheon." Wiggins and her father knew enough French to ask for information, but she noted, "We got in a difficulty with an officer at the palace today over my camera; papa got angry and his French left him."

On July 12, at the Midland Grand Hotel back in London, she described the channel crossing: "I rather like to be locked up in the little compartment cars, we get a congenial crowd together and it's really jolly. We Americans are the only people who speak the English language anywhere near correctly. We can hardly understand the English people, they speak it so badly." A week later, she decried the warm weather as, "the hottest for 14 or 16 years they say," and feeling "tired and warm and lonesome." She continued, "I am so disappointed because I cannot take any photographs. I have carried my camera nearly everywhere I have gone, but I can't snap from a shaky hack and waste a lot of film and work in developing."

Wiggins did not explain why they crossed the channel so many times, but, on July 28, she wrote from The Hague in The Netherlands: "I finally persuaded Papa to go on to Paris and leave me here, and if I had my choice, I would only be in Paris three or four days and spend all my time here. It is simply charming. Papa and I went on our wheels [bicycles] yesterday morning to the coast, about three miles out . . . and today I went alone and made a sketch of an old fishing boat up on the beach." She delighted in seeing the Dutch in their costumes and wanted to go into their homes, but lacked the language skills to ask. She also mentioned that she "was sorry to miss the photo congress, but I would miss more than that to get to stay in Holland and sketch."

While photographing an old windmill, Wiggins met a man who spoke both English and Dutch. He invited her to accompany him by bicycle to visit his country relatives, where she could sketch and photograph the interior of their houses. She described him as a "very nice man, a Christian, and interested in the Y.M.C.A. work, too," so when "he made the offer, I did not hesitate to accept." But, once there, she felt so unwelcome that after taking one view, she left.

Wiggins' photographs illustrated her article, "Alone in Holland," published in the *American Annual of Photography and Photographic Times Almanac* in 1903. She recounted the two week interlude with her bicycle and 4 x 5 inch plate-box camera used to record "snapshots on cloudy days" that "were developed for under-exposure about five months after they were taken." This camera, she noted, "attracted less attention than the folding camera, as with the latter I often had twenty or more children about me; and of all the children in the world, the Holland varieties are the most numerous and the greatest beggars. They seem to rise from the very pavements, and think that because you own a gold watch and a shiny camera you are wealthy. I learned from sad experience not to be too friendly with them, nor to trust them too implicitly . . . of course, I am speaking only of the poorer class." In the article, she included photographs of windmills, canals at Haarlem, The Hague and Delft, and three lone figures with a small sailboat on Scheveningen Beach. The one Dutch interior photograph depicted a young woman working at a hearth with her hair in a single braid and wooden shoes on her feet.

INTERIOR OF DUTCH HOUSE
1900, gelatin silver print
4¾" x 3¾"
Portland Art Museum

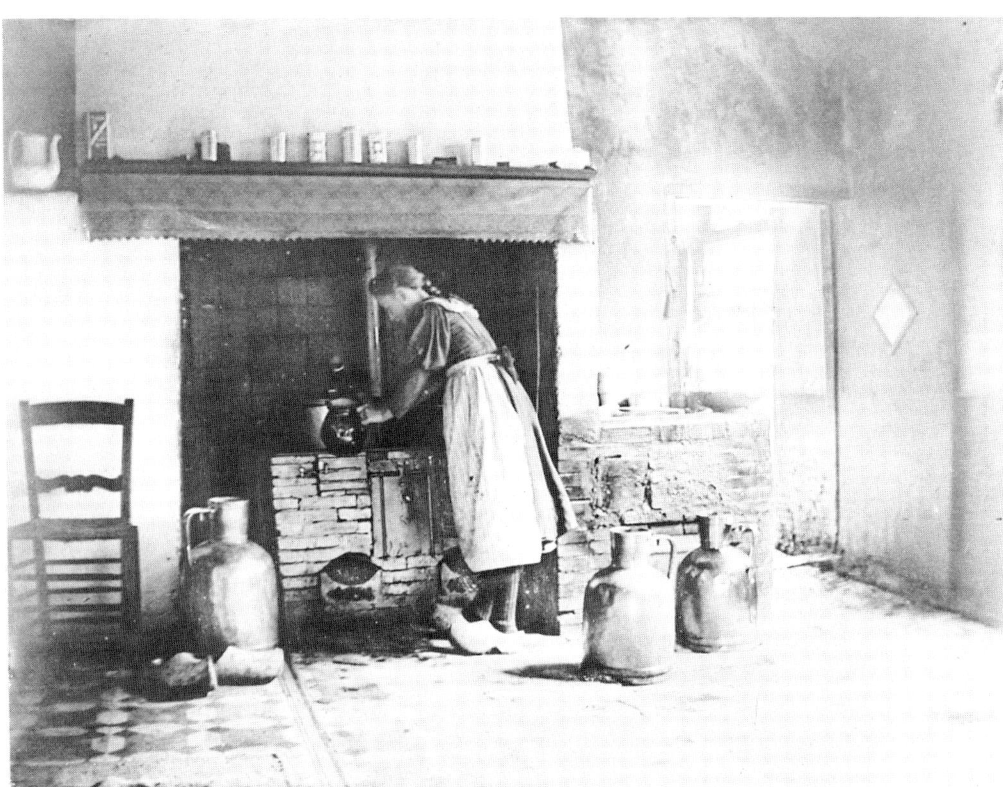

Before leaving Holland, Myra experienced what she called "the narrowest escape of my life." As she explained, "A man was walking directly in front of my wheel, crosswise, and the wind was blowing so he couldn't hear my bell. He finally heard just in time to keep me from striking him, and by that time I was on the street car track, and looked up to see a heavy wagon and horse coming toward me at a very fast gait and almost upon me. I hesitated half a second as to which way I should turn and then it was too late, for the horse's head was over my handle bars, still coming with his head drawn back to keep from striking me. Oh! but he looked like a monster. I thought of a thousand things in that instant, and then jumped, wheel and all, onto the narrow two and one half foot sidewalk without a hundredth part of a second to spare, and then I thought my foot would be run over. I landed on the spokes of my wheel and I tell you I was thankful for that escape. The horse was going too fast to stop, and he would have trampled me to death. My handlebars were twisted, but the wheel was uninjured."

Back in Paris, August 8, and reunited with her father who had spent some time in Germany, Wiggins visited the Louvre where she saw the Venus de Milo and viewed works by Michelangelo, Raphael, and Rubens. Two days later she devoted an entire day to the Exposition Art Gallery where she studied one of Chase's paintings and "nearly all the prize pictures of last year's Salon exhibits in the U.S." In Holland, she had seen paintings by Franz Hals, Rembrandt, and Murillo, whose "Madonna and Child" she "could hardly bear to leave."

On her last evening in Paris, Wiggins wandered through the exposition grounds to take some night photographs. In one of these pictures, street lamps in front of a baroque pavilion are reflected in a quiet pool of water, while the glittering electric lights of the Eiffel Tower, with a spotlight shining from its peak, glow in the distance.

On August 16, Myra Wiggins and John Albert arrived in London en route to New York. The next day she wrote Frances Benjamin Johnston: "I was sorry to miss you in Paris as I had hoped to have the pleasure of meeting you and of seeing some of your work, although I have seen much of it reproduced in the different magazines and it is always a pleasure to study it. May I trouble you to send one of my photos 'Hunger ist der Beste Koch' to Mr. [Snowden] Ward of The Photogram—#6 Farringdon Ave., London as he has kindly offered to have it framed for me and submit it to the Royal Photographic Society's exhibition; not that I am sanguine of its acceptance but there's no harm in trying . . . I am sorry to trouble you—if I had seen you in Paris I should have relieved you of all my heavy photographs. I hope a report of the Congress will be in 'Camera Notes.' I was so sorry to miss it—I was in Holland at the time."

In 1893, Snowden Ward had married Catharine Weed Barnes, co-editor of *American Amateur Photographer* and a noted speaker and photographer. Catharine, who did not take up photography until the age of thirty-five, devoted much of her energy to encouraging and supporting women photographers. She was the first woman to present a paper to the Society of American Photographers of New York. As she traveled and lectured across the country, she openly challenged the attitude that women's abilities were inferior to men's. The Wards moved to London, where they founded *The Photogram* and edited *Photograms of the Year*, an annual international review of the year's best photography. Myra thought Catharine was her second cousin, "I believe her grandmother was my great 'Aunt Emily' who married Thurlow Weed the noted statesman . . . I was later glad to be classed with her and other famous women photographers of America. In London she invited me to visit her and her husband . . . but I couldn't as I was . . . on a schedule."

On August 18, Myra and her father sailed for New York, and reached America a week later. On the ship, she sang in a "grand concert" where she "had the honor of appearing on the same program with the Honorable Chauncey Depew [Senator from New York] . . . We cleared over $300 for seamen and other charities. There was also a professional violinist, the musical director of the Manhattan, of New York. He was the 'star,' I think, he played so beautifully. He was director of the concert and played my accompaniments."

After a few days in New York, they boarded the train for Albany and Montreal, and continued to the Pacific Northwest. Reunited with Fred and Mildred in Salem, Myra must have felt euphoric as she disbursed souvenirs, described museum masterpieces, and related her adventures. As usual, she rushed into her next project—an exhibition at the Chicago Art Institute and the Chicago Society of Amateur Photographers. Wiggins' thirty-seven photographs in the Chicago exhibit included "some royal bromide enlargements, prize winners and salon pictures . . . from London, Holland, Alaska and views from California to the Atlantic Coast." Together with photographs by Oscar Maurer of California and F.H. Worsley-Benison of Great Britain, her exhibition hung for two weeks in the club rooms of the Society before it was transferred to the Art Institute.

Meanwhile, the Ray Camera Company used three of Wiggins' prize-winning photographs in an

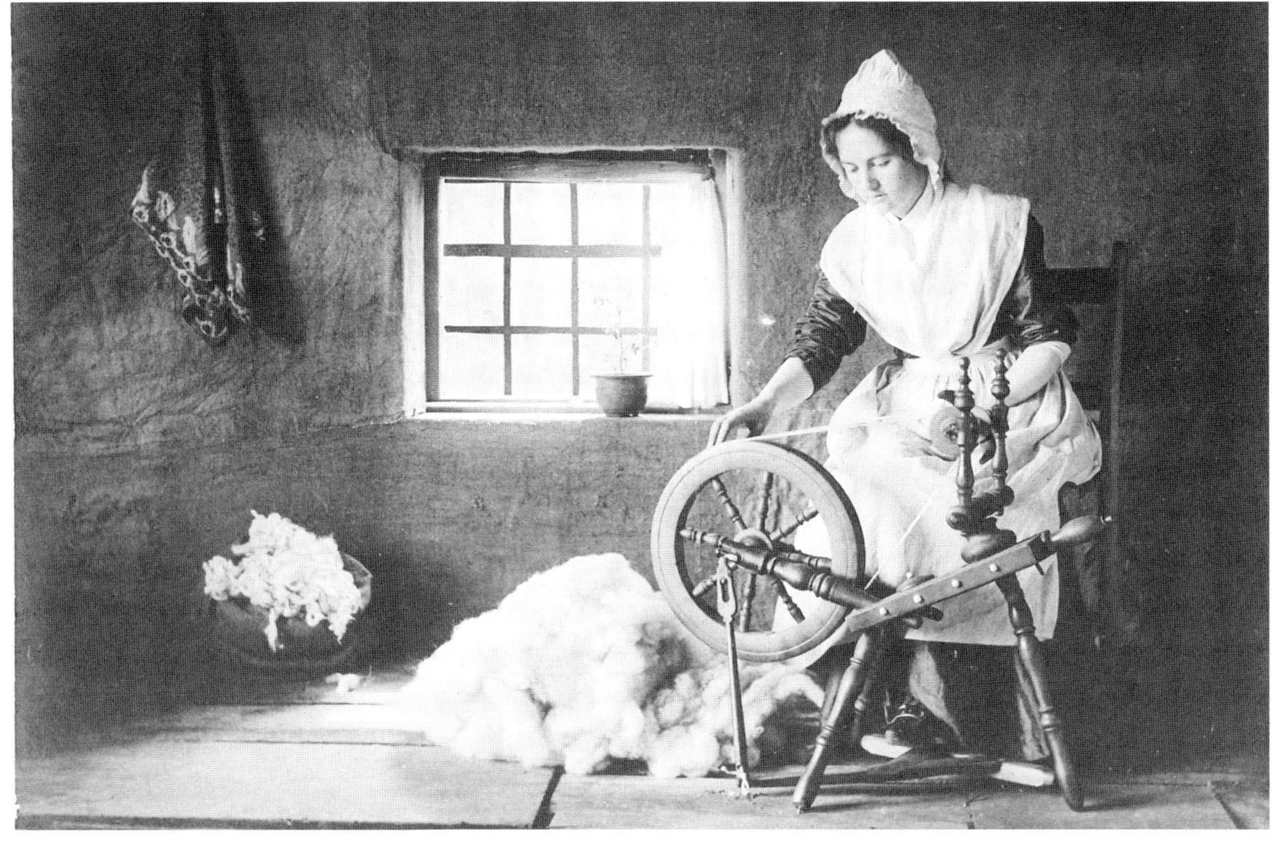

The Spinner
1898, gelatin silver print
7½" x 5½"
Portland Art Museum

advertising brochure of pictures "made with a Ray camera." In one image, "Nursery Rhyme," Alma wears a starched white dress and cap, while sitting in a rocking chair and reading a book by a tall, lace-covered window. On the floor at Alma's knees sits an attentive Mildred, completing an atmosphere of domestic tranquility.

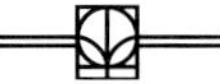

Throughout 1900, Myra achieved one success after another. The fall issue of *Camera Notes* reviewed the Third Annual Exhibition of Prints held the previous spring for New York Camera Club Members. "The Lacemaker" and "The Gathering Mist" had appeared in the show, and Stieglitz selected "The Gathering Mist" to reproduce in *Camera Notes*. The New York *Buffalo Express* published another Wiggins Dutch genre image, "The Spinner," awarded it a $20 second prize in the Figure Class competition for amateur photographers, and commented on the "national reputation" Myra Wiggins and Emma Farnsworth had earned for "the excellence of their work."

Wiggins' greatest photographic coup, however, appeared in *Leslie's Weekly*. Her "Head of the Grand

Court," made with the camera George Eastman presented to her before she left for Europe, earned First Prize for best photograph taken at the Paris Exposition. In the scene, men and women promenade along a wide walkway curving toward an ornate palace, which is fronted by balconies beneath the building's huge arch. Wiggins captured the resplendent grandeur of the Exposition, and, in winning this prize, proved herself capable of generating one award after another.

During these early years of photography, company-sponsored competitions provided talented amateurs with earnings in the form of cash awards and prizes. Traditionally, "no one had ever heard of a girl of a good family making money." However, now Wiggins cultivated an income—already having earned money, cameras, and an overseas trip—that fed her ambition and drive.

By now, Wiggins was recognized as a photographer with remarkable talents. Whether touring Paris, London, or bicycling the canals of Holland; exploring the mountains of Oregon, and the inlets of Alaska; or working in her barn studio, she produced original, high-quality photographs. Her diverse artistic talents set her apart from most other photographers. The iconography of home and domesticity—simple lives amid the growing industrialization of America—became a symbolic alternative to the grab for wealth prevalent at the turn of the century. Yet, this same kind of wealth provided Wiggins with the security and support whereby her talents could be presented to the world. The requisites of marriage, motherhood, and home became tools and resources for imagination and ideas, rather than obstacles. Her life and work embraced creativity and adventure, and Myra remained her own role model.

Ray Special Folding Camera

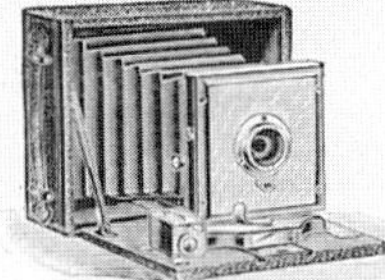

This camera combines all the elements of desirability, practicability, value, and low cost, and has been especially designed for a large number who desire a folding camera at a moderate price.

It takes a picture 4 x 5 inches, made in cycle folding style, and is very compact; best material only is used in its construction, and covered with genuine seal grain leather; equipped with a very fine achromatic lens of an improved Meniscus type; time and instantaneous shutter; reversible view finder; focusing scale; Ray workmanship throughout.

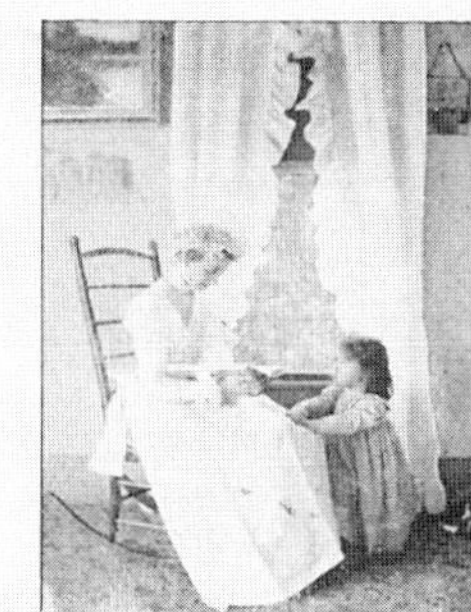

Price

Complete with carrying case and one double holder, . . . $7.00
Ray double holders, each, extra, ... 1.00

16

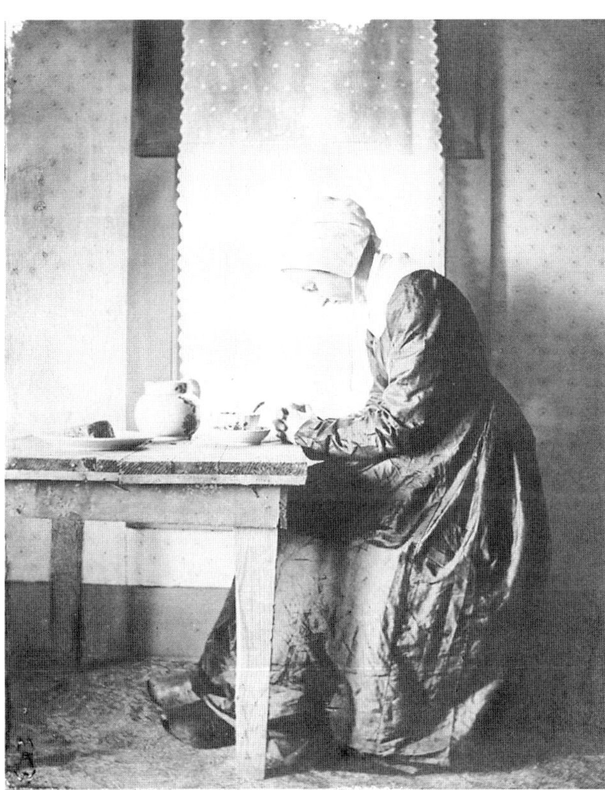

Nursery Rhyme
Ray Camera Company brochure, 1900
Portland Art Museum

Returning Thanks
1900, gelatin silver print
3¾" x 4¾"
Portland Art Museum

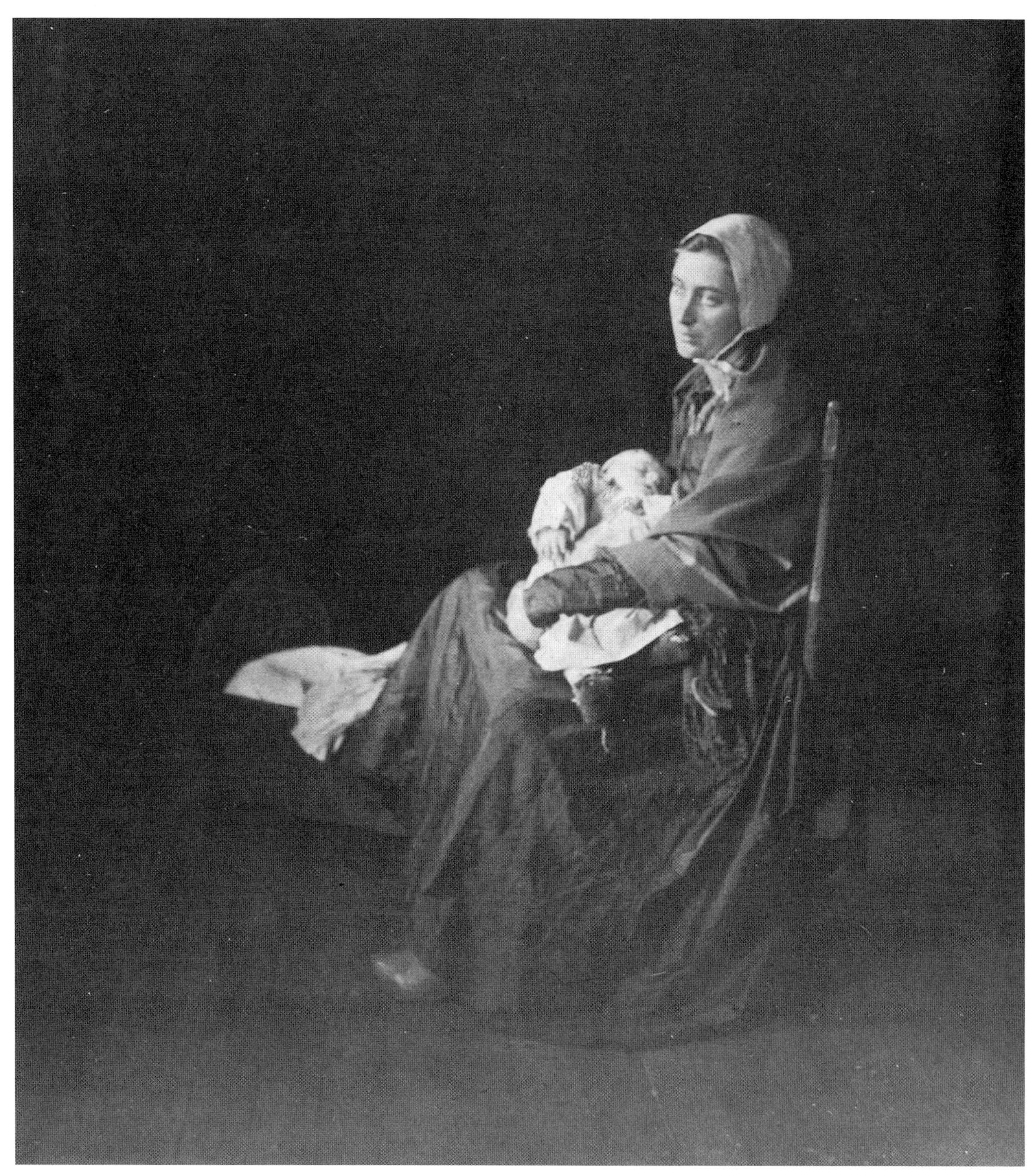

PART FIVE
1901- 1903

In the late nineteenth century, camera clubs provided amateur photographers with the means to socialize, obtain darkroom assistance, and share ideas and information. Organized outings with cameras became popular, sometimes on bicycle or train excursions, and many hotels catered to the traveling amateur by providing darkrooms. Portland's amateur photographers founded the Oregon Camera Club (OCC) in 1895. Both within the framework of the Oregon Camera Club and independently, Lily White and Sarah Ladd pursued their photographic work. In 1900, White demonstrated darkroom techniques to the OCC membership; her presentations included "Negative Taking" and "Preparation of Negatives for Printing." In 1901, the club made White an honorary member.

In 1901, White and Ladd, along with Wiggins, joined the Camera Club of New York. In the spring, Ladd's "Messengers of Spring" and Wiggins' "The Brook, Scheveningen Beach, Holland" were hung in the New York club's Member's Exhibition. In January of that same year, the First San Francisco Photography Salon had opened at the Mark Hopkins Art Institute. The exhibition included work by Wiggins, Gatch, White, and Ladd. Wiggins' "Through the Mist," also known as "The Gathering Mist," earned a second prize bronze medal in the landscape division.

The Bausch & Lomb Company of Rochester, New York, recognized Wiggins' talent for making Dutch genre photographs. In their 1901 competition, they awarded her a $100 first prize for her photograph "The Mother." This solemn interpretation of motherhood, posed in Wiggins' barn studio, depicted a seated Dutch woman whose melancholy face gazes away from the swaddled baby on her lap. The contrast between the light focused on the woman and child and the dark areas surrounding the two figures creates a somber mood.

Wiggins produced her later Dutch pictures in a barn studio. On two occasions, in fact, when the Wigginses moved into houses having empty barns on the rear lots, she converted the barns into studios. She filled her studios with mementos from her art student days and travels abroad, and with decorative items reflecting the Japanese and Dutch motifs popular in the Arts and Crafts movement. Each carefully placed object represented a special memory or significant event in her personal life.

THE MOTHER
1901, platinum print
4¾" x 5⅞"
Portland Art Museum

About the same time that Wiggins won the Bausch & Lomb contest, George Eastman continued promoting the Kodak Girl with *The Witch of Kodakery*, "a little book of verse." This book, according to one reviewer, embodied "the various sonnets that have been evolved in honor of the Kodak Girl, who has become so familiar a figure in the Kodak magazine advertising. The poems are good, and the little book is worth sending for, reading and keeping."

Whether or not influenced by the Kodak Girl, large numbers of women flocked to photography. "Today the woman who does not understand the use of the camera, be it pocket-kodak or of the folding type, is the exception," stated Juan Abel in a 1901 issue of *The Delineator*. Wiggins' work was described in this issue, along with that of Gertrude Käsebier and Zaida Ben-Yusef, in the first installment of a three-part article discussing women photographers and their work:

> The great Northwest has been productive of many brilliant photographers, and in Portland and Salem, Oregon, there is quite a coterie of workers who have made names for themselves in the East. Among these is Myra A. Wiggins, an amateur in the sense that she does not make photography her business. Mrs. Wiggins devotes her attention, when using the camera at all, to genre studies and landscapes . . . Many of her pictures have won prizes in competitions, and others sold to manufacturers of wheat foodstuffs and other things. So successful, in fact, was Mrs. Wiggins that last year she came to New York, stayed some weeks studying art and took a trip to the Paris Exposition and paid the entire expenses out of her prize-winnings of the previous year. And yet Mrs. Wiggins has but little time to devote to photography.

Abel did not expand on what else filled Wiggins' time, but added that she "manages to get into her landscapes a certain softness, or atmosphere as it is called, in her distances which gives them great charm and raises her work well above the average. Her name is well known to all readers of photographic journals." To illustrate her work, Abel used "The Brook" and "Great Expectations," renamed "Hunger is the Best Sauce." Juan Abel's buoyant description of Wiggins indicated her respected status within the pictorial photography movement. She had learned many of her skills from magazines, and now she was positioned to be a mentor to those who wished to join the ranks of pictorial photographers.

At the end of 1901, two new images by Wiggins, "The Babe" and "Heimweih," appeared in the Second Chicago Salon and the Fourth Philadelphia Salon. The *Photo-Beacon* dedicated its September issue as a "Souvenir of the Chicago Photographic Salon." Out of 1,000 photographs submitted to the jury, 129 prints by 58 photographers including Wiggins, Steichen, and Stieglitz were chosen. The editor selected one image from each photographer for inclusion in the Souvenir issue, intending to "present to the photographic world a record of the state of American photographic art at the dawn of a new century."

Wiggins' photograph "The Babe," a variation on "The Mother," shows a seated Dutch woman with a child (Mildred) kneeling at the mother's side admiring an infant bundled in the mother's arms. The composition creates a triangle between mother, child, and babe, but with the same light and dark interplay as in "The Mother." It seemed an appropriate composition since Wiggins was described in the magazine as a photographer who produces "excellent work with strong feelings and pathos."

In December, 1901, *Western Camera Notes* highlighted Wiggins' "Heimweih," or "Homesickness," from the Philadelphia Salon. The magazine ranked "Heimweih" as "one of the best genre pictures in the Salon. It shows a mother and child looking out of the window. The surroundings are modern and American. The garb of the models is foreign and in the pose and the expression is that unsatisfied longing for the home country that tells the story in a pathetic manner and renders the title, while appropriate, wholly unnecessary."

The 1901 Philadelphia Salon proved to be a bittersweet success for Wiggins when Alfred Stieglitz, his circle of photographers, and most international photographers boycotted the salon. They disagreed with the conservative members of the Photographic Society of Philadelphia who felt that besides pictorial photographs, other types of photography also should be included in the show. One critic had lamented how the 1900 Philadelphia Salon had consisted of "one narrow, limited, and rather egotistical school . . . with too few clearly conceived, thoroughly expressed realities; too few real pictures, and too much trash." Despite these reactions, Wiggins still benefited from reviews in the national press praising her work displayed at the salon.

Back home in Oregon, Wiggins swept up more prizes. At the Portland Carnival, she won cash awards in four of five classes of art—a total of $85. The *Oregonian* described her photographs as if they were paintings, comparing them to watercolors, "full of atmosphere," with landscapes "wrapped in the full vapors of heaven."

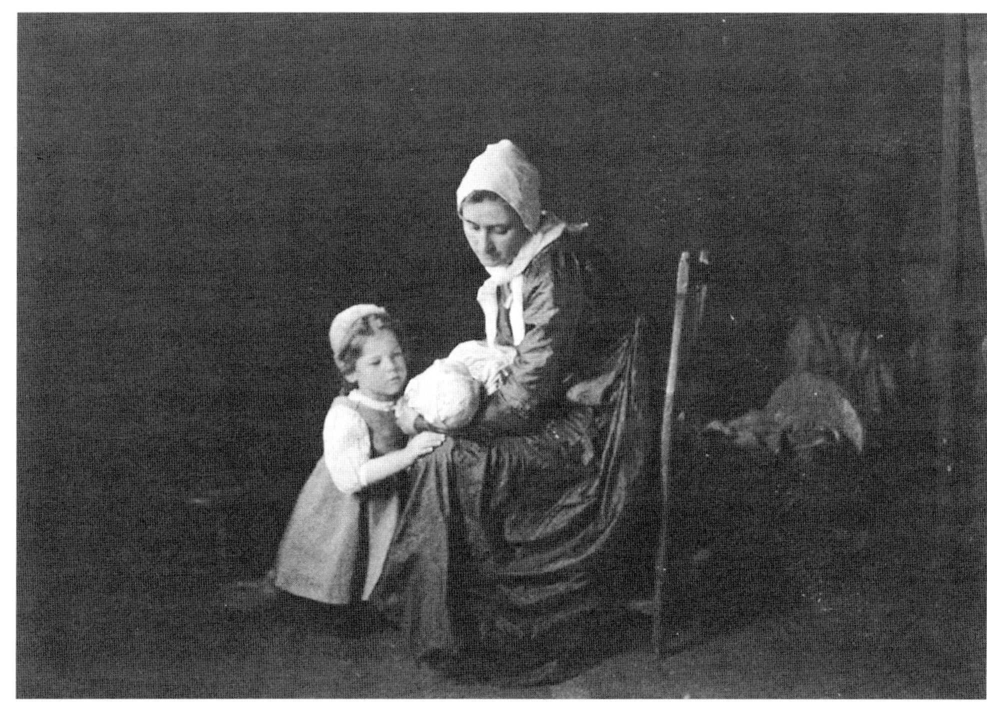

THE BABE
1901, platinum print
7" x 5"
Portland Art Museum

That summer, the Salem *Oregon-Statesman* referred to Wiggins and Helen Gatch as "two of Salem's prominent society ladies" who "have won high honors." The newspaper mentioned their winnings reported in the *Buffalo Express* of the previous December when Wiggins had placed second and Gatch third in a competition in New York. The *Oregon-Statesman* commented, "The *Express* in speaking of these ladies, shows some surprise that a single town would produce two such able artists, but their surprise would no doubt be greater if it were known that these ladies are near neighbors living on adjoining lots."

In January, 1902, *Camera Craft* reviewed the second San Francisco Salon, reproduced "Heimweih," and identified Wiggins as well as White, Ladd, and Gatch (whose work also hung in the

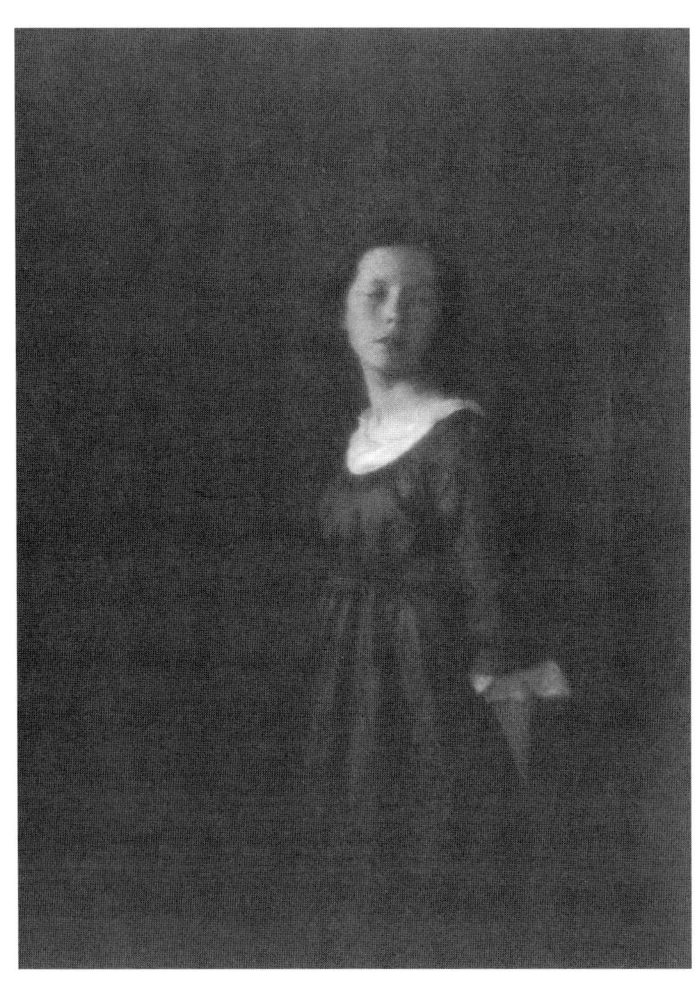

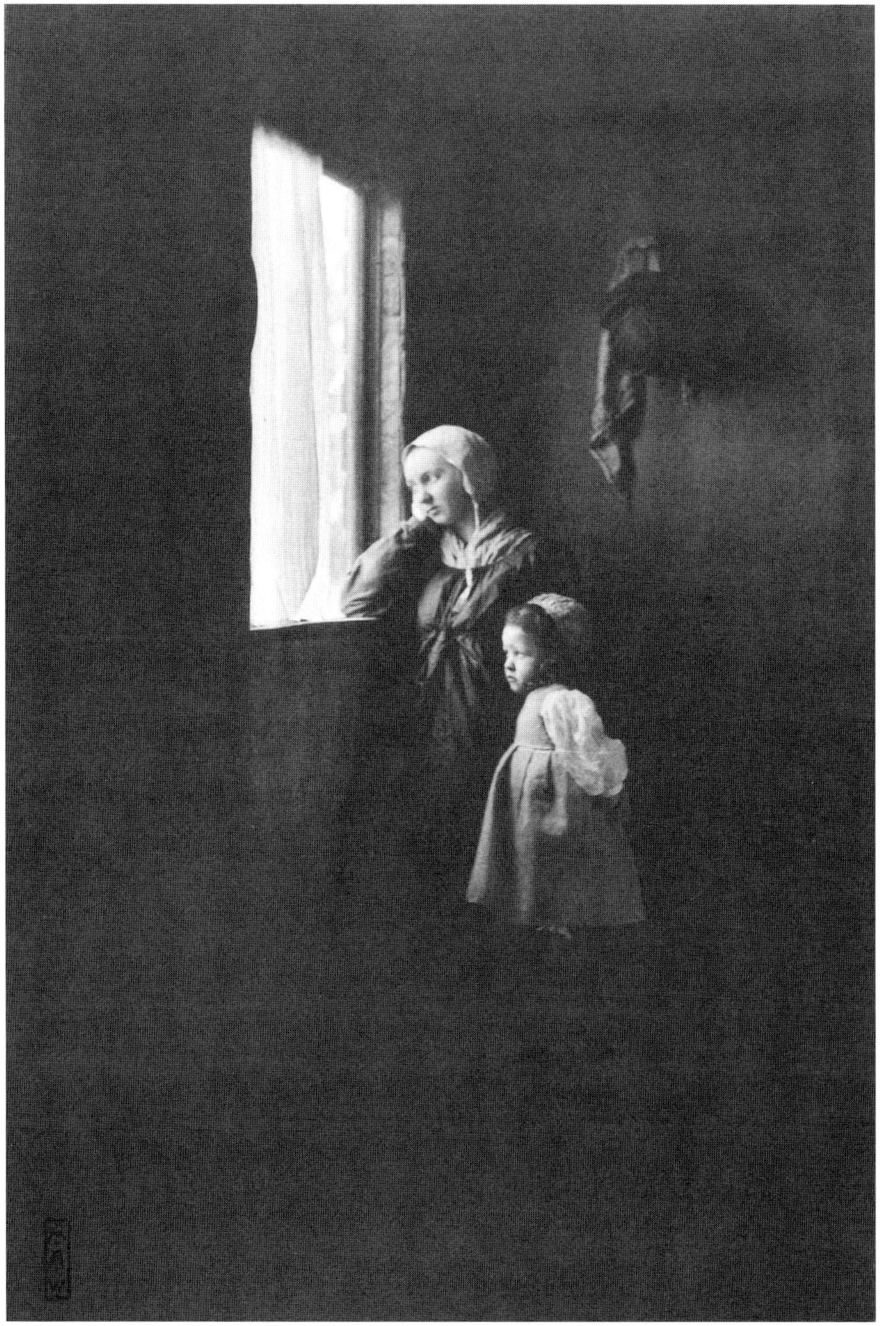

salon) as well-known Western photographers. A few weeks later, the Portland *Oregonian* reproduced "The Mother," describing it as "one of the Oregon art reproductions recently admitted to the San Francisco Salon" that "won the first prize of $100 in the Bausch & Lomb amateur photographic contest last summer."

This string of salon showings, competitions, prizes, and magazine acknowledgments and reproductions positioned Wiggins prominently within the photography hierarchy. She both contributed to and was a product of this establishment, which was created by photographers striving for recognition as artists and the reciprocal interaction of commercial enterprises profiting from supplying them and the general public with photographic materials and equipment. *Western Camera Notes* commented on Wiggins' proclivity for earning money: "Certainly there is no other class of amateur workers in any of the arts who are given so large an opportunity of paying expenses from the proceeds of their work. Receipts from such sources amount to much more than expenses in many cases; witness that of Mrs. Myra A. Wiggins of Salem, Oregon who, we are reliably informed, paid her way on a recent European trip from the proceeds accumulated during a few years from her prize winning photographs."

In the widely circulated *Camera Craft*, author Helen L. Davie recommended photography for women because it took them "out of doors, into sunshine and pure air. Instead of sitting down to her embroidery or lace work of yore, our photographer picks up her camera and starts in search of pictures." While reviewing the work of women across the country, including Käsebier, Ward, and Johnston, Davie mentioned Sarah Ladd and Lily White, "the excellence of whose work is widely known." Davie described Wiggins as a photographer "whose work is probably better known than any amateur on this coast." When it came to glorifying her profession, Wiggins could speak for herself: "There is no one thing which has aided me so much in my study of drawing and painting as Photography," wrote Wiggins, "and it is exceedingly interesting and profitable to study them together. Again Photography has taught me to see things pictorially, for why should one wander far from home seeking subjects, either in landscapes or models? . . . It has . . . revealed human nature to me and has given me valued friends and pleasant acquaintances. It has come to mean the seeking to reveal to others, through its means, glimpses of this world with 'God's great pictures hung.'"

Adding to her success, London's Linked Ring accepted her photograph, "Laverne," in the Tenth Annual Exhibition of The Photographic Salon held at the Dudley Gallery. The Linked Ring, formed in 1892, originally comprised a group of photographers who objected to the Royal Photographic Society's policies of exhibiting all forms of photography together and using painters to judge photographs. The members of the Linked Ring established The Photographic Salon to exhibit photographs "which in their opinion give evidence of personal artistic feeling and motive, quite apart from purely scientific and technical considerations." Here, Wiggins' work appeared with the most accomplished photographers of the United States and Europe. In her personal copy of the exhibition catalogue, Wiggins marked in blue pencil the names of some of her colleagues—Alfred Stieglitz, Eduard Steichen, Gertrude Käsebier, Alvin Langdon Coburn, Eva Watson Schütze, Rudolf Eickemeyer, and Zaida Ben-Yusef.

LAVERNE
1902, platinum print
6⅛" x 8⅛"
Portland Art Museum

HEIMWEIH
1901, platinum print
5⅛" x 8⅛"
Portland Art Museum

The simplicity and softness of "Laverne" were characteristic of the pictorial photographs exhibited in the salon. Wiggins eliminated background detail by blending the darkness of her model's dress and the textured wall, yet skillfully highlighting the neckline and cuffs. Downturned eyes and hidden hands suggest an innocence that contribute to the mood and atmosphere of the photograph.

Interestingly, in this same year Myra's "Heimweih" also hung in the salon of the Linked Ring's rival—the Royal Photographic Society. *Photograms of the Year* reproduced "Heimweih" and noted its appearance there. In expressing her personal style, vision, and technique, Wiggins proved her penchant for success even where battle lines existed between salons.

In December, 1902, Fred Wiggins, while in San Francisco, wrote to his wife (who was visiting Sarah Ladd in Portland) describing his meeting with *Camera Craft* editor Fayette Clute. Clute was "the soul of courtesy, and seemed more than glad to meet the 'Husband of Mrs. W,'" relayed Fred. He was "very much pleased to hear of your late success, and while Eastman has not yet published the list [Eastman's $4,000 competition], they have sent notices to most of the winners. [Oscar] Maurer received two $50 prizes, which so far as they know was the most received in Frisco. They wax loud in their praises of your work. Both Maurer and Genthe have new studios. I may try to see them."

Two days later, Fred wrote again:

> I have just returned from the camera club . . . There were only two men in the rooms, they were cataloguing the prints. They very kindly admitted me, and I looked the prints over. After I had finished I handed my card to one of the men . . . and as I did so I remarked that possibly they might know my wife better than myself. He looked at it and extending his hand introduced himself as Oscar Maurer, and his friend Mr. [William J.] Street. I of course knew them both by reputation and we had a very pleasant chat. Mr. Maurer complimented your work, in fact they both did. He thinks you were very lucky with Eastman . . . He took me down to his studio and showed me some of his work. His work is good. Very good, and he is one of the nicest fellows. You'd be struck on him I know. He was cordial with me, and was anxious to meet you some time. I think I will go up to see Mr. Genthe tomorrow if I have time. It will be a full day.

Acting as his wife's emissary became a sideline for Fred, a role supplemented by his skill as a salesman. Myra claimed five prizes totaling $260 in the Eastman contest, including $100 for her image "Family Cares." (In today's monetary value, that amount would equal roughly $4,000.) Business had brought Fred to San Francisco where he examined the newest line of farm machinery, plows, and bicycles, and test drove the new Knox Mobile, "a fine gasoline machine." In Salem in May, 1901, Fred had bought and consolidated E.F. Parkhurst's wagon and vehicle business and the E.M. Croisan farm machinery store into the F.A. Wiggins Implement House. He sold Studebaker wagons, buggies, surreys, McCormick harvesters, Syracuse plows, cream separators, bicycles, and sewing machines.

In April, 1902, the Eleventh Annual Exhibit of the Toronto Camera Club accepted "Through the Mist," presented an Award of Merit for "Heimweih," and included both Wiggins and Helen

Gatch (also accepted into the show) in their catalogue. *Camera Notes* reproduced "The Babe," elected third choice on the Camera Club Members' Competitive Print Exhibition ballot. Meanwhile, work by Ladd, White, and Wiggins also hung in the Annual Exhibition of Prints sponsored by the Camera Club of New York.

Ladd and White specialized in views of the pristine and picturesque Columbia River Gorge. Sometimes they even attributed an individual work to the both of them. The Columbia River winds its often turbulent, sometimes peaceful, path between perpendicular cliffs to the Pacific Ocean. Lily White traveled extensively in the gorge captaining her own houseboat, "The Raysark." According to one description, the Raysark was equipped with "an up-to-date darkroom with complete photographic outfit, including running water and every necessary detail . . . The Captain of the craft, an expert amateur photographer, was prepared at all times to photograph everything in sight, while the darkroom and all necessary photographic paraphernalia at hand made it possible to turn out at any time a finished picture." With Sarah Ladd and Maud Ainsworth, dubbed the "Hostess" and "First Mate," the three women recorded the beauty and changing moods of the Columbia River for posterity on the rich emulsion of platinum paper.

Spirited women like Wiggins, Ladd, and White were willing to defy the conventional expectation that women's roles in life should only be as nurturers and protectors of the home. Living in the West, however, probably eased their transition into the male-dominated world of work. Although most women willingly accepted the task of being caretakers of home and children, the social structure in the West often was tolerant enough to accept unconventional interests and behavior by females. Women living in the West became land-owners, ranch hands, hotel operators, shopkeepers, barbers, and photographers, and Western female artists, art teachers, lawyers, doctors, and journalists outnumbered their counterparts in the East.

Life in the West often required and allowed for self-sufficiency, independence, and inventiveness. As women such as Myra Wiggins took to the mountains on horseback, or spent time on houseboats on the river as did Lily White, their eccentric, "unladylike" behavior nevertheless probably attracted attention. Although houseboating was a fashion adopted from the East, a woman alone in the

Wiggins' Barn
Studio, Exterior
1901[?]-05, gelatin silver print
8" x 6"
Portland Art Museum

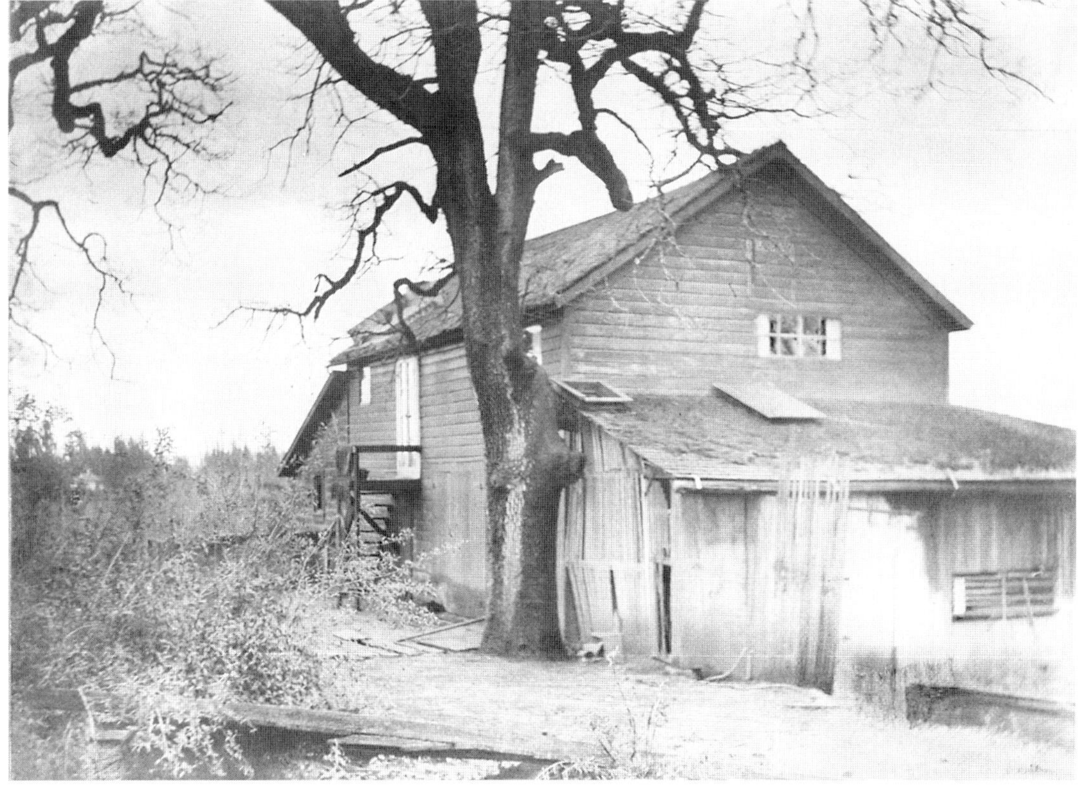

BARN STUDIO, INTERIOR
c. 1901-04, gelatin silver print
8⅛" x 6⅛"
Portland Art Museum

BARN STUDIO, INTERIOR
c. 1901-04, gelatin silver print
8" x 5⅜"
Portland Art Museum

manner of Lily White did raise eyebrows—but that only served to push her to greater self-reliance. As White put it, "a lone woman in a 'power boat' who comes out of the unknown distance up a lonely, wind-tossed river, must have appeared almost too independent . . . When a woman will step into the world of action and do a few vigorous things for herself, she may do all the rest!"

Certainly the results of their "unconventional" behavior came to the attention of Alfred Stieglitz, who was in the midst of his inner and public struggle to move amateur pictorial photography toward general acceptance by the art world. Like Wiggins' early views of Mt. Jefferson, Ladd's and White's skill in interpreting the landscape of the Columbia River was unique. Stieglitz showed confidence in Sarah Ladd's work when he sent it along with a selection of American photographs to an international invitational exhibition in Turin, Italy.

When Stieglitz formed the "Photo-Secession" in 1902, he provided the unique opportunity for photographers to unite in the common cause of promoting photography as art. The name Photo-Secession emerged from an exhibition that Stieglitz organized at the National Arts Club in New York that March. It represented a break from the conservative faction of the New York Camera Club and the Photographic Society of Philadelphia. At first, the Photo-Secession was more of a concept than a reference to a specific group of photographers, but it gradually emerged as a formal organization with Stieglitz as its leader. As the idea became reality, however, the Photo-Secession accelerated the transformation of pictorial photography into an accepted art form.

That summer, disagreements within the Camera Club of New York contributed to Stieglitz's resignation as editor of *Camera Notes*. Meanwhile, Stieglitz penned an appeal to assign photographers, instead of painters, as jurors at photography exhibitions. In the fall, Stieglitz announced his new upcoming serial publication, *Camera Work*, as "devoted to the furtherance of modern photography." These appeals and announcements published in *American Amateur Photographer* undoubtedly were read with great interest by Western photographers. The next pronouncement in January, 1903, defined the aims and the membership qualifications of the Photo-Secession. As Stieglitz explained, the object of the Photo-Secession was to advance photography "as applied to pictorial expression; to draw together those Americans practicing or otherwise interested in the art, and to hold from time to time, at varying places, exhibitions not necessarily limited to the productions of the Photo-Secessionists or to American work."

The Photo-Secession would consist of (1) a council with a director and twelve others to manage the affairs of the organization, (2) fellows chosen by the council, and (3) associates to be elected by the fellows. Associates would be entitled to "submit work to the jury at all Photo-Secession exhibitions" with "interest in the aims of the organization" as "the sole requirement" to become an associate.

Restrictions were placed on members: "In order that the Photo-Secession may exercise a potent influence upon the welfare of pictorial photography, each member will be duly advised by the Council of the attitude which the Photo-Secession will assume toward any important exhibition and whether it is deemed desirable that the members of the Photo-Secession shall exhibit as a body or individually." In a final assertion of authority, Stieglitz directed annual dues of five dollars and all communications to be sent to him at 1111 Madison Avenue, New York.

By this time, Wiggins' work was familiar to such Photo-Secession founding members as Stieglitz, Gertrude Käsebier, Clarence White, Joseph Keiley, and Eva Watson Schütze. Over the years, their work had appeared in the same salons, exhibitions, magazines, and catalogues as had Wiggins'. Not only was Wiggins renowned as a prize-winning photographer, but her Western colleagues, Sarah Ladd and Lily White, also were linked to the Camera Club of New York exhibitions and their photographs had appeared in national publications. Stieglitz's familiarity with the work of Wiggins, White, and Ladd, along with their enthusiasm, talent, and desire for affiliation in the Photo-Secession, led to their election as "Associates" on February 13, 1903.

The first issue of *Camera Work* appeared in January, 1903, highlighting the two London salons. The magazine's layout was designed by Eduard Steichen in a highly stylized Arts and Craft motif. *Camera Work* became a premier publication for avant-garde artists. Supervised by Stieglitz, every installment of *Camera Work* emerged as a work of art—from the quality of the heavy paper to the inserted photogravures. Even the advertisements were elegantly presented. The first issue listed Wiggins with 32 American photographers whose work appeared in the Tenth Annual London Salon of the Linked Ring that "proved in the opinion of all competent judges to have been the most noteworthy of the entire series."

Meanwhile, *American Amateur Photographer* continued as a forum for discussions regarding pictorial photography. In March, the magazine reviewed the proceedings at the annual dinner of

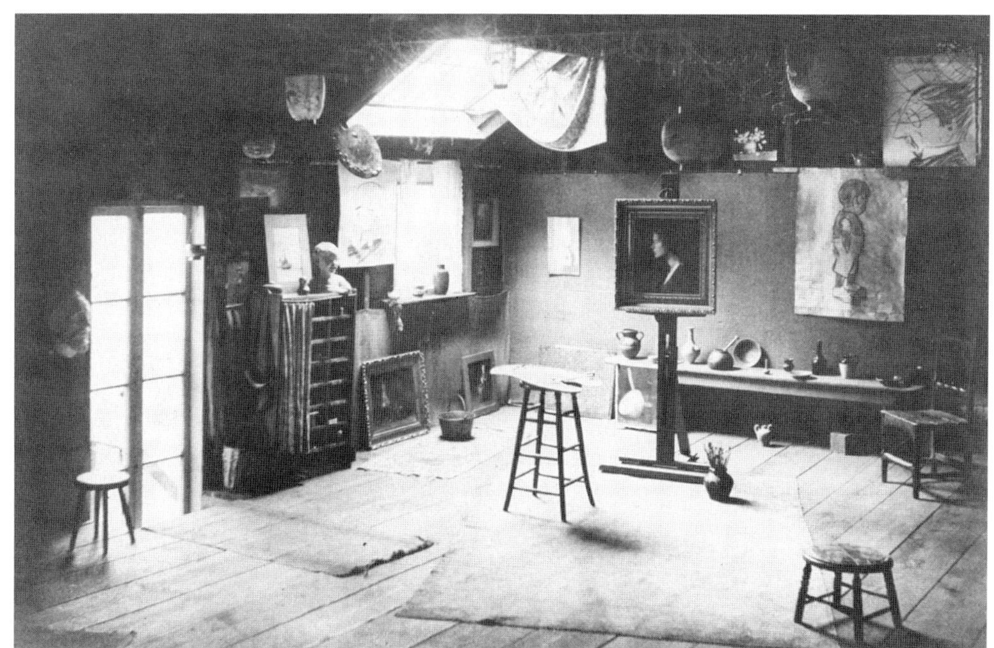

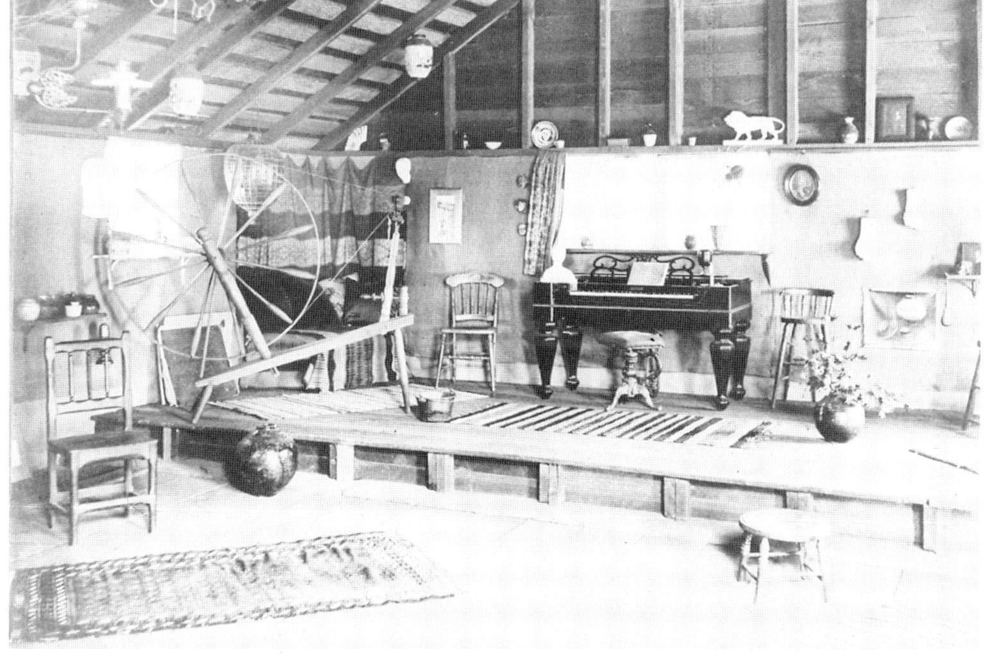

the Camera Club of New York, where Mr. D.S. Plumb, President of the Orange Camera Club, made the "plea that all sides get together so that there should be no need of any Photo-Secession." He recognized "the splendid success of Alfred Stieglitz as being the only American who had broken down the barriers of the Paris Salon against the admission of photographic work as an art or capable of art possibilities." To the applause of those present, Mr. Plumb decried "the so-called Photo-Secession idea; [he] wanted all to get together and work for the upbuilding of photography in its art aspects as well as any other." Clearly, the Photo-Secession was controversial. This same issue of the magazine published Wiggins' photograph "Indian Basket Maker," captioned "Folding Pocket Kodak and Brownie Pictures from Kodak Portfolio." Her photograph, with other work by Steichen and Oscar Maurer, illustrated an article titled "Edinal, an Ideal Developer for Bromide Paper."

In the May issue of *American Amateur Photographer*, a section on the Photo-Secession described the current activities of the group, referring to its work as a missionary effort. The group specified one aspect of its "progress" as "the collecting of the best work of its members for exhibition in all parts of the world." In recent weeks, Stieglitz had received invitations to send collections of prints to exhibitions in Wiesbaden, Germany; St. Petersburg, Russia; the Paris Salon; and Denver, Minneapolis, Cleveland, Rochester, and Toronto: "The Photo-Secession already includes 17 Fellows and twenty-eight Associates—literally extending from Maine to Oregon—three of the former and eight of the latter being women . . . and the best advice we can give to our readers is that they should do their best to become fit for admission into the charmed circle."

The July issue of *Camera Work* clarified the Photo-Secession's position by once again defining itself and listing council members, fellows, and associates. Stieglitz reasserted the group's exclusiveness by stating that associates are "eligible by reason of interest in, and sympathy with, the aims of the Secession . . . it has been found necessary to deny the application of many whose lukewarm interest in the cause . . . gave no promise of aiding the Secession."

The reason why Helen Gatch did not join the Photo-Secession is unknown. Either she did not try to do so, or she was refused admission, which might have created an awkward situation for the two neighbors in Salem. A few years later she rose through the ranks of the Salon Club, organized by Louis Fleckenstein of Faribault, Minnesota, and Carl Rau of La Crosse, Wisconsin, as an alternative to the Photo-Secession for amateur photographers. Wiggins' Photo-Secession membership, however, formalized her relationship, albeit distant, to her East coast colleagues and, at least historically, increased her prestige as an artist.

Myra continued to work at full speed while also conducting art classes in her barn studio. Meanwhile Fred, who enjoyed being in the "vanguard of progress," had a business telephone and sold the first automobile in Salem—a model E Rambler purchased by George Graves in the spring of 1903 for $900. With a six horsepower motor, it could travel up to thirty miles per hour. For his father-in-law (John Albert), Fred ordered a $2,000 second-hand White steamer shipped from Texas to Salem.

About this time, as Fred prepared to leave on a cross-country business trip by train, his relatives arrived from Kansas with the thought of moving to Salem. After Fred left on his business trip, the relatives were entirely in Myra's hands. From Omaha, Nebraska, Fred wrote to his wife: "You are likely hustling around getting ready for church . . . I presume you will have had the folks out to church and tried to 'show off.' Be sure you do not make any brakes at such times my dear. You remember how you tried to show off to the Dutch lady in Holland and how you lost your balance on the wheel."

A few days later, Fred wrote from St. Louis: "Glad the folks are feeling more at home. Don't let Grandpa make you get up at all hours. If he wants to get out and milk the cow, let him, but you need not . . . I almost feel you are worn out darling—you looked so tired and worn the day I left. I wish I could see you and baby . . . You treat me so well."

Five days later from Chicago, he again answered Myra's correspondence in which she had expressed concerns over her housekeeper Alma, who for some reason had become disgruntled : "I am sorry dear that you have been so worn out. I do so wish that you might be able to take it easy. Say, about Alma. You must talk frankly to her and find out what she wants. If it's a question of the laundry or anything of that sort we must have that done out for the present. Keep everything together till I get home and I will fix things up all right."

Again from Chicago, May 8: "Your letter made me more homesick than any I have received yet. You seemed to be so alone in all your troubles. I know you are simply worrying yourself sick about the folks. Now my dear you carried the burden long enough. We have done all we can. Everything will come out all right. If they simply cannot and do not like Oregon you cannot help it. If after 33 years of Kansas cold and heat, drouth and flood, wind and storm, snow, slush and mud, together with chiggers, grasshoppers, cyclones and other attendant pleasures, they still wish and prefer Kansas, we can't help it. I have no fears however and in any case whatever the outcome, it is always alright [*sic*]. I am trying, as I have been for years, to look at everything for the best, for we have not the shaping of our destiny wholly."

Then, from Chicago on May 14 in a letter labeled "Private": "I am glad my dear that you can get away to Eugene [Oregon], and that you are feeling better. If I could get you in my very arms for a minute now wouldn't I love you hard. And my baby girl, the dear sweet baby. How I long for one of her tight hugs . . . I never prayed so hard for guidance in all my life as I have this week, and somehow, while I cannot help worrying, I am strangely calm and confident. I may have to go home without anything, but I am not losing sleep. I have used and am using the light God has given me, and I have confidence in him."

On May 23, from Chicago, in another letter labeled "Private": "My Dearest Little Girl . . . You always tell everything, your joys, your sorrows and all, so naturally that I can read every line and much that's in between. I fear that the presence of all the folks is too much for you. I was so sorry that I had to rush away before everything was settled . . . My dearest little girl, you are the sort that needs lots of love and affection and warmth."

Then on June 1, in Philadelphia: "Saw . . . Stieglitz, Keiley, and Mrs. Toedt in NY. They all were so kind and pleasant. Stieglitz came right down, dropped his work, and sat for half an hour, told me all about his work, about the club, and everything. Will tell you all when I get home." That same day, Fred traveled to Washington, D.C., where he wrote another "Private" letter: "My dear Little Wife and Baby Mildred, I must stick in a line or two, just from my heart. You realized what separation meant, two years ago, but I scarcely did, for I had Mildred. But I tell you I've found what it means to have a dear little wife and baby at the other side of the country, I've missed you so much."

Stieglitz probably talked to Fred about his ideas, hopes, and dreams for his newly formed group of pictorialists. But Myra's life had changed in unforeseeable directions. Far from the costume parties or the carefree times on Neskowin Beach, her days now were filled with domestic responsibilities, a child to care for, a recalcitrant housekeeper, art students to teach, a husband about to return from a business trip empty-handed, and in-laws who frowned upon her independence and life as an artist.

In spite of these distractions, Wiggins continued to successfully enter photographs in national and international exhibitions. In the fall of 1903, *Camera Work* highlighted the American Collection in the Hamburg Jubilee Exhibition of the Hamburg Society Invitational. The list of exhibitors selected by Stieglitz looked like a Who's Who of amateur photographers, including Rudolph Eickemeyer, John Bullock, Alvin Langdon Coburn, Gertrude Käsebier, Joseph Keiley, Eva Watson Schütze, Eduard Steichen, Clarence White, and Myra Wiggins. In addition, the San Francisco Photographic Salon and the Linked Ring's London Salon accepted Wiggins' work.

The British magazine, *Photography*, issued a "Special Number" reviewing the London Salon:

> A closer view of the pictures, leads one to think them not a whit above the average, and worse still, a protracted visit confirms one in the belief that a large majority of these works will not wear . . . Six years ago, this exhibition would have taken the world by storm. Today the world finds it flat, stale, and unprofitable for the most part . . . Even the young and rising contributors seem to be treading in the soiled footprints of men gone the road before them. Freshness, pioneering, and naivity are conspicuous by their absence. There is no youth. The salon is worn out and blasé. Amateur photography of the artistic sort has stuck . . . All things considered, we consider Mrs. Wiggins' picture called 'Polishing Brass,' one of the finest in the whole room. It is certainly the most pictorial, and is exactly like a print after Chodowiecke, both in subject and feeling. A woman is seated at a table with metal utensils of quaint and interesting form. The whole thing is quiet, healthy, and exceedingly well-designed, and beautifully in keeping—an example for hundreds."

In her copy of the magazine, Wiggins penciled, "Best comment I ever had. The highest standard in the world."

In a crowning touch to Myra's achievements, the Bausch & Lomb contest awarded her the $150 first prize in the Dutch Genre category for her photograph, "The Edge of the Cliff." Wiggins regarded this exhibit as the "greatest contest from Art standpoint ever held up to this time." Bausch & Lomb published a 54 page catalogue with reproductions of the work, along with essays by 11 of the participants, including Stieglitz, Steichen, and Wiggins.

In the introduction, photographer Rudolph Eickemeyer, who was one of the judges, stated his belief, "this was one of the first contests of its kind in which a vigorous censorship was placed on the judges, the rules governing the competition being formulated and known to them and to all the contestants before the latter submitted their work." Furthermore, the main object of the competition was "to demonstrate the possibility of our [Bausch & Lomb] photographic lenses from the optical standpoint, that is under the most trying conditions optically." In his essay, Stieglitz, the grand prize winner, propounded his Photo-Secessionist ideals: "In all phases of human activity the tendency of the masses has been invariably towards ultra conservatism. Progress has been accomplished only by reason of the fanatical enthusiasm of the revolutionist, whose extreme teaching has saved the mass from utter inertia . . . those most deeply interested in the advancement of photography along the lines of art have been compelled to register their protest against the reactionary spirit of the masses." Its aim, he said referring to the Photo-Secession, "is loosely to hold together those Americans devoted to pictorial photography in their endeavor to compel its recognition, not as the handmaiden of art, but as a distinctive medium of individual expression."

On the next page, Eduard Steichen professed the qualities needed to create "the true spirit of the portrait, the virility and life that underlie the interpretation of character and personality of the sitter." Wiggins' essay, titled "Genre Photography," appeared two pages later. She asserted, "a picture that 'tells a story' interprets itself to the masses, stimulating the imagination of both savage and civilized." Wiggins then made a few suggestions: "Be sure that the setting is correct. The figures must live where you put them; they must wear their clothing, not simply put it on; they must be physically and mentally engaged in what they are doing—it is fatal to let your subjects hear the click of the shutter. The accessories must belong to the picture, but should be subordinated to the figure or group. Conversation often secures the desired facial expression of the model, and unless this is accomplished all your labor will be in vain."

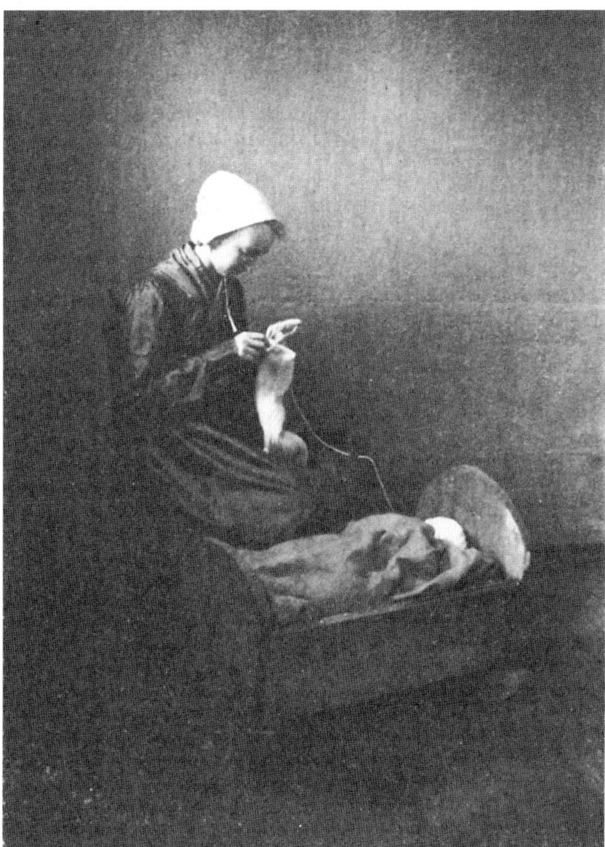

Family Cares
1902, gelatin silver print
12½" x 16¾"
Portland Art Museum

Wiggins' skill in handling her subjects and creating photographs literally positioned her beside Stieglitz and Steichen. In another coup, "The Edge of the Cliff" earned the Grand Award of $100 from the *Youth's Companion* Amateur Photography Competition. Next to "The Edge of the Cliff," reproduced on the cover of the New England edition, Wiggins wrote on her copy: "This was one of my six that won the Grand Award—I worked for it for years." She made pencil marks by the names of Emma Farnsworth, Mrs. Claud (Helen) Gatch, and Nellie Coutant—all honorable mention winners in the Women's division.

Stieglitz renamed "The Edge of the Cliff" as "Along the Cliff," and "Polishing Brass" as "At Work." Wiggins noted, "several of my photos have two titles because I sent them to Mr. Stieglitz to be framed at Of's and I think they were glassed before he noted the title and so he had to re-name them." Her photograph of the Dutch mother gently guiding her daughter along the ocean cliff became an important image for her, as did "Polishing Brass." They appeared in salons and magazines for the next seven years, and served as examples of excellent work in the field of pictorial photography.

The *Library of Practical Photography* used the two images in several of its editions, providing readers and students of photography with technical details about each picture. In "The Edge of the Cliff," the "object of the artist was to pose these two figures of mother and child in a proper setting. A lens of good focal length, with a fairly large aperture was used, and chief attention was paid to the figures. The background was so arranged that its general character was indicated without any one feature standing out assertively to divide attention with the mother and child. The result is that the figures stand out in bold relief and are not confused with the background. At the same time, there is no mistaking the general character of the cliff used as a setting for the figures. The white dress of the child contrasts well and balances the dark garments of the mother. Looking into the picture one feels that there is some appreciable distance from the foreground to the vanishing point in the background."

Another edition mentioned, "the weather was quite cloudy, and exposure was made late in the afternoon. The lens used was a Bausch & Lomb, with an open diaphragm. For exposure a cap was used, and made as quickly as the lens could be uncovered and covered. The plate used was a Cramer Medium Isochromatic; developer used was pyro, and the plate was controlled entirely in the developing, with no after manipulation. The print was made on a sepia platinum parchment."

"Polishing Brass," according to Myra, was "made with a north light near an ordinary window in my art studio. The exposure was made in the morning; lens used, Bausch & Lomb with an open stop; exposure given, 2 seconds; plate used, Seed, developed in Pyro with no after manipulations, printing process, Sepia Platinum, mounted on sepia-brown followed with salmon-color."

Wiggins left little to chance when creating her photographs. She paid careful attention to details, she knew her equipment and chemistry, and thoughtfully planned her compositions. She often printed on variant materials from negatives, ranging from heavy sepia platinum papers to delicate Japanese tissue prints. Even her choice of colored mounting papers contributed to the unity of the images.

As 1903 ended triumphantly, 1904 opened with equal success.

In January, "The Edge of the Cliff" and "Polishing Brass" hung in a Photo-Secession Exhibition of more than 150 photographs at the Corcoran Art Galleries in Washington, D.C. In February, the exhibit was doubled in size and moved to the Carnegie Art Institute in Pittsburgh.

"The Photo-Secession Exhibition in Pittsburgh is indisputably the most important and complete pictorial photographic exhibition ever held in this country," wrote art critic Sadakichi Hartmann. "I consider it a privilege to have viewed it." Within three weeks, about 11,000 visitors visited the 312-print exhibition.

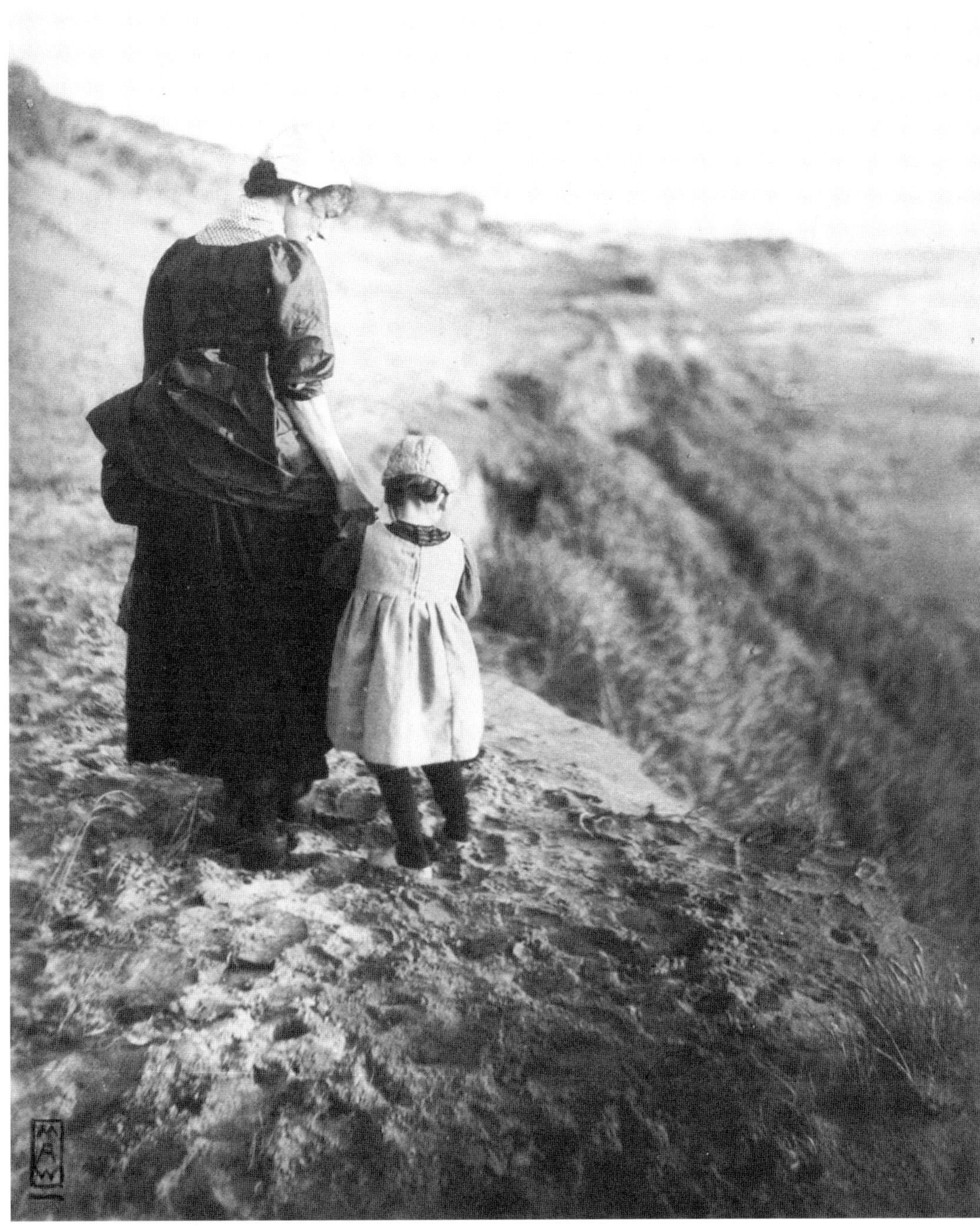

The Edge of the Cliff
1903, platinum print
6" x 8"
Portland Art Museum

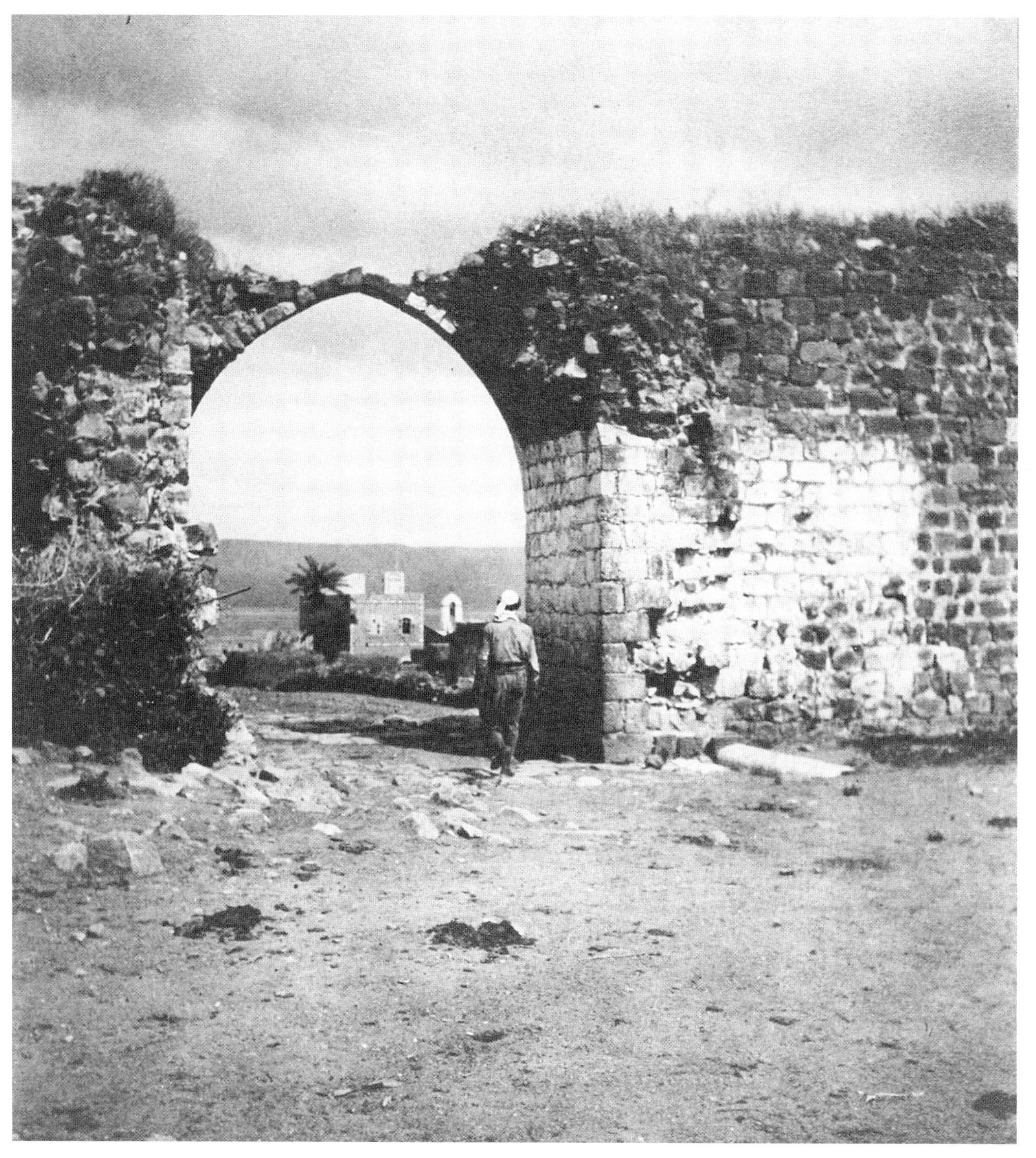

Part Six
1904

Myra Wiggins, always a cautious spender, saved her earnings and prepared to sail abroad once again—this time to the Middle East. One of five Oregon delegates on a "Cruise of the Christians," she would attend the World's Fourth Sunday School Convention in Jerusalem, April 18-23, 1904. The meeting was billed as a "crusade" that "will result in a vast spread of information concerning the ancient peoples and the Holy Land." Another delegate from Salem, Mrs. Lucille Park, a Bible teacher and instructor at Willamette University, accompanied Wiggins. On March 8, they sailed from New York City.

Wiggins' letters home were edited and printed as installments in the *Oregon-Statesman*, although about three weeks lapsed before the mail reached Salem from the Mediterranean. Excerpts from her unedited letters reveal her style of working and mode of traveling at the time, her concerns and anxieties, and the self-confidence that supported her desire for independence. They also indicate Wiggins' continuing business association with the Eastman Kodak Company, which by this time had established subsidiary offices around the world.

While in New York, she had searched for her Photo-Secession colleagues, as she explained in a letter to Fred written the day after embarkation:

> [March 9, 1904] One day out from New York . . . We had our salt water bath this morning and will sign for one every morning . . . Be sure to forward Fan's letter—did Mildred get hers from Fan? Fan [Frances Freiot Gilbert] and Frank [Gilbert] both nearly took my head off so to speak because I didn't bring Mildred . . . I think I will send you a bill of what I bought in N.Y. and you can put the amount in a letter to me can't you? . . . Lucille [Park] and I started to find Stieglitz—we went to the Camera Club first and did not find him, tried the telephone too but without result—the janitor told us to go to Steichen's just half a block away, but he was at the framers Of's so we tried Käsebier's next just a block away. She was away in Boston but we got a glimpse of her artistic studio. We then went to the framers and found Steichen but he could give me no definite dates for the foreign exhibitions—but he said that he would have Stieglitz write me. He was just sorting over the pictures from the Pittsburgh exhibit to ship that

Tiberias
1904, gelatin silver print
7¾" x 9⅞"
Portland Art Museum

day I think to Dresden—he showed me mine—"The Edge of the Cliff" with the glass all smashed so of course it won't go. He said Stieglitz had not seen the last I had sent him yet. He said the Salon at Haarlem, Holland was going to be a very important one also the Dresden one—I will strike the one at Paris too, then there is to be one at Bradford, England also. Steichen looks a genius. Hope to see his studio when I return.

Myra continued her frequent letter writing in the following days, revealing a wealth of information about her journey:

THE PARTHENON
1904, gelatin silver print
7¾" x 10½"
Portland Art Museum

[March 12, 1904] Saturday Evening, Aboard the steamer *Kurfürst*: We have just heard tonight that there are 804 passengers on board and 385 men running the boat including the stewardesses. I loaded up my new camera today and am using up a six exposure film to try it. I snapped a picture of Dr. Jessup, an old white-haired man who gave us a beautiful and practical talk on how to behave ourselves in the foreign countries to which we are going. He was 49 years a missionary in Syria . . . we also heard from Miss Jesse Ackerman . . . this is her sixth trip around the world. We have prayers every morning now in a room in the front of the ship where there is a piano. Eastman's goods are on sale in that room; haven't found the darkroom yet.

[March 16] I had a nice letter from Eastman and they allowed me $30 worth of goods instead of $20 which they owed me—were exceedingly polite at the branch office.

[March 17] A man took a snap at us with Papa's camera, but we were in the shade, so it may not be good. Eastman told me that I could get all the film I wanted aboard but for fear that I couldn't I bought about 6 or 7 rolls and it is a good thing that I did as I haven't been able to buy a single roll on board but can get more in Constantinople. I want to develop some tomorrow to see if my new camera is all right. I used both at Madeira.

[March 18] I haven't told you about a friend of ours who sits at our table—a Mr. Lorenz of Dayton, Ohio. He is a publisher, just music I think. He is a composer also; he gave me some songs to look over the other day and when I get home he is going to mail me some copies of them. They are very pretty and he wrote one of them. He likes my voice. Don't be frightened. He is a gray haired man and has four children. We saw their pictures. Mrs. P. asked him to come to our room to see a few of my photos which I have with me and he was "impressed." He has two cameras with him, one 5 x 7 . . . My arm has been all right since I left home, only it is weaker than the other one and two or three times I have strained it lifting something too heavy and then the old pain comes back for an instant. I think so many times how fortunate it was that I had it fixed that day, for I suffered almost constantly with it before especially at night.

[March 22] On the Mediterranean, between Algiers and Malta: We usually take a nap after luncheon as we don't get enough sleep (set watches forward 1/2 hour every night), but today I hurried to my room to develop so that I could finish by 2:30 when we have choir practice. I developed two rolls of film and was just five minutes late to practice. Then afterward I went back and tended to the negatives which were soaking . . . My films did not turn out very well today as I expected it was too dark on the narrow streets and the focus on my new camera bothers me. Papa's camera has something the matter with it too—every film has a partially unexposed streak at the side, on some it shows very plainly, on others faintly—think it is the bellows . . . I can hardly stand it not to see my husband and baby and not to even hear from them is almost unendurable but I just don't let myself think of it. I wish you could have seen us yesterday wandering around the streets of Algiers with the natives and I would have given a good deal for a picture of Mrs. Park as she sat on a bench in the park where I left her when I wandered in the square to take pictures—on the same bench with her were Arabs, negroes, Turks and regular tramps, but it was in the shade and I couldn't take the picture, however, I had a good laugh at her.

[March 26] I have seen the Acropolis! It is too wonderful for description . . . I have been wandering all morning over the ruins taking snapshots, which is very difficult to do successfully with small cameras as neither of them has a sliding lens board, therefore I have to lift them up a little to get the high columns . . . Of course, the Parthenon is the gem. Its majesty is indescribable even in ruins and what must it have been in all its glory!

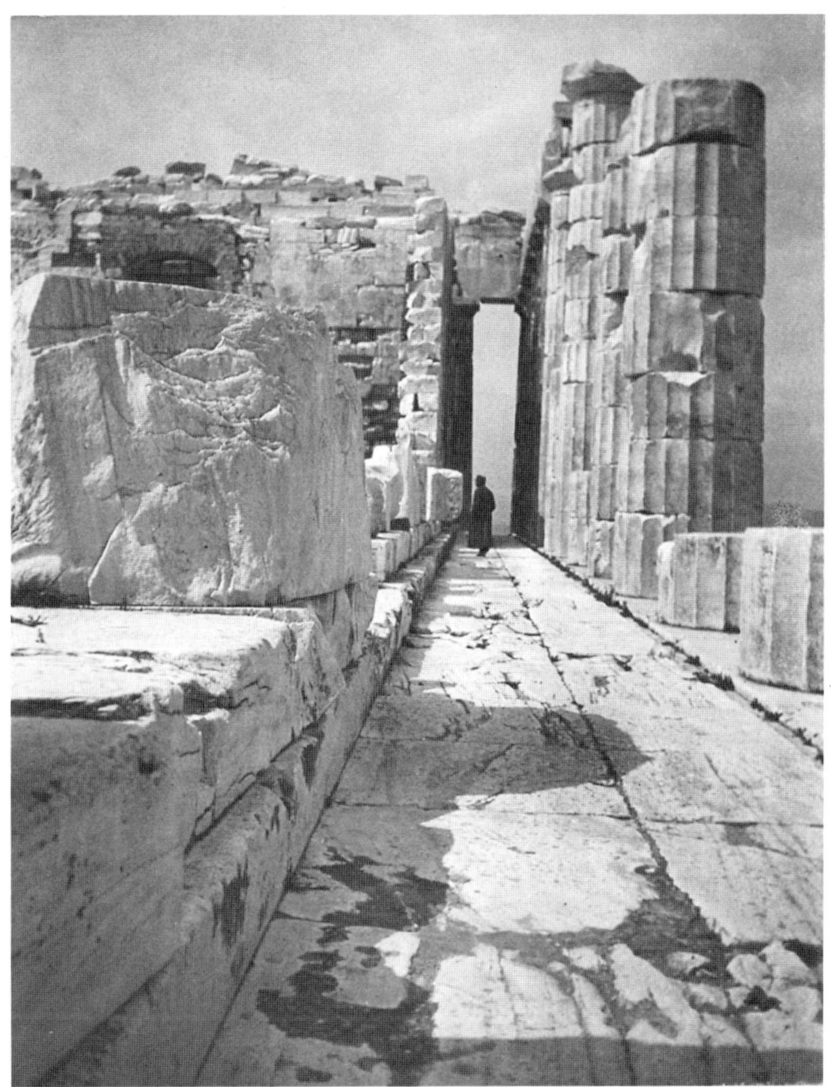

[April 2] On the Mediterranean Near Rhodes—[In Constantinople] We first drove to the Kodak shop where I bought 14 rolls of film paying about 10 cents more a roll than at N.Y., the regular price being about 15 cents more. I gave the man $20 and such a time as I had getting

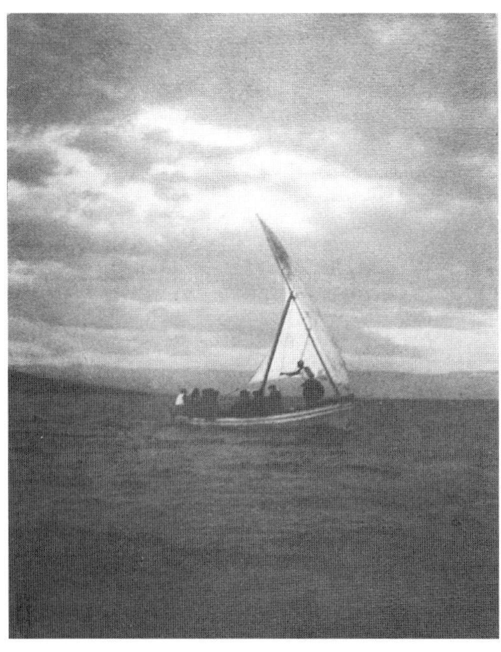

SEA OF GALILEE
1904, gelatin silver print
7¾" x 9¾"
Portland Art Museum

the right change; the guide stood in with the man and I stood for my self and stuck to it. The men I think were honest but did not understand the value of their money in English or American coin. It happened to be next door to "Cooks" so we waited till they opened (about half an hour) as the shop keeper was willing to let Cook's man settle the question—It paid to wait even if we did have to pay carriage hire, as I gained nearly $3 by it. After purchasing the films, which by the way I was so glad to get as it was impossible to get them on board and I had just about run out with practically all my trip before me.

[In regard to a Turkish rug she had bought from a vendor, she wrote:] It was very hard to bargain with him but I finally did get it $3 cheaper than his price. Mrs. Park said that "nobody could have done it but Mrs. Wiggins" . . . It was raining and everybody looked discouraged, especially those holding Ephesus side trip tickets, as we had been warned the evening before by Mr. Warren that it would be a very hard trip; about 5 miles of walking after we reached there . . . Mrs. Park and I with two or three hundred others decided to "do or die" and how glad we were . . . Ephesus; it is grand! . . . A caravan of camels was in Ephesus that day and I got some of the latter to pose for me. I wandered off into a field where they were—set up my tripod (for it was a dark day) and took portraits of the camels. Mrs. Park said they actually looked like they were posing for me. Twice they thought that I got a little too close and took after me. Of course I yelled, grabbed my camera and ran, greatly to the amusement of a group of Arabs . . . but it was no fun running for the ground was covered completely with squares of marble and stone . . . I wandered alone, when all of our crowd had started for the station, and got along all right till I took a picture of a hut, when a youngster picked up a big rock and threatened me, I motioned to him that the girl had given me permission. I threw him a penny then retraced my steps because I was afraid to go on. It was well that I did for when I was almost at the top of the hill above the huts nearly all the inhabitants began yelling at me and wanted money . . . I do hope some of the time pictures will be good for I couldn't take snapshots. When I told Mrs. Park my experience with the natives she said I could never get rid of her again, for she saw that she must take care of me; but I told her I could run and climb as fast as any of them. However I shall not do it again.

[Sunday, April 3, Easter] It is almost unbearable not being able to hear from you. We have wished so many times that we had told you to cable. You are just about having your Easter services now in the morning and I am praying for you all, for my heart is with you now and not here, and my dear baby too. I hope that God will keep us all safely and permit us to meet again.

[April 5, describing an excursion in a cavalcade of 23 carriages: Haifa] My three friends were all middle aged men with grey hair and I may as well confess that we all had a good time. Two of them were S.S. [Sunday School] superintendents and when they discovered that you were one too, we shook hands all around . . .

We had not gone far till we saw one of those primitive plows made of a crooked stick and pulled by two oxen. I was not about to miss my chance so I grabbed my camera sprang out of the hack while it was going, ran to the field took a snap shot and was returning on the run when the man at the plow took after me for "Backsheesh" (meaning "money" or "a present"). Well, I have never heard the last of it for of course, the whole cavalcade witnessed it and several of them said that they would give a good deal for a picture of me with my coat flying out behind and the man after me. I returned to the hack, jumped in while it was going, as I did not want to stop the whole line and was greeted by one of my friends thus, "Well you're a brick, you're worth a whole dozen of them" . . . We went out of our way a few rods to water our horses at the first well we passed. There were a number of girls there getting water and I tried to get a picture of them . . . I must write to Mr. Ward of London and ask him about the exhibitions as I am so afraid that I will not hear from Mr. Stieglitz in Rome.

[April 14] Jerusalem, Palestine: When we arrived at the Tomb of the Kings I first ran up the road to take a picture of some camels, then caught up with the party in time to light my candle and descended into the tombs (sort of catacombs). I left them there and came out, took a snap of the entrance then went up above and sat down; soon a man came along and sat down; soon a man came along and paid a woman to grind meal so that he could see the operation and I took a picture of her and the hand mill and a little later snapped her cooking at the fire outside. If they see you taking a picture of them you can't get away without paying "Backsheesh" and I can fool them nearly everytime for I cast my eyes high or to one side till they think I am taking it over their heads or to one side of them, and they never know it. One gentleman said, "Why you get more out of this trip than anybody I know of." It's hard to work though for if I want to get any pictures at all I have to keep ahead of the crowd all the time and we have a favorite guide who lets me do it; an old man named Solomon; he is as wise as his ancestor too, for when he sees me snap right and left without attracting unnecessary attention he plods along as if nothing had happened, with a shy wink at me. Another guide would perhaps tell the person in Arabic that he

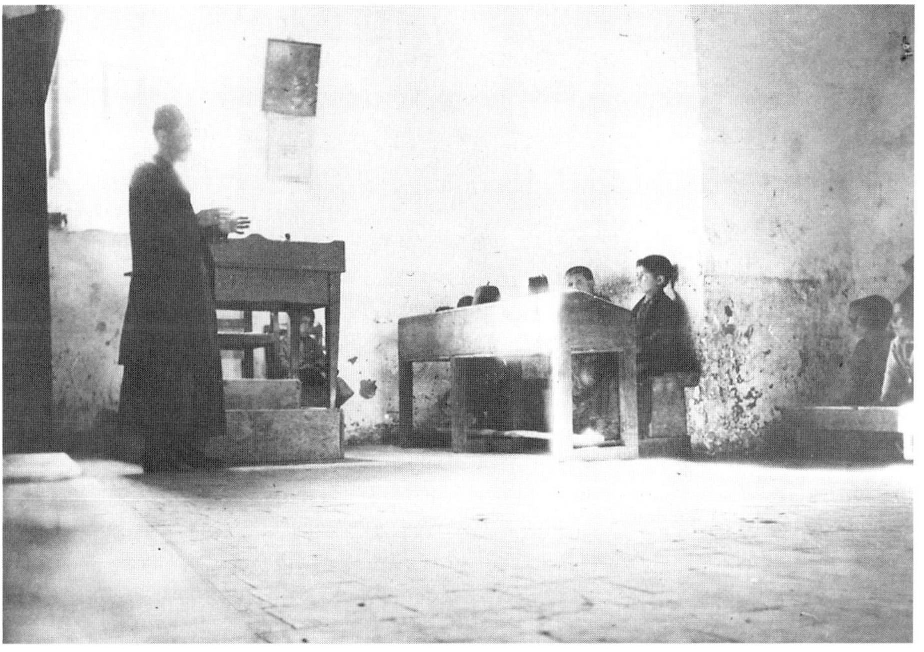

Arab Classroom
1904, gelatin silver print
9⅝" x 7"
Portland Art Museum

IN VENICE WATERS
1904, gelatin silver print
9⅜" x 6⅞"
Portland Art Museum

VENICE
1904, gelatin silver print
9½" x 7⅝"
Portland Art Museum

had been photographed or turn and stop or attract attention in many other ways . . . [Saturday morning] . . . bought $9 worth of films for Papa's camera . . . could not get one to fit mine, they were all taken; had to pay 90 cents each for all I bought, they sell regularly at $1.00 here . . . [Tuesday afternoon] I attended the convention this morning and took some pictures. The best session of the convention yet was yesterday morning. We learned so much about Jerusalem from native pastors and missionaries; they are doing such wonderful work.

[April 23, in a letter to Mildred from the Grand Continental Hotel in Cairo:] I want to tell you about a little girl that I saw at Nazareth . . . she bothered me very much begging at first, then she stopped begging and took hold of my hand and walked clear to the hotel with me—she tried to talk to me and I tried to tell her about my little girl away off in America . . . My little girl will soon be eight years old, I will send you something for your birthday, maybe from Rome. I hope that you are a good little girl and help Grandma all you can try and not be a bother to any of them for they are so kind to you—you must not let them spoil you with kindness either for Mamma wants to find the same sweet little girl when she returns . . . You must take good care of Papa and not let him get too lonesome.

[May 4, on the train from Rome to Naples] We drove to the Roman Forum—a place full of interest especially on account of the recent excavations within the last two years. The work is going on all the time; modern churches and houses are being torn down . . . I planted my camera on a rock to take a time picture . . . when a guard came running up to me telling me by signs that it was forbidden to take pictures of the place—I caught up with the guide and asked him about it and he said it was only the new excavations which photographers were forbidden to take pictures of. I took snapshots of some of the fine old columns and arches which are standing among the ruins . . . we drew up in front of the Catacombs of St. Donitilla . . . and all went through them with lighted candle. One enthusiast took a flashlight picture of a lighted altar and the rest of us with hand cameras seized the opportunity and aimed, too, but the result depends upon whether or not our cameras were perfectly steady. When going through those narrow, dark passages I could not help thinking how thankful we ought to be for our religious liberty . . . I forgot to say that the morning before I called for letters and only rec'd one, from Alfred Stieglitz, notifying me of foreign exhibits.

[May 13, Venice, Grand Canal Hotel] Yesterday morning after we returned from Cook's we hired a gondola for an hour and a half at a franc (20 cents) an hour, giving orders to be taken through the smaller canals and it was just fine. I enjoyed every minute of it. Of course, I took some snapshots, but the high point of our gondola was in the way most of the time and the gondolier could not always turn to one side on account of other boats passing . . . Mrs. Park returned to the hotel and I went in search of a brass and copper store which we visited yesterday with our guide, but I preferred to bargain without him and save the commission. I bought such a pretty old brass tray, a bronze knocker (for future use), and a small copper pot, and I am so pleased with all three. After luncheon Mrs. Park took a nap, and I gathered together my sketching materials, hired a gondola and started out. I selected a pretty spot, dismissed the gondolier and started in. I was not without an audience from the first, but they were quite useful to me. From one I hired a chair, another, unasked, emptied my jug of water and brought me some fresh, two or three others shook from my umbrella the dust and ants of the bridge, another brought me some refreshments, and still another acted as critic.

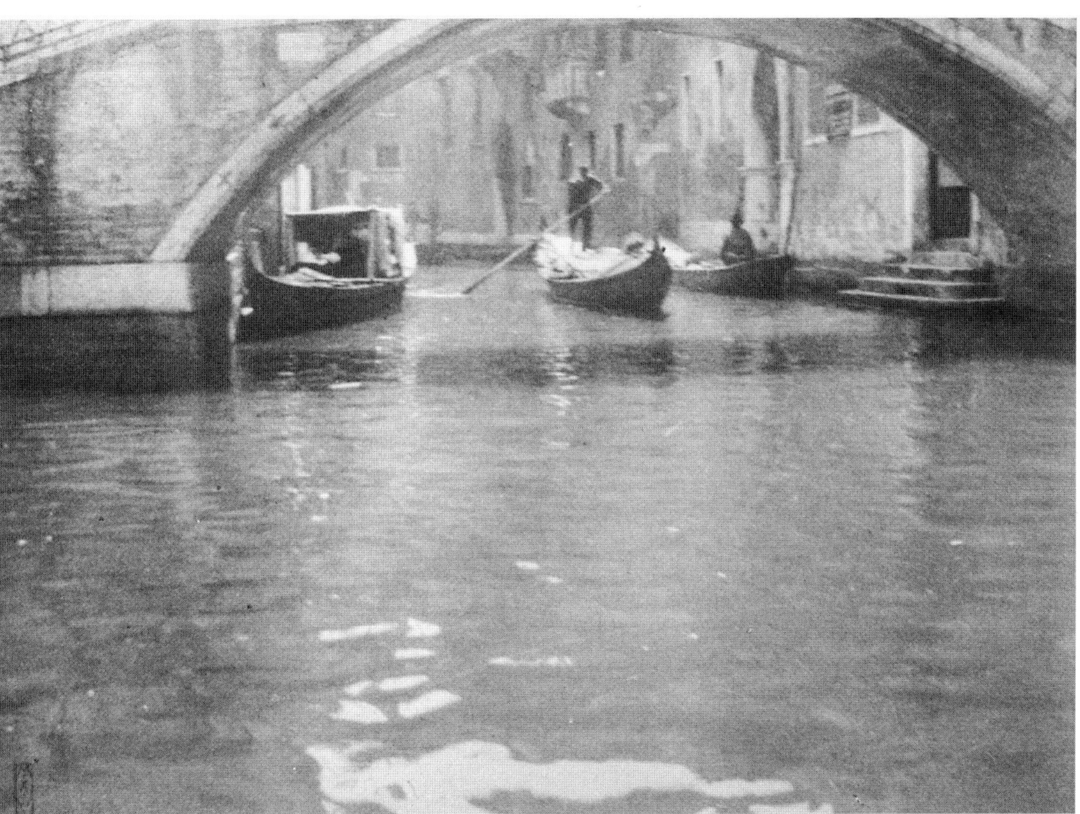

[May 26, Midland Hotel, Bradford, England] We are spending the night here at Bradford where we arrived at four-thirty this afternoon. I came to see the Photographic Exhibition, as it was an important one . . . Lets see, the last letter I wrote you was at Paris Sunday afternoon . . . Monday morning Mrs. Park took the Cook's drive . . . I had the same drive four years ago with Papa. I first hunted up the "Photo Club de Paris" and there learned that the Photographic Salon was being held in the Petit Palais . . . what was my surprise and delight to learn that the great yearly Salon (of paintings) was on . . . well I was there from ten to two o'clock and had a thoroughly good time . . . After taking luncheon in the building . . .
I crossed over to the Petit Palace, to the Photographic Salon and there I stayed until it closed at six o'clock. As I paid my franc and entered I

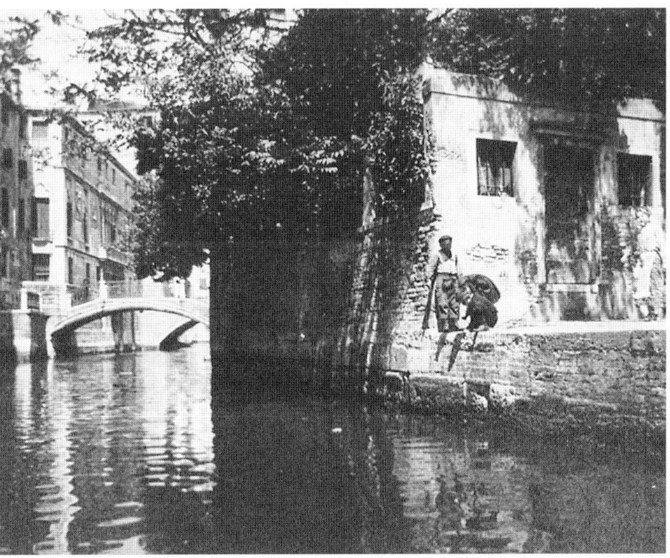

picked up one of the catalogues which were for sale near the door and in my best French asked the girl if the American work was listed in it, she answered yes, so I bought one and started in. You can imagine my surprise when I found that two of my pictures were hung and catalogued. I did not recognize them by their French names at first but soon puzzled out "Still Life" and the other one, "The Edge of the Cliff" the girl found for me. I think Mr. Stieglitz did not tell me, just for a surprise. The American work was splendid, ahead of everything, as usual, and it was the first real photographic Salon I had ever had the pleasure of visiting.

[June 6, *Kaiser Wilhem II*] Only one more day and we are due in New York! . . . my trunk is simply full of brass, copper, and green jugs.

When aboard ship for two months and while touring the Middle East and Europe, Wiggins juggled photography, singing, drawing, and writing—dashing from one activity to another. She seemed to enjoy the attention her talents received from her fellow travelers. Ironically, after eleven years as a photographer and with her work frequently appearing in exhibitions, catalogues, and publications, she had, for the first time, a chance to actually view a major photography salon when in Paris.

After Wiggins returned from this trip, which would be her last one abroad, she made 200 lantern slides, tinting many of them, and printed an album of large pictorial photographs taken during her travels. Also, small personal snapshots, many of Mrs. Park and Myra in various locales, were tipped into individual copies of Myra's book, *Letters From a Pilgrim*, published in December, 1904.

Wiggins rarely entered her travel photographs in competitions or submitted them to Stieglitz for exhibition although they stand out as finely composed, mood evoking examples of pictorial photography. When using her camera during her travels, Wiggins became the quiet observer, looking for the unique moment and place. "Arab Classroom" depicts children and their teacher in a natural setting. The seated children are dwarfed behind their desk and by the instructor beside a podium. His hands are blurred by the camera's slow shutter speed. Stone walls and floors infuse texture, while a square wall hanging creates a triangular connection with the children and instructor. In "Venice" the viewer's eyes are drawn over the water, past three children at its edge, and beyond to overhanging foliage and a bridge connecting the two sides of the image. A portion of the next bridge suggests a continuation of the scene. In "The Parthenon," a man standing among the columns provides a true sense of the height and grandeur of the ancient ruin. The pictorial elements in "Sea of Galilee" present a moody scene with dense atmosphere, churning water, and silhouetted men.

On a couple of occasions in December, 1904, Wiggins presented her lantern slides to the public. After the second presentation, a Salem newspaper stated:

> The second entertainment of Mrs. Myra Albert Wiggins at the Presbyterian Church last evening was attended by a larger audience than the first one a week before. Mrs. Wiggins showed views at Athens, Venice, Rome, in Egypt, Switzerland and Ireland, and the United States. Her explanations of the places and buildings and ruins and her own experiences in

securing the photographs were intensely interesting and vivid. Many of the plates were colored. This was done by Mrs. Wiggins herself, and could not be better done elsewhere. When she threw on the screen the view of the Sea of Galilee she held it there while she sang "Blue Galilee." When she came to Loch Lomond in Scotland, she did the same, singing "Loch Lomond" each time to the delight of her most interested and sympathetic audience. There was not a single person in attendance who was not highly entertained and instructed. The book by Mrs. Wiggins, entitled "Letters From a Pilgrim" describing her trip in company with Mrs. Park, is just off the press, and it will be on sale at the Statesman office and at the bookstores today at one dollar a copy.

In the midst of Myra's energy-filled routine, young Mildred adapted to her mother's unusual lifestyle. While her mother traveled and worked, Alma and relatives, including Myra's parents John and Mary Albert and her sister Blanche, helped care for Mildred. Mildred recalled that she visited Alma's mother in Turner, Oregon, about ten miles south of Salem, while her mother went to the Paris Exposition in 1900. "I liked that. I thought that was lots of fun because my bedroom had eaves to it and I liked to look out the eaves, through the windows that were slanted."

Mildred remembered cooking—particularly helping her father with breakfast, or preparing dinner—when she was eleven years old. "I liked to cook. It just seemed natural to me"—a sharp contrast to her mother who was uninterested in cooking and not one to invite people to her home for dinner. Mildred recalled, "If my mother had something else that was pending—that she had to do right away—we knew her art had to be taken care of. That was the way it was for my father and me. If my mother had things to do in connection with her art, that would be it, of course." Mildred helped her mother with negative and print developing in their bathroom. "We had a red light which when she wanted to develop anything I remember she had to make the room very dim."

Fred continued in his supportive role of his wife's career. Besides visiting Myra's photography colleagues during his travels, he handled her correspondence during her absences, helped hang her shows, and transported her paintings to exhibitions. "My father certainly helped when my mother had to have paintings taken some place for an exhibit," recalled Mildred. "My poor father; I can just see him helping her get somebody to get it shipped to a certain place at a certain time." A family member commented, "he was probably the best salesman for her art because he . . . was always putting her best foot forward, not always his, but hers. Fred was a marvelous salesman." As Fred wryly stated, "The only thing worse than being a lady artist is being married to a lady artist."

Fred gave Myra a most valuable gift. He allowed Myra to be Myra. On the surface it might appear they shared little in common. Fred grew up on a Kansas farm in a family that lived by a strict Protestant work ethic and considered art a frivolity. Myra came from a wealthy, more free-spirited family devoted to art and education. Fred began working at fourteen, whereas Myra went to New York and studied art for three years. Fred sold farm implements. Myra had no knowledge of farming. While Fred slept at night, his wife was a night owl, retiring to bed at four or five in the morning. In mid-life,

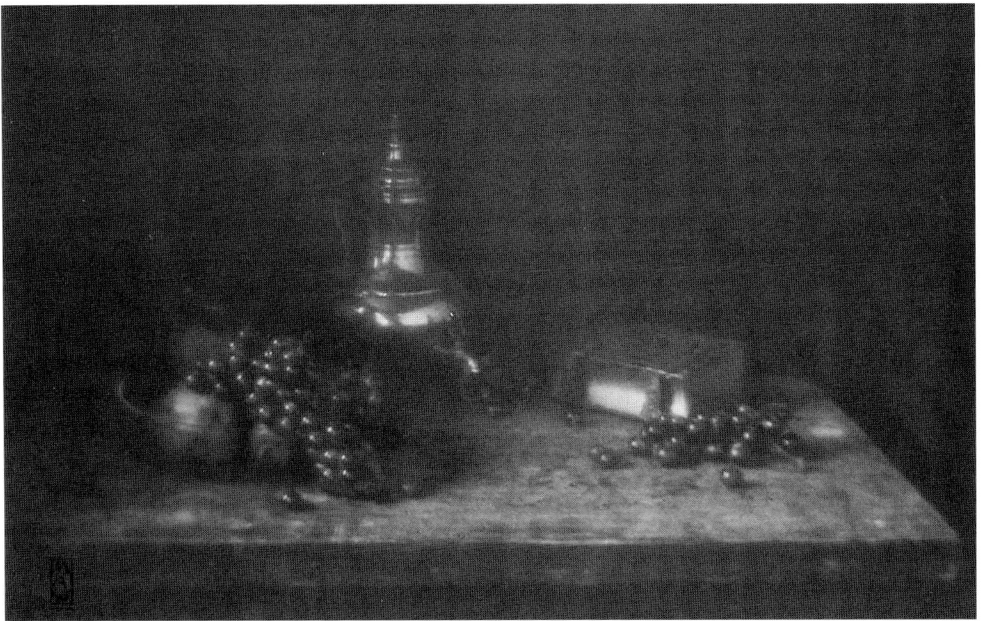

Still Life
1905, gelatin silver print
7⅜" x 4¾"
Portland Art Museum

Fred entered the nursery business. Myra admitted she knew nothing of gardening.

On the other hand, each was inventive and enthusiastic about life. Fred was a grand story-teller; Myra always had a twinkle in her eye. Although their careers absorbed their lives, they were devoted parents to Mildred. Both found comfort and strength in their Christian faith. Myra and Fred valued their independence and granted it to one another. Alone and together, they crossed the country by train dozens of times—Fred took over 100 trips.

Myra did not hesitate to voice her opinions or stand up for her beliefs. Her willingness to be argumentative became evident during her journey home from abroad in 1904. While in New York, she read an *Oregon-Statesman* editorial that was critical of the Oregon Building at the St. Louis World's Fair. Later in the week, at the St. Louis fair, Wiggins' visit to the Oregon Building prompted her to write a letter to the newspaper. She declared that the Oregon Building, instead of being a "poor forsaken looking log cabin, [was] the most artistic little building on the grounds. The whole of it was genuine, and, certainly showed it, in contrast with the sham on every side." She continued, "What was my surprise and delight upon entering our building, to find more than half a dozen comfortable rocking chairs, a couch, and in the center of one wall, a splendid old stone fireplace, which gave the room such a home-like air. I must mention, too, a great shaggy, black bear skin, which hung on one of the walls; this to me, was far more interesting than a whole room full of mediocre exhibits, such as so many state buildings show . . . I found the mud all and more than the editor found it, but for the rest, I feel it my duty to thus publicly disagree with him. Yours, for Oregon, Myra A. Wiggins."

After Wiggins' return to Salem, a number of publications and exhibitions featured her work. In August, *Photo-Era*'s special "Mother and Child Number," showed Wiggins' *Youth's Companion* grand prize-winner, "The Edge of the Cliff." In September, *The Photo-Miniature* used "The Edge of the Cliff," "Heimweih," and "Polishing Brass" to illustrate the article "Practical Methods of Development." "The Edge of the Cliff" appeared with the work of twelve other photographers in the German portfolio, *Die Kunst in Der Photographie* (The Art of Photography, 8th Edition). This portfolio, renowned for its high quality reproductions, was published quarterly between 1897 and 1908.

In 1904, Stieglitz sent 200 photographs representing the Photo-Secession, which included works by Myra Wiggins and Sarah Ladd, to the Hague International Photography Exhibition. *Camera Work* lauded the salon as "the first really important photographic exhibition held in Holland," and reported that "the Secession collection more than held its own and received universal praise." Around the same time, Wiggins independently submitted her work to the London Salon. Unfortunately, because of a misunderstanding by the hanging committee, her work—though approved by the jury—was neither catalogued nor hung.

Another Wiggins photograph, "Song of the Sea," illustrated Fayette Clute's article "The Western Workers in the United States" in *Photograms of the Year, 1904*. Clute asserted that Maude Ainsworth, Sarah Ladd, and Lily White "show such a variety in their work that to describe it would be almost as fallacious as it would be futile." He acknowledged that, "in Myra Albert Wiggins and Helen Gatch, both of Salem, Oregon, that State has two workers of whom it may well be proud. No exhibition is complete without a representation from them." Clute also discussed the formation of a Western Division of the Salon Club of America.

The Salon Club of America had emerged in December, 1903, out of a desire by pictorial photographers around the country to examine each other's photographs and ideas and to promote the work of new photographers. One activity of the club was to circulate a portfolio of the members' work for criticism and comments by other members. Recipients added a photograph of their own and sent the portfolio on to other members.

Under the leadership of the somewhat abrasive Curtis Bell, who was willing to challenge the potentate, Alfred Stieglitz, the Salon Club announced in March, 1904, that it was seeking submissions to the First American Photographic Salon, to be held in New York. On June 28, the American Federation of Photographic Societies emerged as an umbrella organization for the Salon Club, the camera clubs of Washington, D.C., Chicago, and Philadelphia, New York City's Metropolitan Camera Club of which Bell was president, and, soon, the Portland Society of Photographic Art. The group formed "for the purpose of a common exhibition on a nationwide scale" and elected Curtis Bell its president.

Wiggins had just returned from her trip abroad and was still in New York in June when Bell visited her and "tried to ensnare me," as she put it. "I was leaving New York for Oregon in fact, just packing my suitcase—when Curtis Bell called on me—he used all his powers of persuasion and even followed me to the elevated station in his endeavor to get me to join their ranks; he was so persistent that I finally was forced to give him a 'piece of my mind' and told him exactly what I thought of his club and of my club. I think Mr. Hartmann sent him to me."

Sadakichi Hartmann reviewed the Salon Club portfolio at Zaida Ben-Yusef's studio in New York. "The work is very promising," Hartmann wrote in *American Amateur Photographer*. "It is not yet exactly what the French call *arrivé*. The majority of the Salon Club members is still experimenting and searching for a manner of expression in which the characteristic qualities of photography may be most perfectly exhibited." He concluded by proclaiming that the formation of this group "sounds like an open revolt. And there may be an opposition! A duel between Messrs. Alfred Stieglitz and Curtis Bell would prove indeed a great attraction."

As critics like Hartmann fueled rivalry between the two groups, Stieglitz fired off a memorandum to Photo-Secession members urging them not to participate "in the so-termed First American Salon which is to be held in New York City this autumn."

In the September issue of *Photo-Beacon*, Stieglitz felt "compelled to thus publicly announce that the proposed exhibition will be of such a type or character that neither I nor the Photo-Secession can have any connection with it nor be represented therein."

Meanwhile, Helen Gatch represented her corner of the country as a member of the Salon Club Committee. In October, the salon's portfolio traveled to Salem, Oregon. The *Oregon-Statesman* announced its arrival at Gatch's home where it could be viewed the next week. Gatch would be adding one of her prints before sending the portfolio to the next location. Sarah Ladd's name also appeared on the newspaper's list of Oregon contributors, but Lily White and Myra Wiggins did not participate.

SONG OF THE SEA
1903, gelatin silver print
6" x 8"
Portland Art Museum

The next day's paper printed an article simply attributed to "Anon" that questioned why Wiggins was not included in the portfolio. When Myra was asked, "she explained that although invited by the promoters to participate, as a member of the Photo-Secession of New York she in common with the members of that organization, felt obliged to decline on account of certain principles for which their organization stands." As the account proceeded, it seems likely that Wiggins actually had a direct hand in the "Anon" article, which continued with, "The Photo-Secession of New York is an organization of pictorial photographers whose sole aim is the advancement of photography as an art. Mr. Stieglitz, said to be America's best known photographer, is the director and all work passed through his hands is accepted in any European photographic salon. In fact no foreign exhibit is considered complete without an exhibit from the Photo-Secession, and these collections are in such demand that the director is compelled to refuse more than half the requests."

The writer continued by listing numerous foreign locations where Secessionist work had appeared, and then suggested that "it is possible for the Lewis and Clark [Centennial Exposition, 1905] management to secure a Secession loan exhibit if the right steps are taken . . . The Metropolitan Camera Club of New York, a large organization with Curtis Bell at its head, stands in opposition to the Photo-Secession and it is said by the photographers to be unfortunate for the interest of photography that these two bodies cannot unite." The identities of "the photographers" quoted here—possibly Wiggins and Gatch—unfortunately are not mentioned, but the quote does seem to express a desire by them to resolve conflict.

Interestingly, in his *Photograms of the Year* article, Fayette Clute, also a portfolio participant, mentioned the need to limit Western Division members to thirty of the "best workers." His list of seventeen photographers invited to join included Helen Gatch, Sarah Ladd, and Myra Wiggins. If the *Statesman*'s list of participants was correct, then Sarah Ladd must have overlooked Stieglitz's objections. It is clear that Wiggins was invited to participate in the Western Division of the Salon Club, but declined on the basis of loyalty to the Photo-Secession. For Helen Gatch, the Salon Club offered the opportunity to participate in a national organization—an honor that Wiggins already had achieved.

The First American Photographic Salon, which included two of Gatch's pictures, opened December 5, 1904, at the Clausen Art Galleries in New York with lukewarm reviews from the press and extreme criticism from Stieglitz. On February 4, 1905, Wiggins wrote Stieglitz, "Am looking forward with pleasure to receiving the next number of Camera Work; have been so amused by the different reports on the 'American Salon' and hope that Camera Work will have something to say on the subject, as otherwise I will never know the true state of things."

The salon traveled next to Washington, Chicago, Boston, Toronto, San Francisco, and Portland (Oregon), where in April, 1905, it was honored as the first exhibition to be shown at the city's new art museum. The *Oregonian* suggested that "anyone having had misgivings as to photography being an art will have them dispelled upon visiting this Salon." A Second and Third American Photographic Salon were held later, with Gatch's continued involvement. However, many of the Salon Club's members eventually switched loyalties and joined the Photo-Secession. In March, 1907, Wiggins still quizzed Stieglitz: "What do those people of the American Salon and Met. Camera Club think of the Photo-Secession and its exhibitions etc. by this time."

Although conflict existed between the leadership of the two groups, the extent of any antagonism in Salem, Oregon, is uncertain. Myra's allegiance to the Photo-Secession and Gatch's to the Salon Club probably created some personal difficulties and awkwardness for the two women, despite having been friends and neighbors for years. Meanwhile, Wiggins and Sarah Ladd continued their interaction, and they, as well as Gatch, continued to make pictorial photographs in spite of the friction between Stieglitz and Bell.

Years later, writing in 1926, Wiggins recalled Gatch as being her friend and colleague. Perhaps Wiggins and Gatch simply were unwittingly caught up in a circumstantial situation beyond their control and larger than they desired.

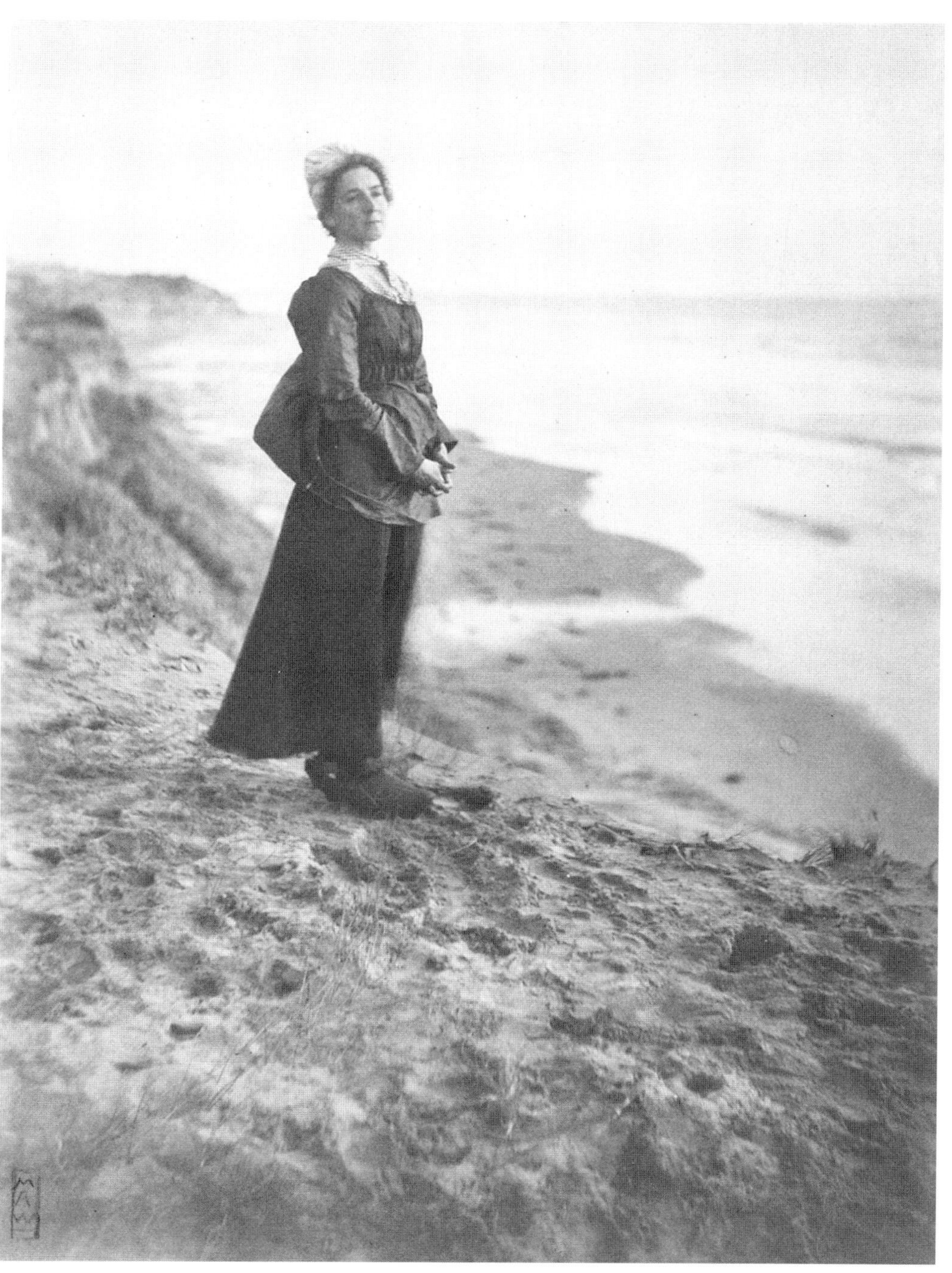

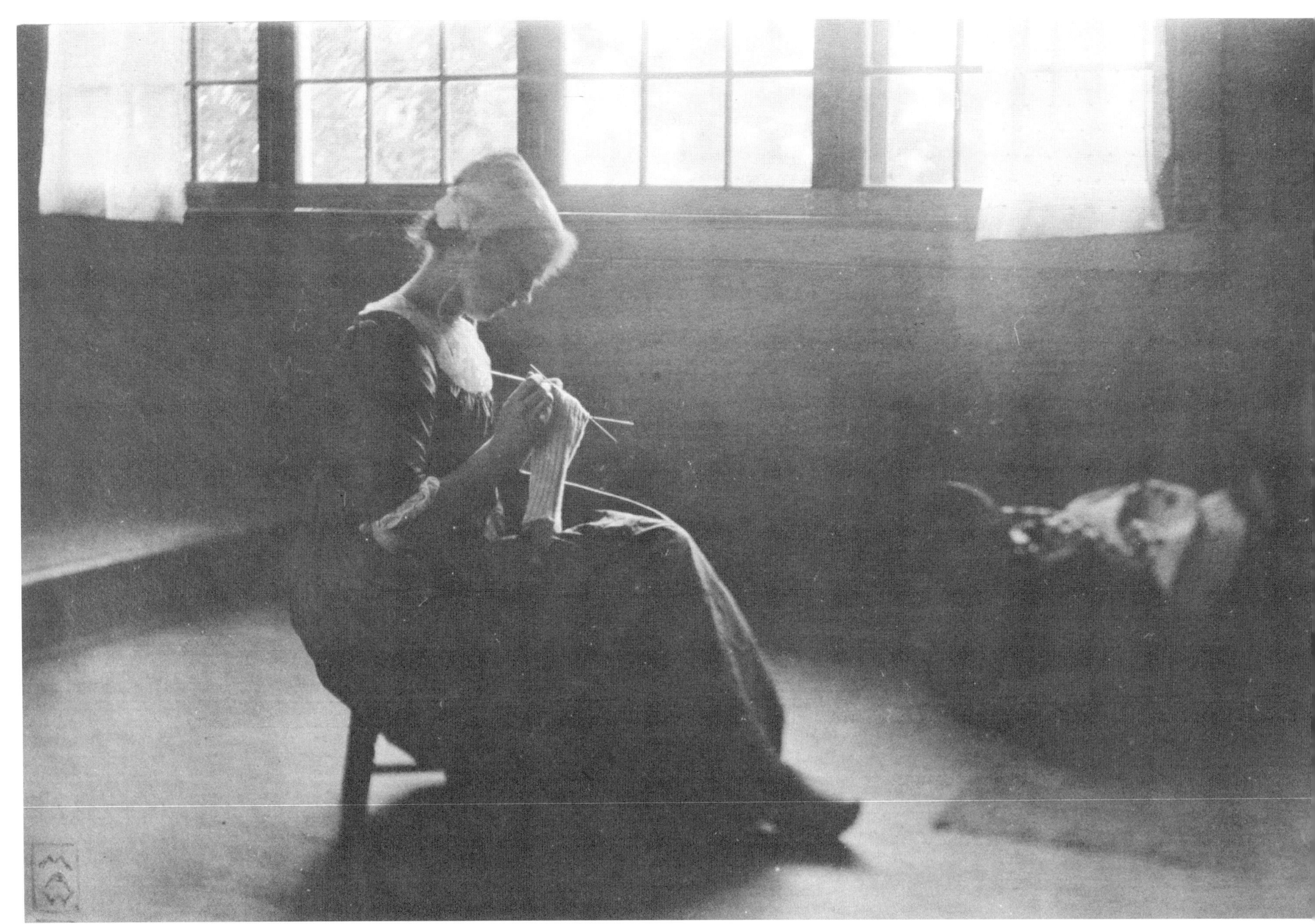

Part Seven

1905- 1910

In the United States and abroad, Myra achieved much of her success independent of the Photo-Secession, which both helped and hindered her ambitions. However, she responded with loyalty when Stieglitz expected it, although sometimes it was not in her best interest. "Even out here," wrote Wiggins to Stieglitz, "I have to suffer for the 'cause' when misleading items are published in the newspapers or my name doesn't appear in certain catalogues . . . then my friends look with pity upon me and I keep silent." She probably was referring to the friction when the Salon Club portfolio arrived in Salem and local newspaper accounts fueled a rift between the Salon Club and the Photo-Secession. Yet, for Wiggins, Photo-Secession membership signified her acceptance into the pictorialist fold and gave her the chance to participate in something bigger than what was available in the West.

Over the years, Catharine Weed Ward continued to support Wiggins' work. In *The Photogram,* Ward penned a column, "Women in Photography," commenting: "A worker whose results are models of composition and technique is Miss Frances Benjamin Johnston, best known here and in America by her figure studies, taken at home and in the studio. The magazines claim much of her work. She has been rivaled in the past few years by Mrs. Myra Albert Wiggins, who does exceedingly clever figure work, showing keen artistic perception, and her name is in more than one English catalogue."

It was during these years that Wiggins interspersed portrait work with her Dutch genre photographs. Again, she turned to friends and family as subject matter, creating likenesses stylistically similar to her published work and complete with her monogram applied to the lower corner. Her rendering of Harry Wentz conveys the quiet dignity of this remarkable Northwest landscape artist. The inverted white triangle of his shirt provides contrast to Myra's characteristic use of a dark background and opens up to his slightly uplifted face and pensive gaze. Wentz studied at the Art Students League shortly after Wiggins had attended there. He was a student of Frank Vincent DuMond, and soon became a fine instructor in his own right, as well as director of Portland's Museum Art School. In contrast to Myra's romanticized portrait of Wentz, her more sharply focused portrayal of her husband, Fred, depicts him as a dignified businessman:

Shadows
1905, gelatin silver print
6⅞" x 4½"
Portland Art Museum

his watch fob, textured three-piece suit, and relaxed pose suggests prosperity and leisure time.

In "Margaret," Myra's niece Margaret Rodgers portrays the emotional tenderness of childhood. With averted eyes and hands in pockets, she epitomizes the coyness and innocence of childhood, but also emanates sadness. In "My Pupil," a portrait of Genevieve Hailey, a shaft of light emphasizes the girl's bent arm supporting a palette. Genevieve gazes at the palette as if looking into a mirror.

In 1905, Stieglitz included Wiggins' "Still Life" in a Secessionist exhibit in Vienna, where "its collections were met with full appreciation and dominated the exhibition." Meanwhile, "Shadows" and "Hallowe'en" each won a $10 honorable mention in a 1905 Kodak Competition. Kodak published a catalogue of this exhibit, gleaned from over 28,000 prints submitted from around the world. The object of the Kodak exhibition, claimed the brochure, was "to show the charm of photography . . . the simplicity of the present photographic methods . . . and the art possibilities of photography." Kodak pointed out the versatility of the camera "for nature lovers, educators, parents, and travelers . . . for these, too, there is Witchery in Kodakery." Enchantment and ease of operation embodied the message Kodak relayed to consumers, and the competition format offered the means and encouragement for reaching these goals.

In 1905, Portland sponsored the Lewis and Clark Centennial Exposition commemorating the 100th anniversary of the Lewis and Clark Expedition's journey across the continent and arrival at the mouth of the Columbia River. The planners of the exposition were prominent men from throughout the state and included Myra's father, John Albert, who served as the fair's state commissioner from Salem. The centennial was the first international exposition under the patronage of the U.S. government to be held west of the Rocky Mountains. The exposition's authorities hoped to "bring to the attention of the rest of the world the present achievements and the splendid promise of the Pacific West in a form never before attempted."

Frank Vincent DuMond, the well-known New York painter and Wiggins' art teacher, directed the fine arts section of the fair. He planned to bring the best art in the country to Portland. DuMond had made frequent trips to Oregon to teach summer art classes and married one of his students, Helen Xavier, a native of Portland. As a great artist familiar with Oregon, DuMond was a sensible choice as exhibition director. But, much to the disillusionment of local artists, DuMond did not include Northwest art in the exhibit. Instead when he selected and installed paintings by the likes of Camille Corot, Mary Cassat, James Whistler, Kenyon Cox, William Merritt Chase, Gustave Courbet, and Claude Monet he created a sensational exhibit of work previously seen only in the East or Europe. DuMond felt this type of exhibit would prove that the West was not the crude and backward place many Easterners perceived it to be. "The proportion of works by masters is far higher than that of previous smaller events," DuMond stated, "and the standard of excellence is, therefore of necessity superior."

The photography section of the exposition was arranged at the last minute. *Camera Work* described the process in its July issue: "As we go to press, the Lewis and Clark Exposition in Portland, Oregon, opens. A great feature of this Exposition, is to be its art section which under the management of the painter, Mr. F.V. DuMond, of New

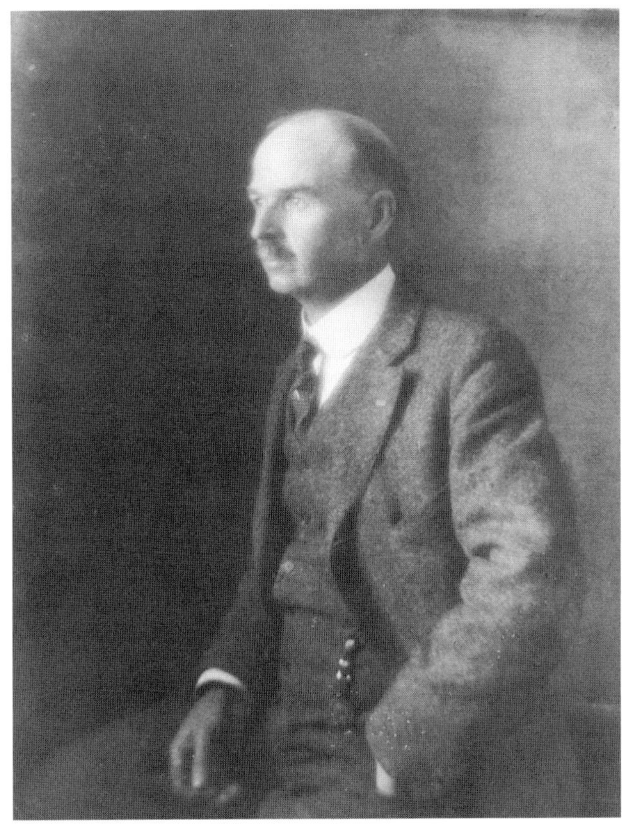

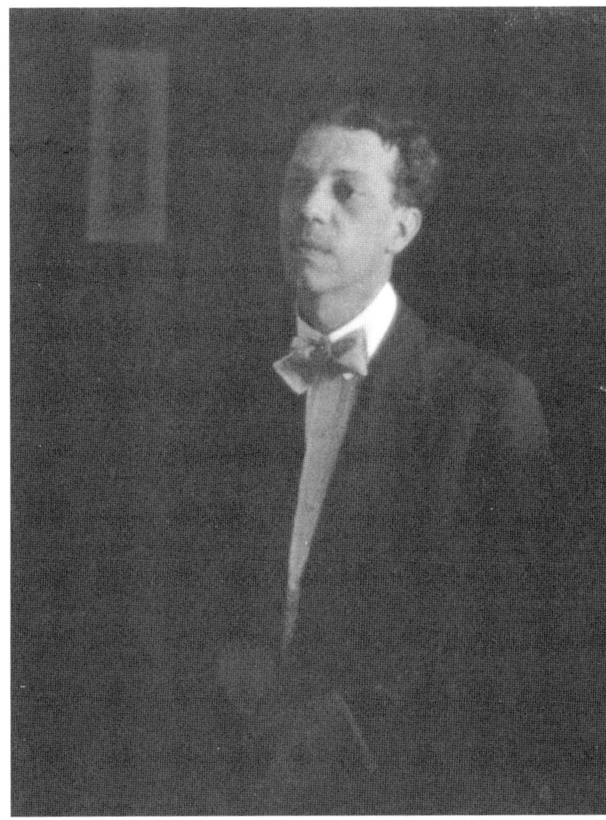

Portrait of Fred Wiggins
no date, gelatin silver print
6" x 7⅞"
Portland Art Museum

Wentz, the Artist
c. 1905, gelatin silver print
6¼" x 8¼"
Portland Art Museum

York, is by invitation only. A section of this exhibit has been devoted, under the same rules, to Pictorial photography. Mr. DuMond having appointed Messrs. A. Stieglitz, F. Benedict Herzog, president of the Camera Club, N.Y., Eduard Steichen and Joseph T. Keiley a committee to select 25 photographs worthy of exhibition . . . Naturally the task of the committee was unusually difficult, as not only did the invitation come at the eleventh hour—as inevitably seems to be the lot of photography—but the very limited number of twenty-five frames left no great scope."

The four members of the committee included their photographs in the exhibit along with the work of twelve others. Photographs by three women—Gertrude Käsebier, Sarah Sears, and Mary Devons—comprised only four of the 25 images. Four of the sixteen photographers were not Secessionists, including Herzog and Rudolph Eickemeyer, making it more a pictorial photography exhibit than a Secessionist one. They included one image by Seattle photographer Edward Curtis. The fact that the exhibit included no Oregon photographers probably reflected DuMond's personal vision of

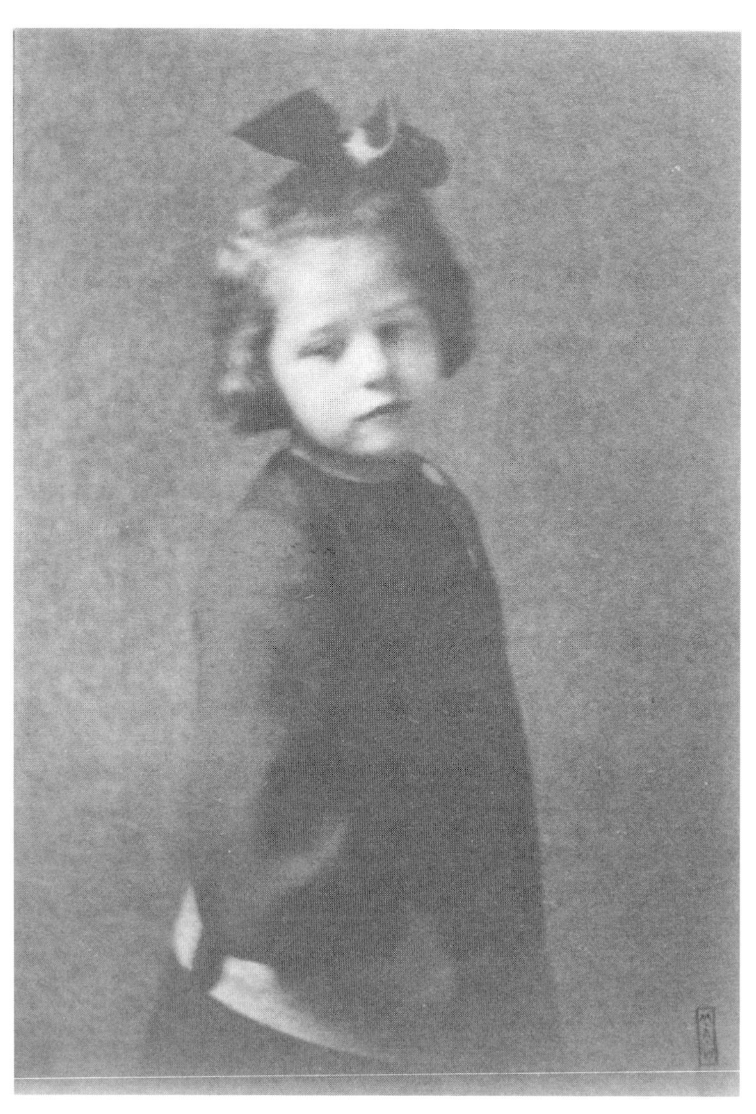

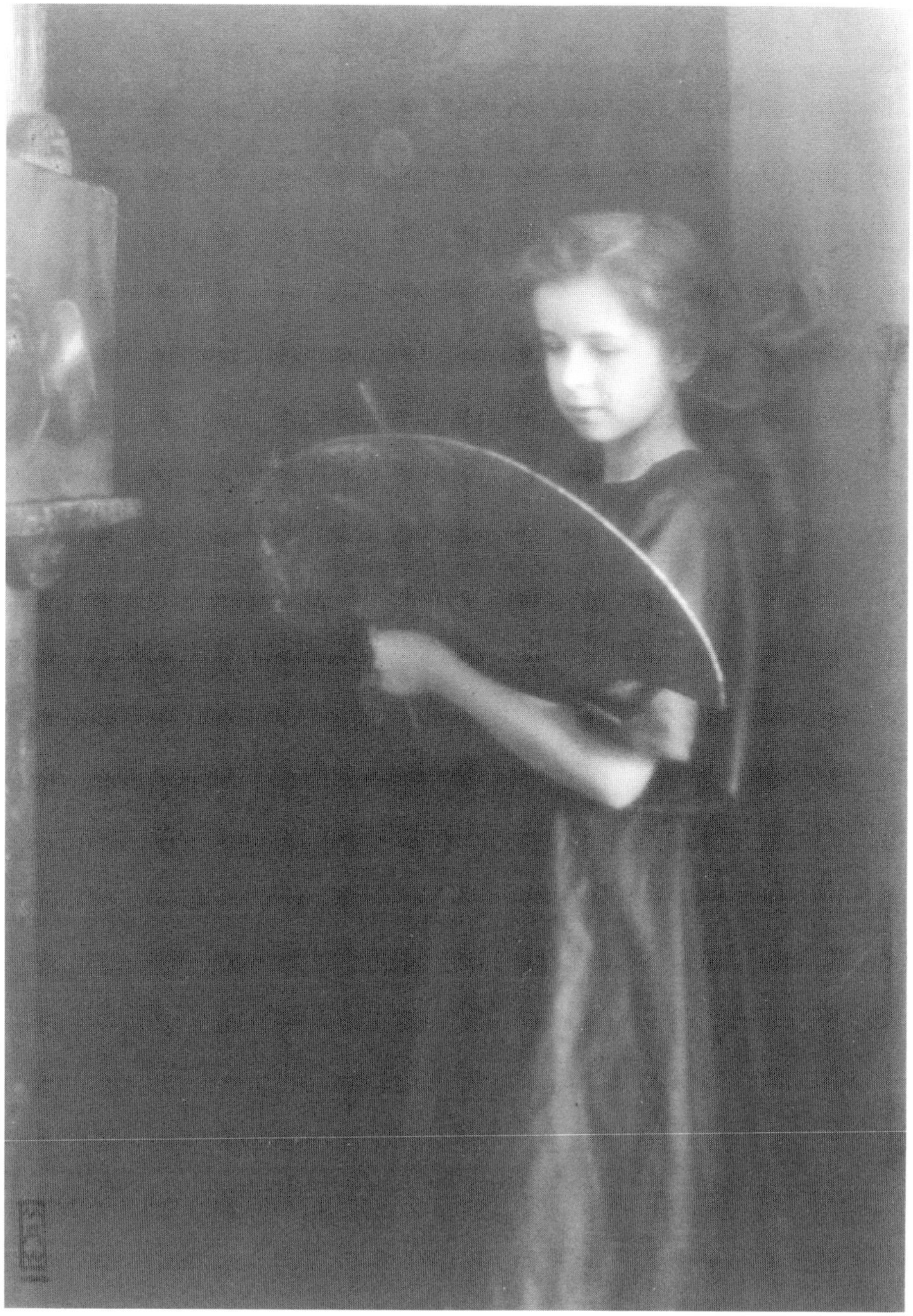

what the art section should be. Since no record exists of Wiggins' reaction to this exhibit, one can only imagine her disappointment at her exclusion.

In early July as the exposition attracted summer crowds, Myra's parents, John and Mary Albert, and their son Harry's wife, Stella, went for a drive in John's steam driven automobile. About eight o'clock in the evening in the Eola Hills outside Salem, they drove up a rocky incline leading to the old Rynearson rock quarry. Suddenly the car stalled, then began to roll backward, and the emergency brake failed. To avoid racing uncontrollably down the steep grade, John steered the car onto the uphill side of the road, but the car rolled over on its side throwing the three occupants onto the rocky ground. Stella and John escaped injury, but Mary sustained fractures of the right collar bone, three upper ribs on the right side, and the lower jaw bone on the left side. She also suffered severe bruises on the face. The doctor regarded her injuries as painful but not serious, and predicted a recovery in spite of her "delicate health." The expectation she would recover left family and friends all the more shocked when Mary Albert died two days later.

After the funeral on July 10, as mourners paid their respects and letters of condolence poured in, Myra's artistic disappointments must have seemed petty next to the grief for the loss of her mother. "My Dear Myra," wrote a friend, "It is not with the idea that I can lessen your grief I write this but only to let you know I am thinking of you daily and sympathizing deeply with you in your sad hour of trouble. Having lost a dear devoted parent myself I can feel for you and can realize how hard it is to give up your dear mother. But Myra we are given extra strength to bear these troubles and we must only think of them as gone ahead of us. I loved your mother dearly, she was so kind and lovely to me always. Time will reconcile you to your great loss so be brave dear girl and bear your burdens of sorrow as best you can . . . Your true friend, Agnes."

In November, Stieglitz wrote to Wiggins: "Thanks for your kind letter. I am sorry to hear that you have had so much trouble. It's life, I suppose, to be continually tried in some manner or other. A print or two of yours is to be put on our walls in the Secession Galleries. Our members interests are always well taken care of, I assure you, but not at the expense of Secession aims or ideals! Shall see to it that the desired prints are returned to you. Our little galleries are not quite in shape yet, due to strikes, etc., so the opening has been postponed until Nov. 20th."

Stieglitz was referring to the "Little Galleries of the Photo-Secession," later called "291" because of its address at 291 Fifth Avenue, New York. The gallery formally opened on November 24, 1905, with an exhibition of 100 photographs by Photo-Secession members. The exhibition catalogue did not list Wiggins as an exhibitor, nor did she ever mention the show in her records. If Stieglitz did omit Wiggins' work from the exhibit, it never seemed to affect her support for the Photo-Secession.

Stieglitz did not hear from Wiggins again until February 22, 1906, when she wrote: "I am sending you in this a draft for six dollars for my membership dues and one dollar extra to be used for the return of any of my prints which you may be through with . . . Has my print 'Early Morning' which I sent framed been shown at any exhibition? I am inquiring for the lady who owns it. What is the paper placquette which came from Holland—did every exhibitor receive one? Also the bronze plate from Vienna Photo Club—did every exhibitor receive

MARGARET
1903, gelatin silver print
6¼" x 8¼"
Portland Art Museum

MY PUPIL
c. 1900, gelatin silver print
5¼" x 7½"
Portland Art Museum

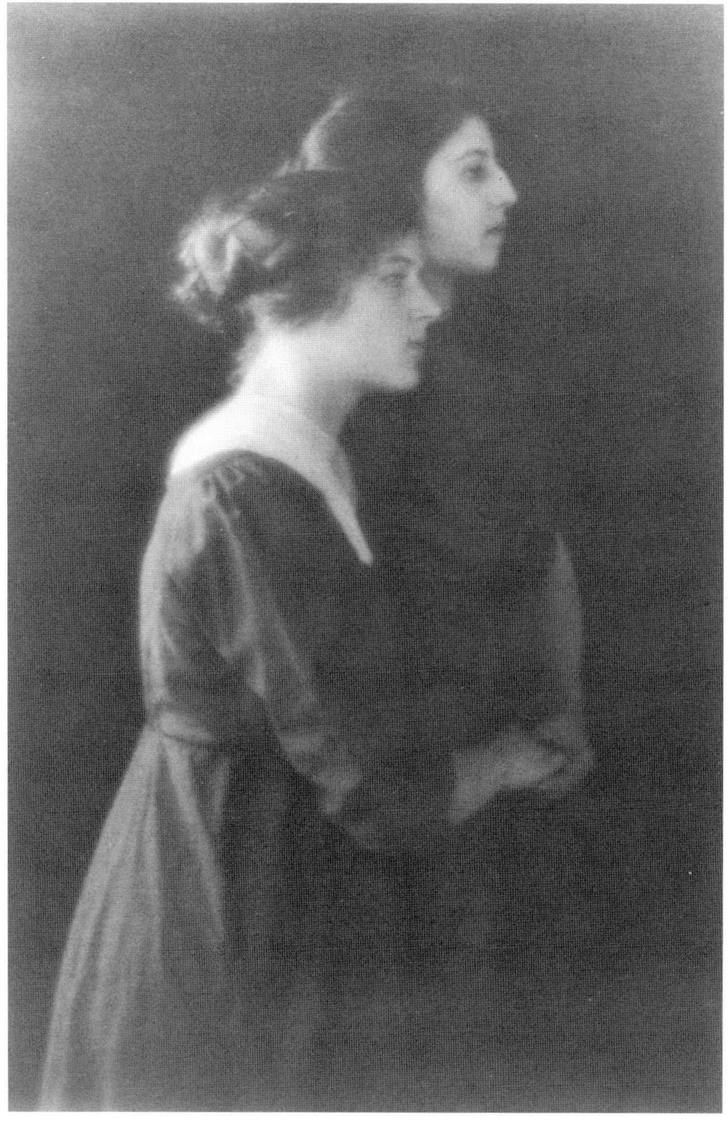

Friends (Mildred Wiggins and Margaret Ferr)
c. 1912, gelatine silver print
5¼" x 8⅛"
Portland Art Museum

one? . . . Am sorry that this letter requires an answer and I thank you for your last one. With thousands of others I appreciate the great work which you are carrying on almost alone."

By now, Wiggins' inquiries to Stieglitz indicate that a feeling of isolation began replacing her earlier enthusiasm and sense of belonging to the Photo-Secession. At the same time that she plied Stieglitz for information, she was apologetic for imposing on his time. Ignoring the fact that communication from Stieglitz was sparse, she did continue her support of the Photo-Secession. In characteristic fashion, despite her distress, she carried on, with her friendships and family offering her sustenance.

In March, 1906, Sarah Ladd wrote to ten-year-old Mildred: "I should like so much to come and see . . . you . . . but now I have been away five weeks, and there is much to look after. Miss White and the First-Mate are still away and will be for two weeks longer. We have a new launch now and we call her The Lark. Isn't that a pretty name? She is a big one—twice as big as the other, and has a cunning little kitchen or galley on board. Someday you must have a ride in her. She goes so much faster than the other, that we shall often use her for going to town. Tell your mother I have fourteen rolls of films to develop, and give her my love." Years later, Mildred recalled her excitement as a child when she "heard we were going on the houseboat."

An invitational exhibit, "The Work of the Women Photographers of America" organized by the Camera Club of Hartford, Connecticut, opened in April, 1906. This exhibition of "the leading women photographers of America," boasted a Hartford newspaper, was "the first time in the history of 'New Photography' that the women photographers have been invited to hold an exhibition exclusively of their own work." This show was the first of its kind since Frances Benjamin Johnston had organized the women's photography exhibition for the Paris Exposition in 1900. The organizers hung 154 pictures by 26 women, including Wiggins' "Polishing Brass" and "Early Morning," as well as work by Helen Gatch, Jesse Tarbox Beals and Alice Boughton from New York City, and Annie Brigman from

Oakland, California. Sadly, the exhibition never traveled beyond Hartford, Connecticut.

As the months passed, Wiggins felt more disconnected from her Eastern colleagues. Stieglitz did not need to reciprocate the loyalty he received from Wiggins. Moreover, her geographic isolation and growing domestic and financial distractions contributed to her current peripheral standing in the Photo-Secession. Whereas Helen Gatch at least had the opportunity to contribute to a traveling portfolio, Wiggins had no equivalent opportunity. Wiggins projected her frustration in an October letter:

> Dear Mr. Stieglitz, Enclosed please find $6.50 for my subscription for Camera Work for 1907. I have just learned of the members exhibition next month and am sending you today by express 5 platinum prints . . . I have also just learned through the Photographic Times that a certain size mount is desired but as it is so late I cannot remount now, however you are at liberty to have any of my prints remounted or framed at my expense. If I had been notified I could have sent them 2 weeks ago.
>
> This is the first work that I have done for more than a year and I miss the criticism of a true artist as there is no one here to whom I may show my work. I know you are too busy a man to give this criticism but it would be very helpful if some member of the Secession could do this for the members who are so far away from the art centers and keep them informed on exhibitions as to whether or not the Secession would show as a whole and then we would not attempt to show individually when the Secession had an exhibit. It does not seem right that you should have to attend to the correspondence and I thank you heartily for every letter that you have written me . . . P.S. Congratulations on the Little Galleries exhibitions!"

As a postscript, she listed "Prints—2 of 'Edge of the Wood,' 1 of 'Maidenhood,' 1 of 'In Venice Waters,' and 1 of 'Irene.'" Stieglitz hung "Edge of the Wood" in the Little Galleries Members Exhibition, November 10 to December 30, 1906. "Edge of the Wood," which is emblematic of Arts and Crafts convictions, depicts a soft focused group of carefree, playful children dancing in a timeless sylvan setting.

About this time, Fred Wiggins sold his implement store. With two Salem partners, he organized the Washington Nursery Company near the town of Toppenish in central Washington. Fred left Salem for Toppenish in 1906, with Myra and Mildred following in the next year. In March, 1907, Myra wrote Stieglitz: "We are moving away from Oregon and after April 15th my address will be Toppenish, Washington—Indians and sagebrush must hereafter be my inspiration, with now and then an irrigation ditch for variety—however we shall endeavor to make the desert 'blossom,' at least in spots as Mr. Wiggins has gone into the nursery business there."

The lack of enthusiasm in Myra's letter is not surprising. She had to leave behind her support system—friends, family, broader cultural opportunities, widespread regional artistic recognition, long-settled communities, a beautiful coastline, and mountains—the foundation of her personal and artistic life. Mildred felt "sure that my mother didn't want to come here. It was a strange place—she'd rather stay in Salem."

It was about 325 miles by train to Toppenish. From Salem, they probably stopped in Portland to

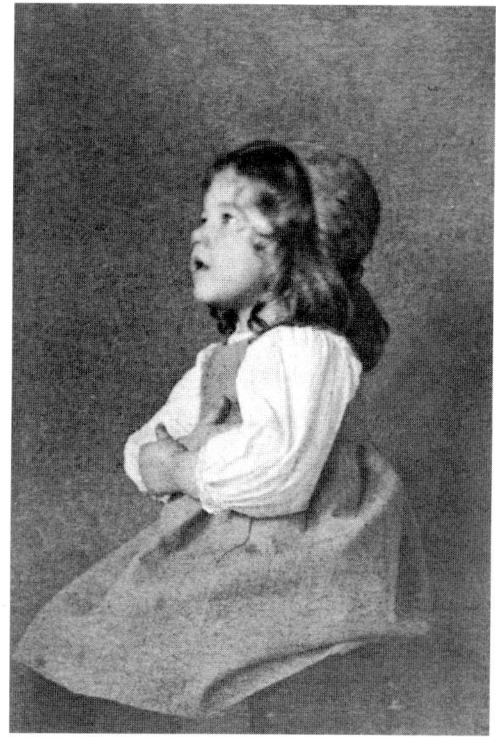

Portrait of Mildred (age 4)
1900-01, gelatin silver print
4⅛" x 6¼"
Portland Art Museum

EDGE OF THE WOOD
1906, platinum print
8" x 6"
Portland Art Museum

EARLY MORNING
1906, platinum print
8" x 6"
Portland Art Museum

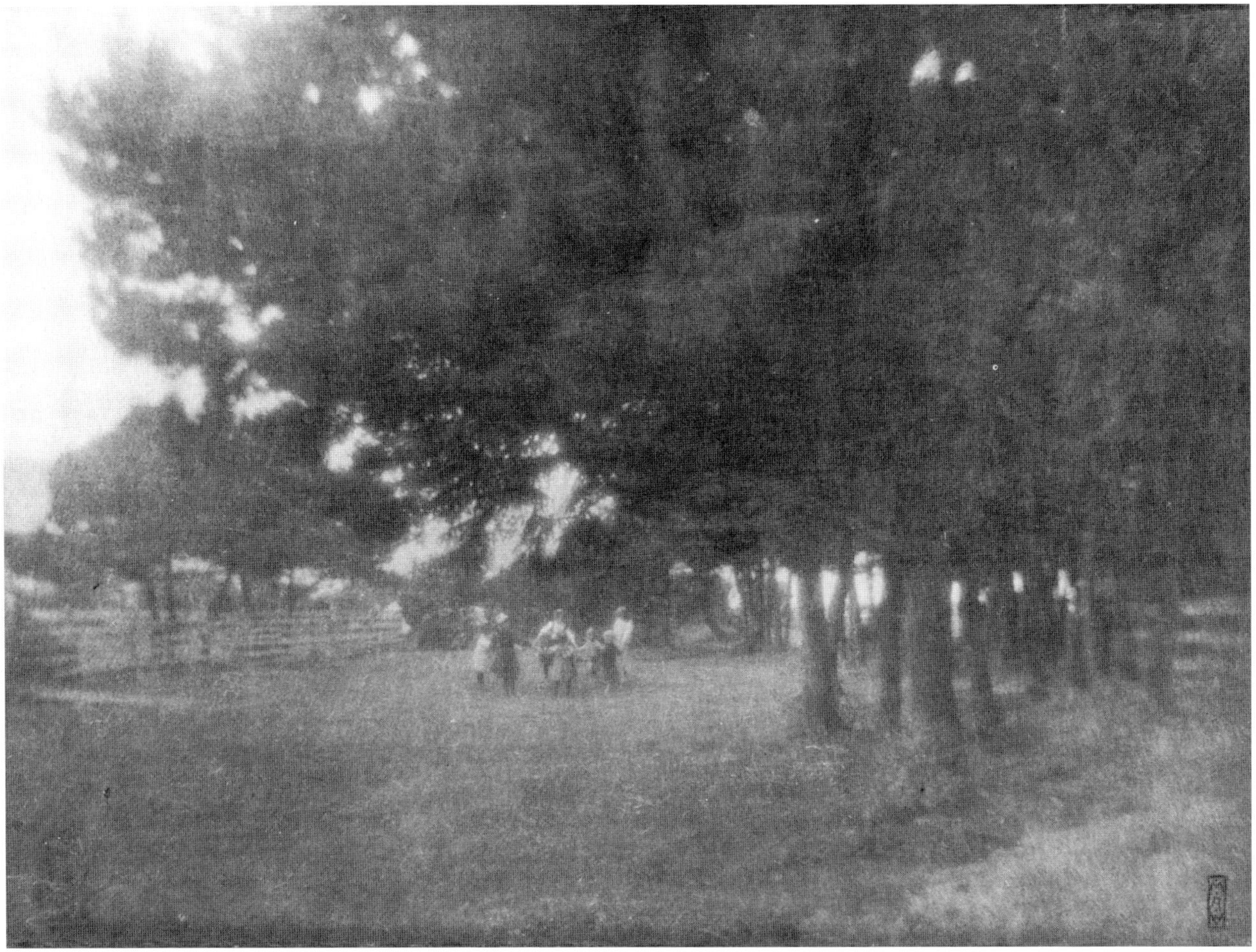

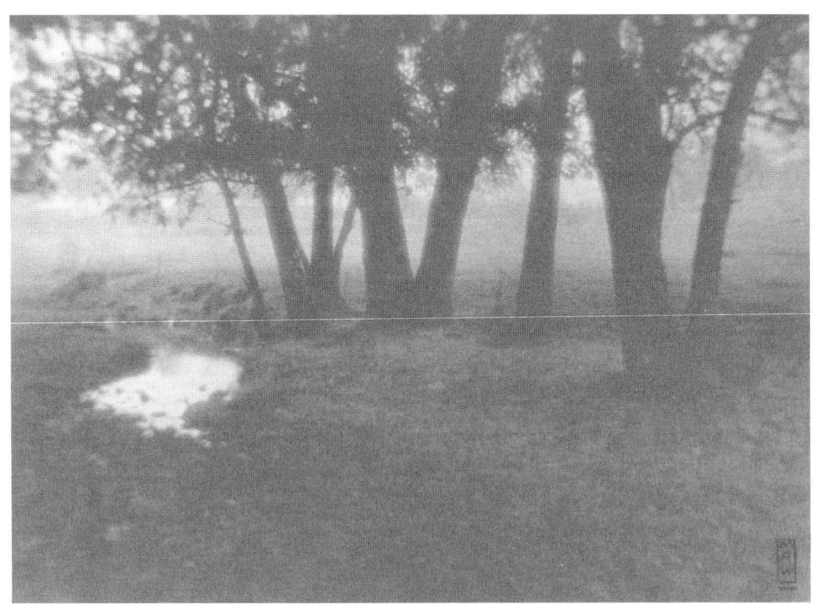

visit friends before boarding for the journey up the Columbia River to Pasco, Washington. At Pasco, the river curved north and the train crossed a bridge spanning a narrow point in the river. They continued on the Northern Pacific Railroad northwest up the Yakima River another 75 miles to Toppenish.

Ten years earlier, one observer had unfavorably described central Washington as "drab isolation and endless miles of sagebrush." Like other settlers, the Wigginses encountered scorching winds, blinding glare, dust, and suffocating heat. But Fred dreamed of turning the desert green. Back in the 1880s, while Myra was learning photography, few people lived in central Washington; but that changed after the Northern Pacific Railroad established the new town of North Yakima (now Yakima). The powdery soil proved fertile, but lacked water. To irrigate the desert, private developers constructed the two-mile-long Sunnyside Canal with headgates at the Yakima River. Within three to five years, apple and pear trees produced fruit, and soon hops, grain, and melons were added.

In 1905, the Washington State legislature "passed a new irrigation law that gave the United States government the right to acquire lands for canal and reservoir sites through a process of condemnation." In granting the right to acquire water necessary for any project, the federal government wrested control of the Sunnyside Canal system and opened the way to development of the Yakima Valley. Talk of high yields and quick profits encouraged entrepreneurs to move there and enter business, as Fred Wiggins did with his Washington Nursery Company.

The first year in Washington, Myra and Mildred lived in Yakima, twenty miles northwest of Toppenish, while their bungalow style house was being built. Wiggins found a barn where she painted and conducted classes. When they moved into their Toppenish home, the Wigginses waited another year for electricity. Summer brought blazing heat and dust storms as tumbleweeds rolled down the streets and rain created a muddy disaster. Fred "always felt sorry for [Myra] because the dust bothered her so much and she had hayfever." For the first years, Myra's new pioneer life left her with little time for art.

Still, despite life's distractions, magazines continued to feature Myra's work, but the pace slowed as her time became filled with other concerns. "Hallowe'en" appeared in *Western Camera Notes* as a sample from the 1907 Kodak exhibit. *Photograms of the Year* published "Shadows" to illustrate "a field that is being very successfully worked by a number of American women," according to Snowden Ward. "It is especially suited to women's interests and opportunities, to her keen sympathies and intuition, and in this genre of home life, she should be able to teach much to mere man."

Again, Fayette Clute in an article, "Work in the Western States," recognized the Salem colleagues: "A Westerner is a pioneer or the descendent of a pioneer; his natural inclination is to break new ground . . . Myra A. Wiggins and Helen Plummer Gatch, both of Salem, Oregon, continue to improve in the breadth and forcefulness of their work. The very few examples I have seen since writing last year indicated that there has been very little radical change except that there is less regard being paid to petty details and more to that strong human interest that can only be secured by the best of understanding between model and artist."

Clute's statement perceptively described Myra's style of work, which required careful thought and

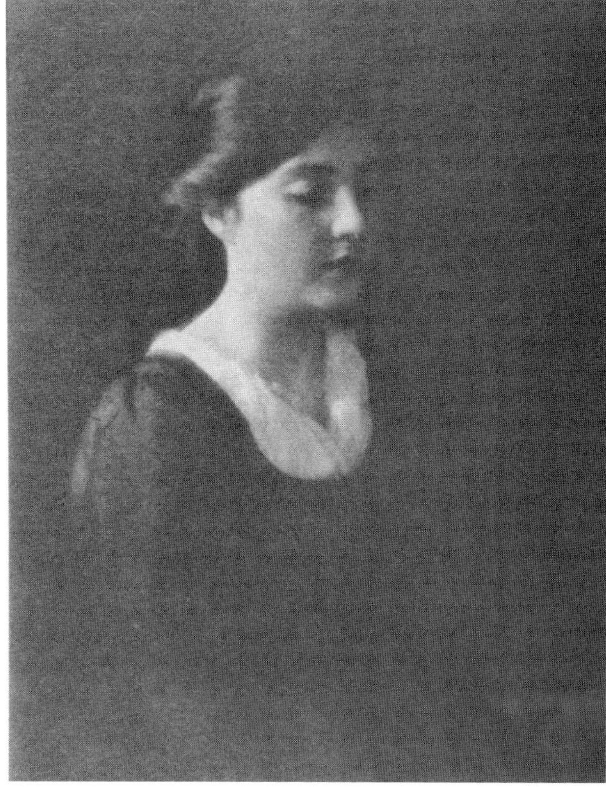

Irene
1906, platinum print
6" x 8"
Portland Art Museum

Nymphaea
c. 1908, gelatin silver print
6" x 8"
Portland Art Museum

preparation. For instance, Myra described the Dutch dress seen on so many of her models as "simple in design so that it does not attract attention, and the models look as if they really wore it, not simply put it on." She advised photographers not to "'dress up' your models," since "many a fine picture is ruined because this is too apparent." Besides using Mildred and Alma as models, Wiggins' students, friends from the beach, or even strangers with the right photogenic appeal often were subjects. In Salem, Wiggins had held Saturday art classes in her home and one of her students became the Dutch woman in "The Spinner." At Myra's parents' beach home in Newport, their neighbor Edith Ballinger and her daughter were the figures in "The Edge of the Cliff."

Wiggins saw the model she wanted for "Nymphaea" (the Latin name for water lily) on the train while traveling to the coast on an annual outing:

> I watched this beautiful young girl as closely as possible without attracting notice and was fearful at every station lest she should leave the train. Arrived at our destination, the very last moment I lost her in the crowds of summer tourists, and daily I searched for her, meeting the boats and at the post office until at last my search was rewarded and I quickly gained her permission to pose for me. When preparing to take this particular picture . . . on this occasion I left the cottage with a retinue of about half a dozen helpers. And through the path in the woods we marched single file to this beautiful little lily pond, which I had accidentally discovered one day; the spot always made me think of gnomes and fairies. My helpers were all loaded down with supplies. We carried two or three cameras, a large tripod, two costumes, Dutch caps, hats, scarfs of different kinds, scissors, pins, a hatchet to use in case shrubbery or trees would have to be cut down for the right point of view, long ropes to tie around the children's waists when wading in the pond to get for me the necessary lilies, (and it may be needless to say that this was accomplished with much bribing and weeping for there were snakes in the pond and several attempts were made accompanied by much screaming before success resulted.) So after passing through all this that I have related, my model shows unusual ability to enter into the spirit of the picture.

Photograms of the Year, 1908 published "Nymphaea" noting, it "loses much in its translation from the original warm brown to black, but even in our version is a pleasing portrait fantasy."

In November, 1907, Stieglitz hung "The Lily Pond" in the Photo-Secession Members Exhibition at the Little Galleries. Wiggins no doubt was pleased to have her work shown, but some members had up to nine photographs hung in the 95 picture exhibit. One example hardly represented Myra's work adequately. After that, Stieglitz never again showed a Wiggins photograph in his gallery. (Today, a copy of "The Lily Pond" cannot be located. Possibly Stieglitz had renamed one of Myra's other photographs and catalogued it with the new title.)

Exhibitions on the West Coast, however, still provided Wiggins an opportunity to show her work. In 1908, two of her photographs hung in the Arts and Crafts Exhibition at Idora Park in San Francisco. In a review, fellow Photo-Secessionist Annie Brigman pointed out how Wiggins "invariably infuses her work with an atmosphere of tender sadness." Brigman did not mention which image she was referring to, but Wiggins' distinct and recognizable Dutch genre pictures were not easily confused with the work of other photographers.

Slowly, Wiggins' pictorial work was coming to a halt. In October she wrote Stieglitz:

> Enclosed please find money order for $6.50 and $5.00—the former for another years subscription for Camera Work and the latter for Photo-Secession dues. This I should have sent months ago. Each year Camera Work grows more beautiful and it is the very last magazine that I could do without. Am a busy housekeeper these days and cannot find time for other things. Am very

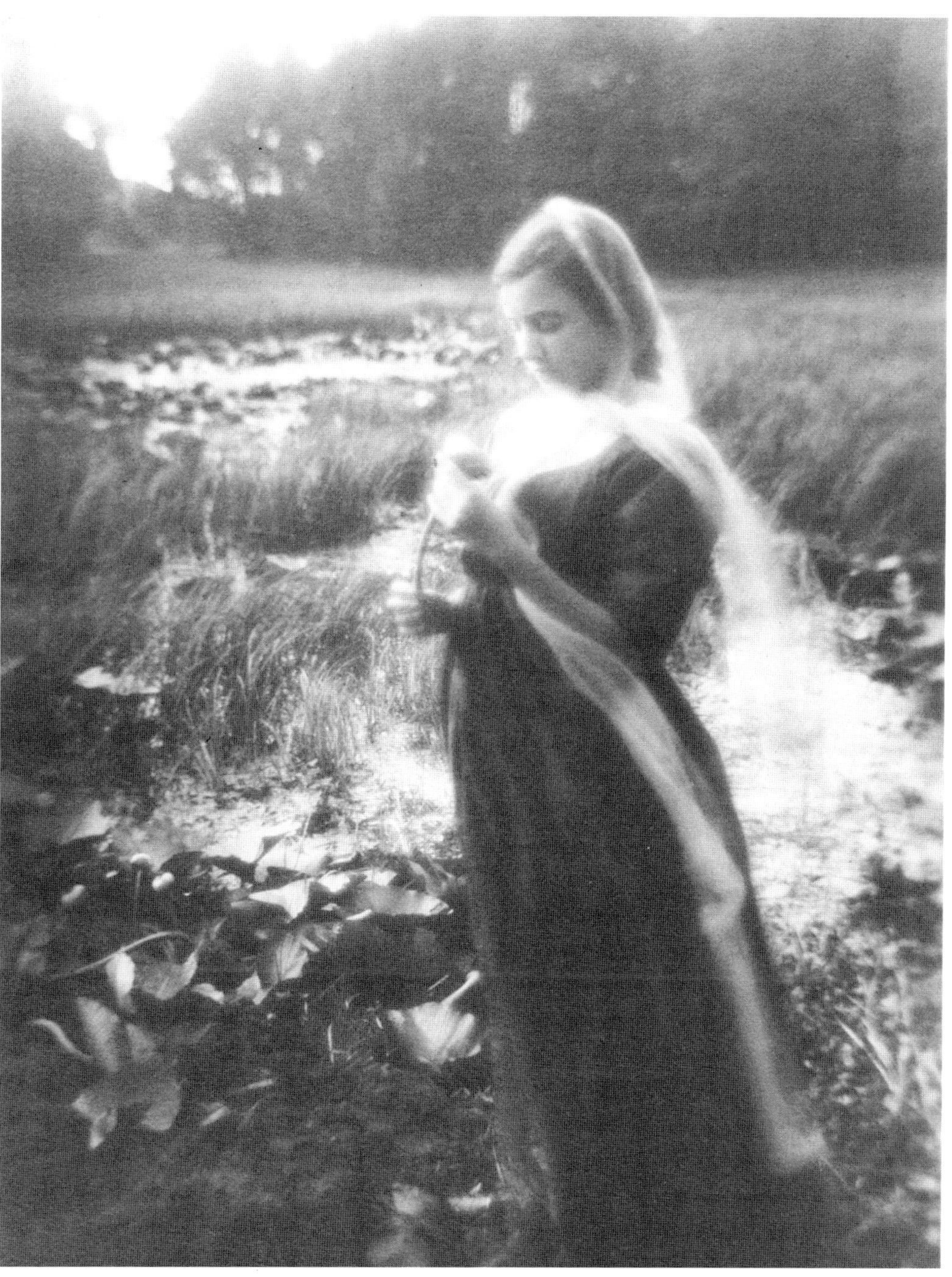

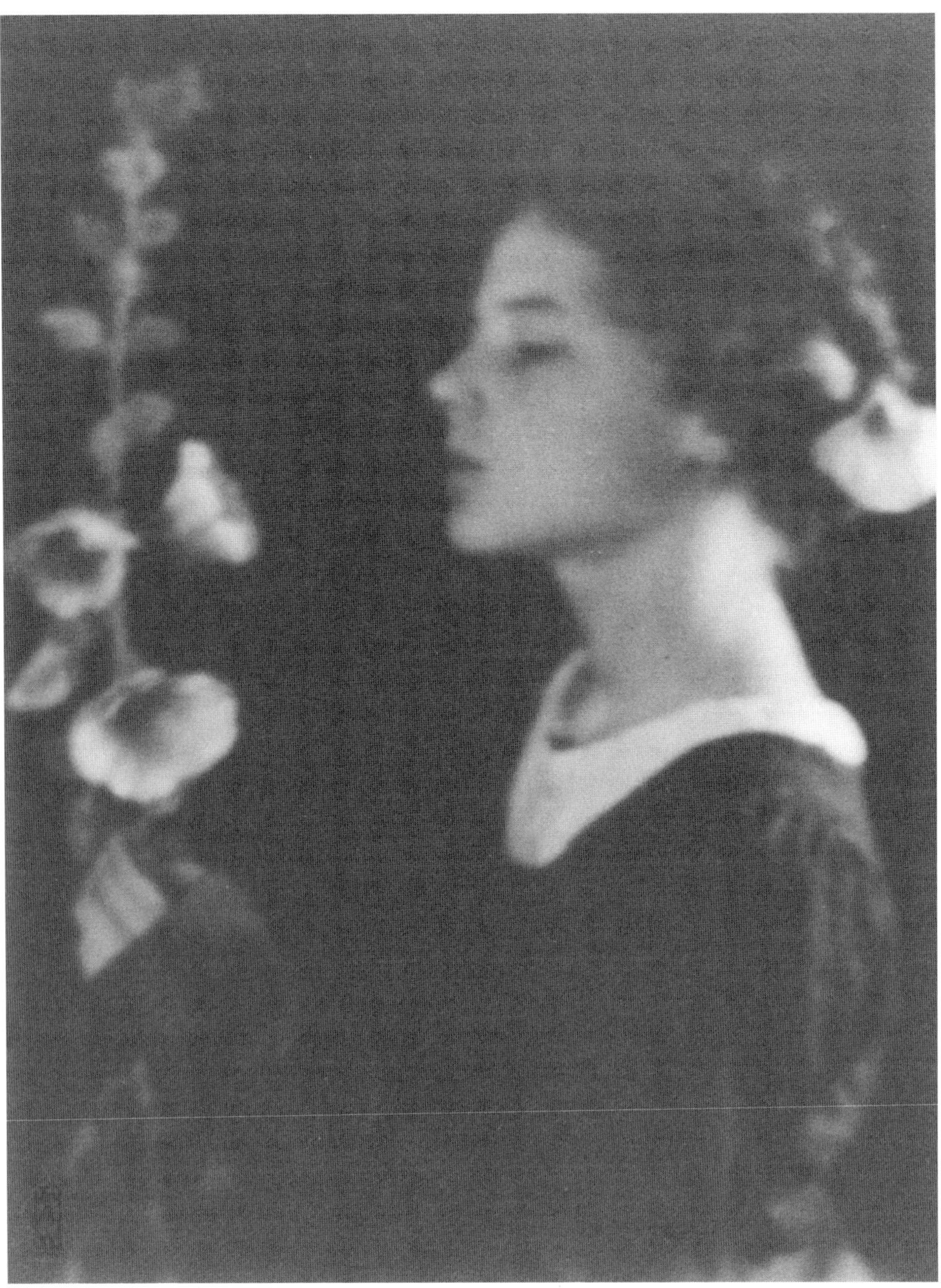

much interested in your experiments with color photography, and if differently situated would love to take up the work in connection with lantern slides. I have a stereopticon lecture on Palestine, Egypt and Athens which I give occasionally and I have enjoyed tinting some of the slides. My address is simply Toppenish, Wash. leave off all the rest. We are holding an annual Indian Fair here this week. The Indians, wearing their richest garments and blankets come from the surrounding States. They are exceedingly picturesque, but I am afraid of them. I tried to take a snapshot of one of them and was rewarded with a lash from a whip. If you have any old Secession Exhibition catalogues of members work would like very much to have some—have not had any for two years.

Wiggins' veiled reference to a lack of money, her isolation in central Washington, and her diminishing connections to the East reveal the beginning of a shift in her artistic life. She maintained her Photo-Secession membership, although Stieglitz's interests had turned to the modern art of Marius De Zayas, Marsden Hartley, John Marin, and Auguste Rodin. In the next few years he introduced the work of Pablo Picasso, Max Weber, Henri Matisse, and Paul Cezanne, and exhibited the photography of Baron Adolph de Meyer and Paul Strand.

In June, 1909, Wiggins again wrote Stieglitz: "I may be able to send you some photographs this next Fall, but I cannot tell as other cares are crowding so, and good help is impossible to get here so I have very little time outside of my home. I am surely an unworthy member of the Secession and wish that I could help such a splendid cause with more money and better work. Your hard labor is now showing results not only in this country but in many countries and it must be a great satisfaction to you. No magazine yet equals Camera Work. We had hoped that you would visit the Seattle Fair—and stop off to see us on your way (on Northern Pacific) but I see that you are going abroad. We leave next week for Seattle and our summer outing at Newport, Oregon." A naive expectation at best, but what hope it must have given Wiggins to think even for a moment that Alfred Stieglitz would venture West and be her guest.

Wiggins was referring to the Alaska-Yukon-Pacific Exposition—Seattle's answer to the Lewis and Clark Centennial Exposition held in Portland four years earlier. In addition to the usual displays promoting American ingenuity, the exposition featured an art gallery with paintings by the Old Masters, American Impressionists, and French artists. In a switch from Frank Vincent DuMond's policies in Portland, work by Northwest artists appeared at the Washington State Pavilion and the Women's Building.

The Washington State Federation of Women's Clubs sponsored the Women's Building to "showcase the accomplishments of women." They displayed "female cultural achievements," such as watercolors, needlework, poetry, and music, "while providing hospitality for women's groups that convened in Seattle" for the exposition. The women offered nutritious meals, and childcare was provided by trained nurses so mothers could enjoy the exhibits. The exposition awarded Wiggins a bronze medal and certificate for her watercolors and photographs.

As the heyday of pictorial photography began ebbing, Wiggins exhibited one print in the International Exhibition of Pictorial Photography at the National Arts Club of New York in early 1909. *Camera Work* proclaimed, "This exhibition demonstrated for the first time in a comprehensive manner that pictorial photography is the one and only new contribution made to the art of the world by America, and furthermore that it is the only other art movement of modern times that can be compared in significance and importance with the Impressionist movement."

Hollyhocks (June Idyl)
c. 1910, platinum print
6" x 8"
Portland Art Museum

Hallowe'en
1905, gelatin silver print
3½" x 3½"
Portland Art Museum

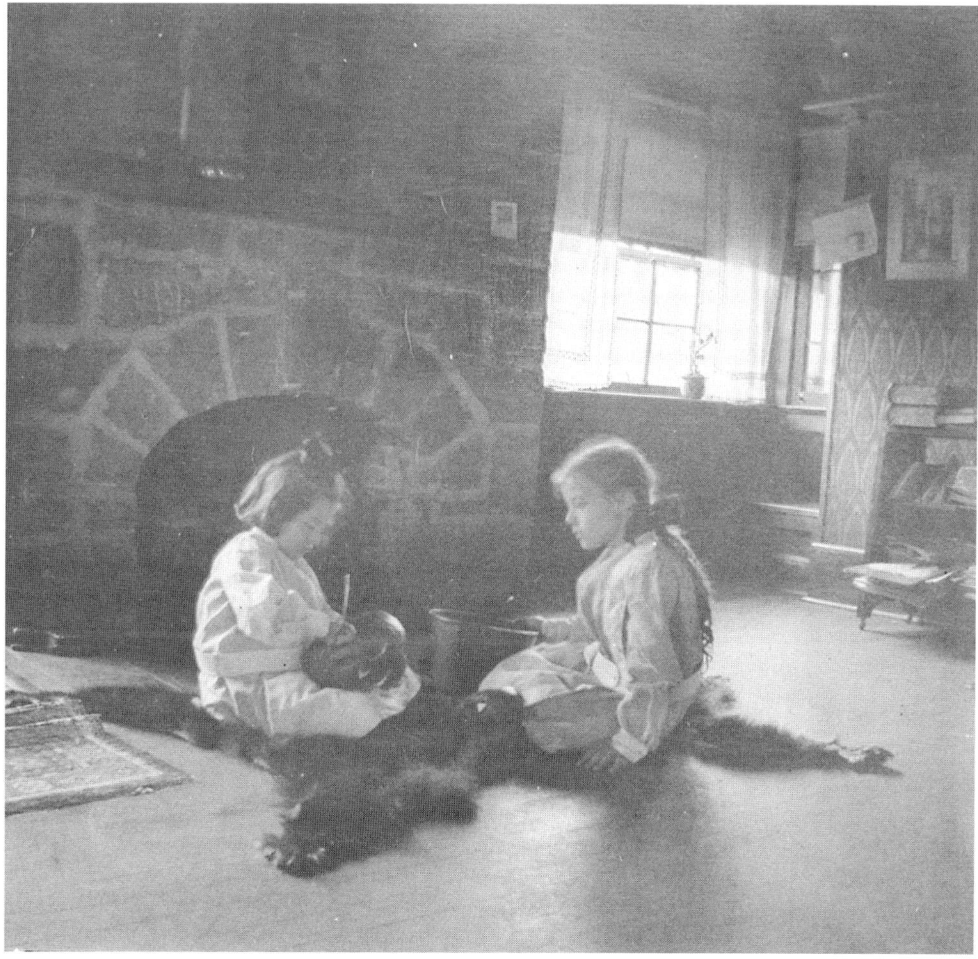

In June, 1910, while "Polishing Brass" hung in the Sixth Annual Pictorial Photography Invitational in Seattle, plans were made for the Photo-Secession show at the Albright Art Gallery in Buffalo, New York. Photographs would be hung in two sections—an invitational section with pictures selected by the Photo-Secession and an open section where submitted prints would be judged by the Photo-Secession.

In another rebuff, Stieglitz did not select Wiggins' work for the invitational section that included 560 images by 37 photographers. However, "Polishing Brass," "The Edge of the Cliff," and a new image, "Hollyhocks" (also titled "June Idyl"), were chosen to hang in the open section which included 124 pictures by about 30 photographers selected by Stieglitz, Clarence White, Max Weber, and Charles Caffin. Of these, 12 were members of the Photo-Secession. One reviewer noted: "The open section was added to this exhibition to give all American photographers an opportunity of being represented, and such of their work was selected as proved to be of a sufficiently high standard to link it with the spirit and quality of the Invitation section."

It did provide Wiggins with the opportunity to receive public recognition along with her colleagues. A number of persons, however, thought the open section "relatively unimportant—probably because of a common idea that outsiders were not wanted." They called it "somewhat of a mistake." The well-known names that once accompanied Myra's in catalogues and exhibitions constituted the invitational section. In spite of this, Myra always regarded her participation as a personal victory and the fulfillment of two decades of photographic work.

Fifteen-thousand people visited the Albright Art Gallery in what would turn out to be the final, major presentation of pictorial photography by the Photo-Secession. The exhibit also represented the conclusion of Stieglitz's efforts in the pictorial photography movement as his focus on art shifted in a modernist direction. (In fact, Stieglitz as early as 1906 had felt that his efforts to advance the cause of pictorial photography had been completed.) The Albright Art Gallery, in acknowledgment of photography as art, purchased photographs from the exhibit for its permanent collection. "Polishing Brass," bought by pictorial photographer and publisher Spencer Kellogg of Buffalo for $15, was one of 65 photographs sold at the exhibition.

Although always proud of her admission into the Albright Art Gallery exhibition and her connection with Stieglitz, Wiggins nevertheless was included on a marginal level. She had achieved greater fame through her own self-promotion than Stieglitz ever accorded her. Wiggins' Photo-Secession membership did affiliate her with the movement that forever changed photography, but her own independent contributions to pictorial photography far outweigh any of her achievements associated with the Photo-Secession.

In following years, the Photo-Secession slowly dissolved as quarreling between Stieglitz and some of the members resulted in defections. *Camera Work* continued publication until June, 1917, by which time only 36 subscribers remained. Many years after Wiggins' death, Mildred sold her mother's complete set of *Camera Work* to a collector for a substantial sum. Although the Photo-Secession drifted from its early sense of purpose and Stieglitz moved on to new pursuits, Myra Albert Wiggins remained loyal until the end.

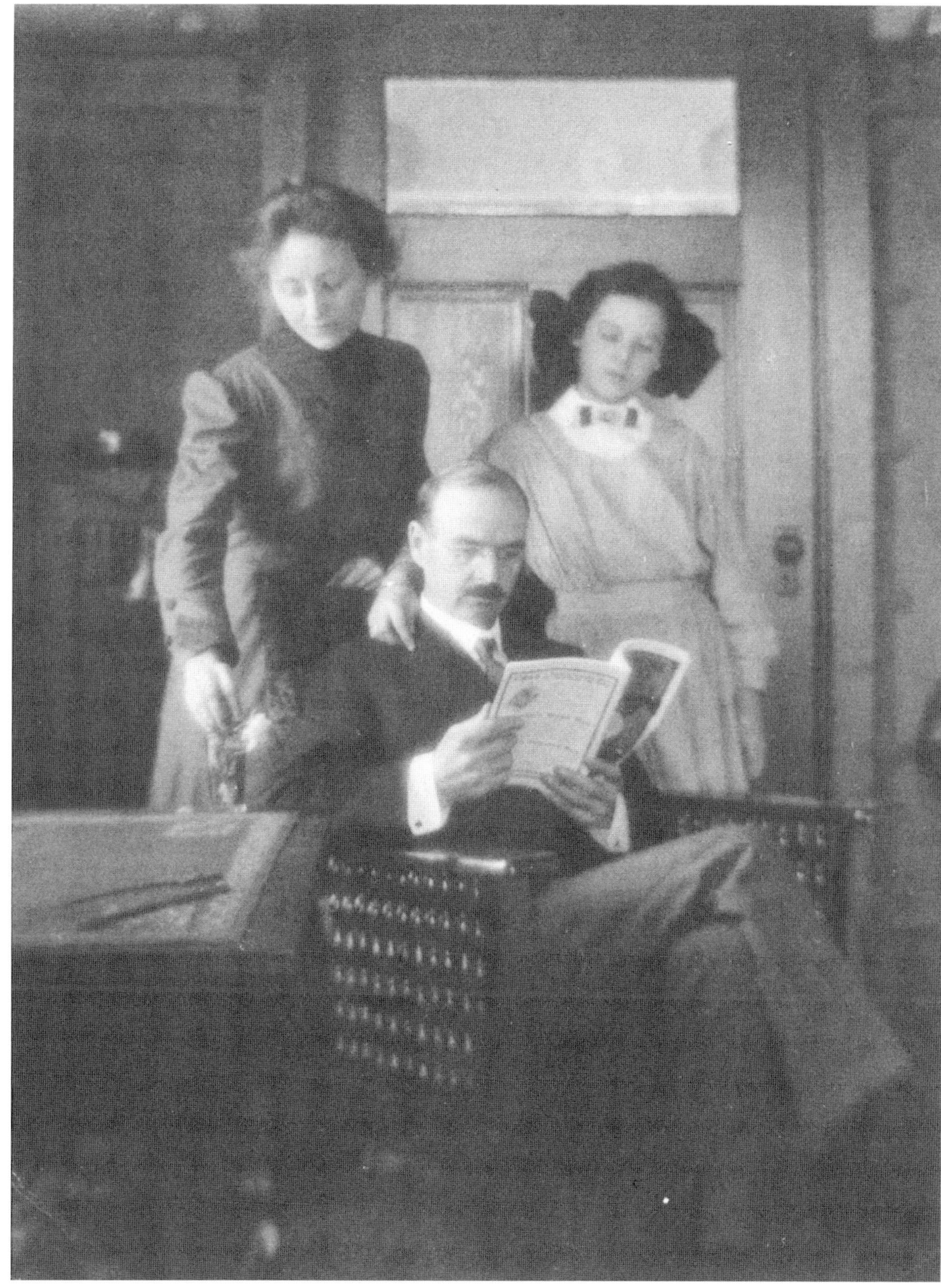

Family Portrait, Toppenish
"about 1909," gelatin silver print
5¾" x 7⅞"
Portland Art Museum

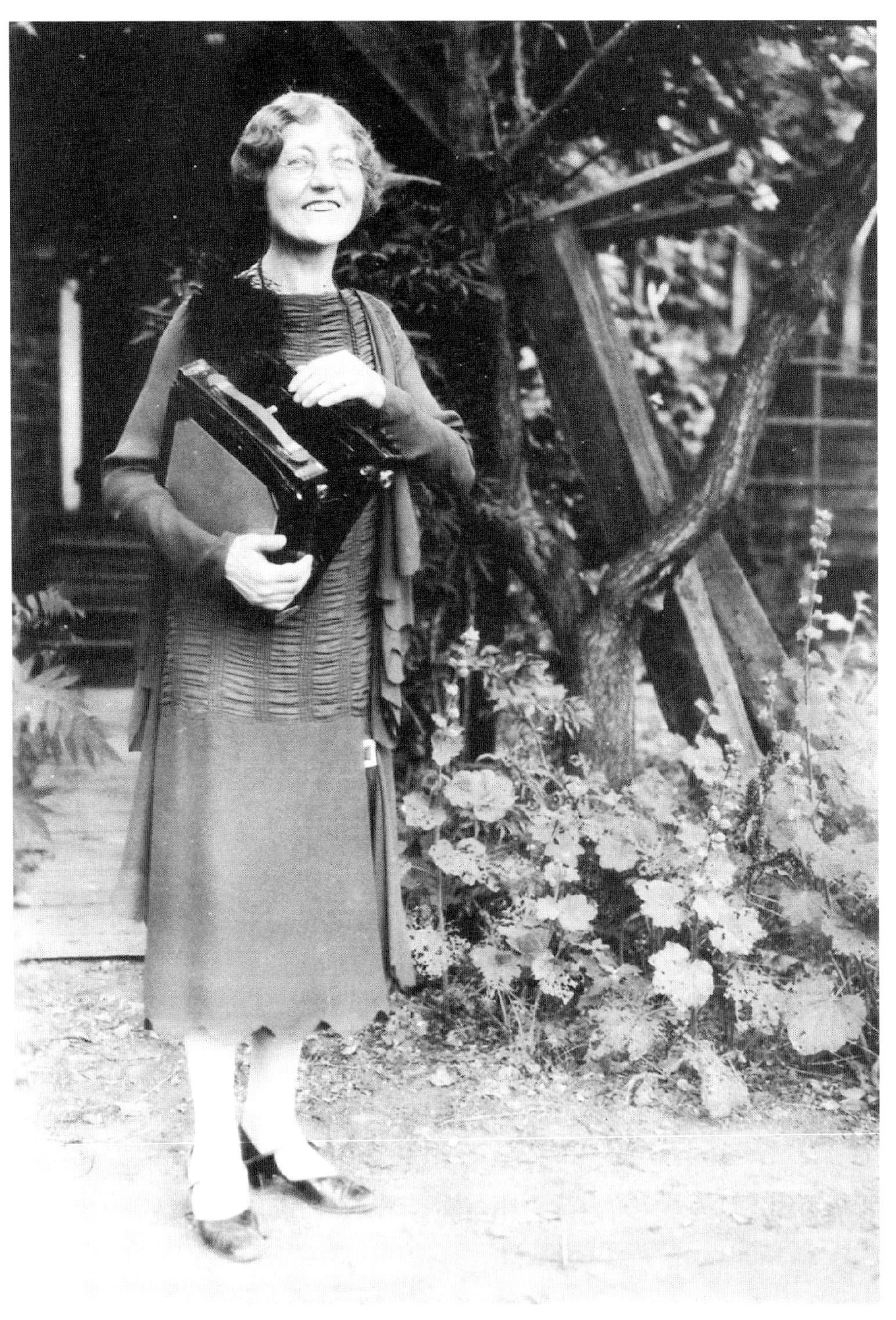

Part Eight

1911- 1956

After 1910 came a period of experimentation and exploration for many artists. Some looked to the abstract geometry of forms seen in random things and places. Modern industrial objects such as smokestacks, automobiles, and bridges, as well as urban skylines and factories, became subject matter. Often, photographers emphasized mechanical purism with unmanipulated, sharply focused images. Others blended these new ideas with the old, producing graphically designed compositions that rendered familiar objects in unusual ways—often with the creative use of lighting and shadows. However, many across the country retained a keen interest in pictorial photography, and clubs and annual salons continued to showcase this kind of work. The salons, though, tended to be more inclusive, rather than elitist as in the past. These salons could include prints exhibiting modern subject matter and techniques alongside the manipulated, soft-focus imagery of mother-child scenes or rural landscapes.

During this time, Stieglitz seldom exhibited photography in the 291 gallery or published it in *Camera Work*. For Stieglitz, artists like Pablo Picasso, Henri Matisse, Arthur B. Dove, or Marsden Hartley prompted more enthusiasm. In 1917, Stieglitz produced the last issue of *Camera Work* and closed his gallery, having concluded with Georgia O'Keeffe featured in her first one-woman show. In doing so, Stieglitz signaled the end of an era that had transformed photography and art. He continued to photograph, of course, creating a series of cloud scenes called "Equivalents" and a prodigious collection of prints of Georgia O'Keeffe, whom he married in 1924. He did not present contemporary art to the public again until he opened the Intimate Gallery in 1925, which was followed by An American Place from 1929 to 1946. Mostly painting and sculpture were exhibited. During this 21-year span, he displayed photography only seven times, and three of the shows were of his own work.

Meanwhile, Myra looked to Seattle, 150 miles west of Toppenish, for her artistic opportunities and connections. In Seattle, several organizations had been formed to promote the arts and to sponsor exhibitions. These included the Society of Seattle Artists (1904), the Washington State Art Association (1906), and the Seattle Fine Arts Society (1908). In 1913, Myra's "Polishing Brass," "Edge of the Wood," and "Still Life" hung at the Annual

Myra Wiggins, Toppenish
c. 1925, platinum print
3⅛" x 4¼"
photographer unknown
Robert and Shirley Benz Collection

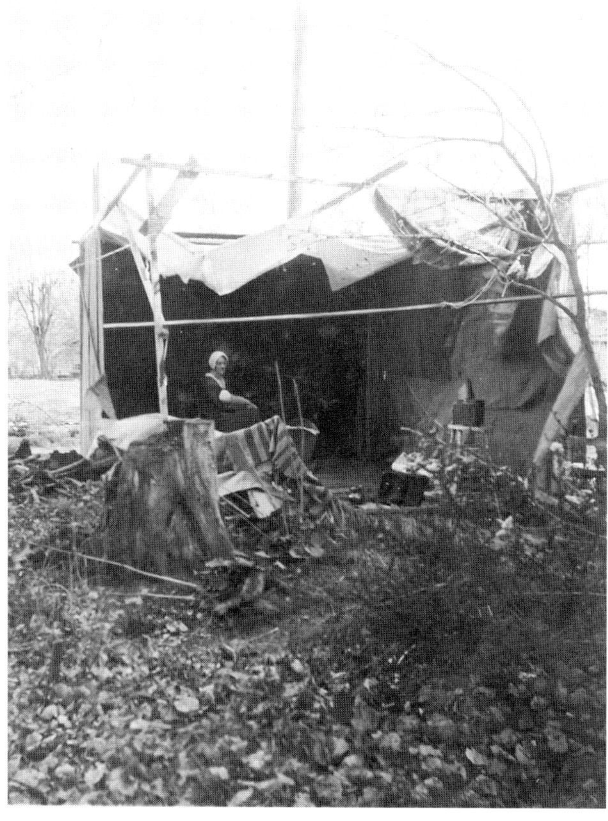

My improvised Photo Studio in our alley in Toppenish
1929, gelatin silver print
3⅛" x 4⅛"
Robert and Shirley Benz Collection

Exhibition of Photographic Art in the museum galleries of the Washington State Art Association. This exhibit, featuring 17 Washington artists, appeared alongside Indian and Chinese art, as well as paintings from New Mexico. In 1914, the Seattle Fine Arts Society sponsored its first Northwest Annual Exhibition, which became the most important art competition in the region for many years.

Myra established a studio in their new Toppenish home—a modest, comfortable, two-story bungalow. Students drifted in and out of her home and she occasionally gave vocal lessons. Probably late at night, with domestic responsibilities aside, she wrote poems and sometimes set them to music. Mildred recalled her father cranking up their old "tin lizzy" automobile that could act "stubborn as a mule." The Wiggins family took frequent trips to Yakima on the "Sunny Jim" train for cultural events, usually concerts by singers or pianists.

Judging from Myra's letters to Stieglitz, her first years in Toppenish were largely consumed by household responsibilities. Opening the nursery strained the Wigginses' financial resources. Besides her home studio, Myra maintained a studio in Yakima where she taught art, providing much needed additional income. By 1915, Mildred had graduated from high school and decided to attend Willamette University. Her great grandfather, Joseph Holman, had endowed a scholarship fund for his grandchildren to attend the college.

In September, 1915, while Myra and Mildred visited George and Blanche Rodgers' home in Salem, Joseph Albert surprised his sister by offering her a trip to the Panama-Pacific Exposition in San Francisco. Wiggins protested that she could not go because, "I haven't any clothes and I have to finish Mildred's sewing and I haven't my furs." After some coaxing, she relented; Blanche loaned her a coat, while Joseph's wife, Jessie, loaned her furs.

"Isn't this a grand surprise," wrote Myra to Fred. "Joe pays all my expenses. More later on steamer if am not sick."

Myra's concern over clothes was not frivolous, but reflected the Wigginses' financial troubles. On board the steamer, she wrote Fred:

> I went to work on my black net dress in the afternoon, for I thought if I were around where father was that I might have to go some place in the evening and my waists were soiled and 2 of

them actually wearing out in the elbows and under the arms, but I had to come as I was and I will buy a waist in San F. instead of in Seattle as I intended doing. I had not received any check from you at all when I left and we were really embarrassed—I gave *my* last $2.00 to Mildred to take to school and I borrowed $3.00 of Margaret [Blanche's daughter]— be sure (if you have not already done so) to send a check to Mildred and send me $10.00 Inside Inn c/o father . . . and if you can spare it I would like to have some of my *own* money as I now owe myself $12.50—$8.50 of that was spent before you arrived at the coast—do try to sell one of my lots so that Mildred can have what she needs this winter. What will we do if we can't rent the house . . . I have that building and loan to keep up—you must tell the prospective renters that it is easily heated in winter.

References to "my" money indicated Myra's proclivity for earning an income—her source and proof of her independence. But, it also became a phrase aimed at her husband in response to his apparent lack of business proficiency. "How I wish we could have gone together," she concluded, "and Mildred too—but sometime we will I know. We will just have to keep up our courage which is our only 'stock in trade' at present—and God has been very good to us after all, hasn't He. Dearest love—and God bless you my dear husband."

In the Seattle Building at the San Francisco exposition, Wiggins viewed her watercolor "The Pines," selected from a state-wide exhibit by the Seattle Fine Arts Society. Besides enjoying the art exhibits, she probably encountered the "Electriquette" battery-powered wicker chair, drank pineapple juice at the Hawaiian pavilion, or saw demonstrations of wireless telegraphy, radio, and Henry Ford's assembly line. She might have explored the exposition's Joy Zone containing 25 theaters offering "light opera, vaudeville, and movies," or dined for the first time in a cafeteria.

At this point in time, many details of Myra's and Fred's life remain unclear. In 1917, Fred's business must have taken him on the road. A November 21 letter to Myra from Fred at the Davenport Hotel in Spokane, Washington, rendered these sentimental thoughts: "I came to my room at 5 minutes of 8 this evening and turning to the Gideon Bible on the table, I read 'seek ye first the kingdom of God and his righteousness and all else shall be added unto you.' I thought that a happy reference, intended for me—so at exactly 8 o'clock I knelt in

THE WIGGINS HOME,
TOPPENISH, WASHINGTON
Robert and Shirley Benz Collection

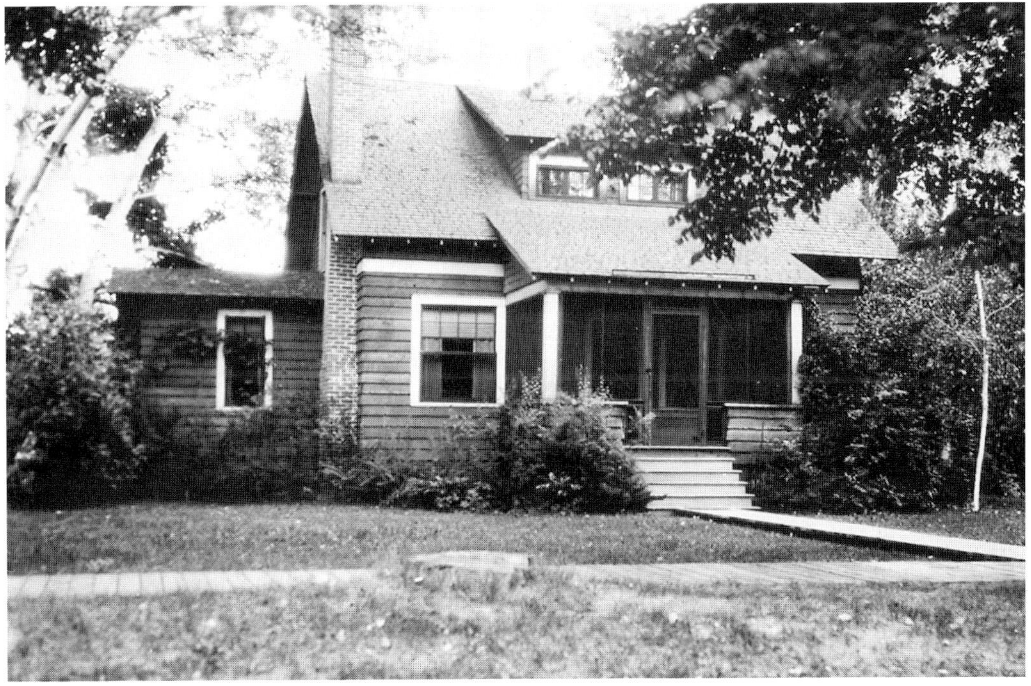

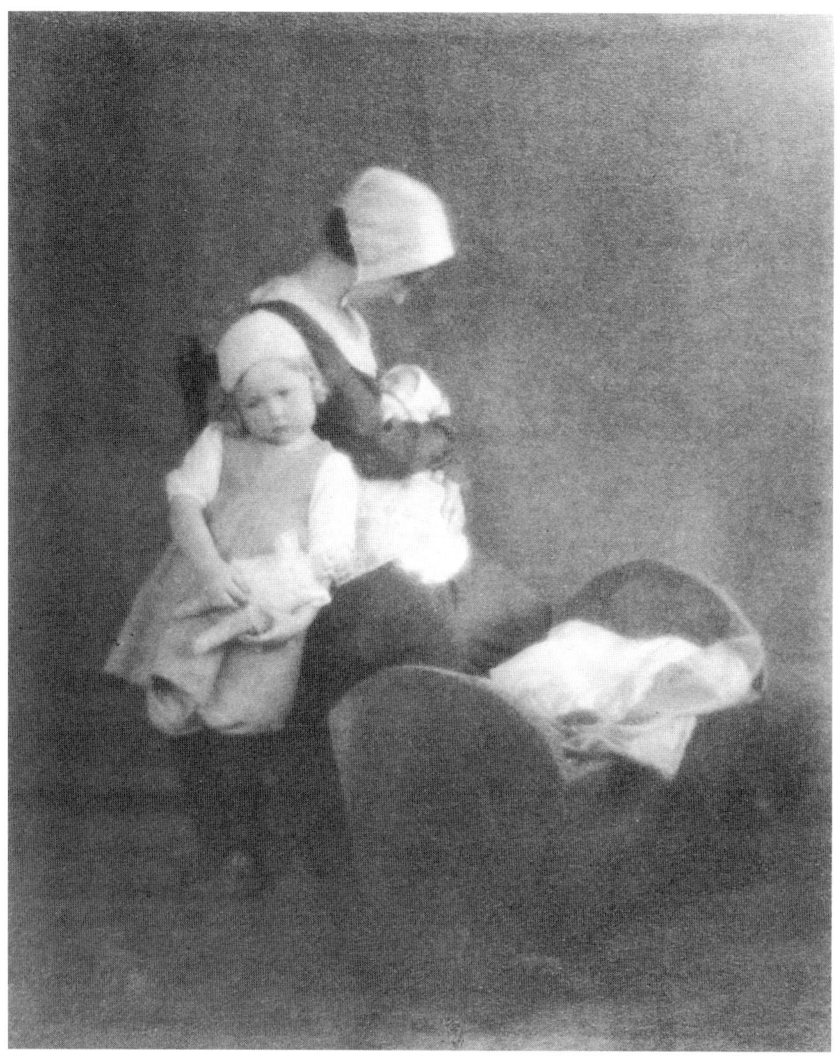

prayer for 5 minutes for you and our dear little girl and myself. There in the box [in the lobby] just placed was your letter—our anniversary letter—and I thought what a happy coincidence to receive it at just the minute we were pledging our vows 23 years ago . . . I have thought of you many times today my dear, and prayed for God's blessing on you."

During the 1920s, while the nursery business demanded Fred's attention, Myra continued to teach art. She also sang alto solos in their church choir, accompanied by a young organist named Reuben Benz. Mildred had inherited her mother's vocal talent. After graduating from college she joined the church choir in Toppenish where she met Reuben. Mildred and Reuben soon were married in the Wigginses' garden, and settled in Yakima where Reuben prospered in the apple business. They had two children, Mary Elizabeth Benz and Robert Benz.

In 1924, encouraged by Fred, Myra again pulled out her camera equipment and created Dutch genre scenes. As she described it, "After several years of putting aside any thought of serious work, though a grandmother, I tried my hand at it again, inspired by my little granddaughter, Mary Elizabeth Benz, and the resurrection of the old wooden cradle which I had made so many years ago." Several workmen built a rough Dutch interior under the outside shed of a neighboring barn. After several days in the heat, Wiggins succeeded in making a picture called "Dethroned."

That year, "Dethroned" appeared in the Seattle International Photo Salon in the Frederick and Nelson Department Store gallery and was printed in the rotogravure section of *The Seattle Daily Times*. In "Dethroned," Wiggins used Dutch domestic iconography and the triangular composition with diagonals that had worked so well for her in the past. The heads of the mother, baby, and child form a smaller triangle inside part of a larger one that includes the cradle carefully placed on a diagonal plane near the doll held by granddaughter Mary Elizabeth. The lighter tones of clothing contrast with the dark background and wood cradle.

In December, 1928, the Seattle Fine Arts Society sponsored Myra's final photography exhibit. The exhibition brochure, featuring "Hollyhocks/June Idyl" on the cover, listed 23 photographs ranging from "Hunger ist der Beste Koch," to "Edge of the Wood," to "The Forge." On the walls were Wiggins' most celebrated photographs, including her personal favorites. Of her genre studies, she considered "Polishing Brass/At Work" and "The Edge of the Cliff" her best. She chose "Edge of the Wood" and "Early Morning" as her most important landscapes. "Hollyhocks" she ranked highest for portrait studies, and "Still Life/Grapes and Brass" was her favorite still life photograph.

The four years between the 1924 Seattle International Photo Salon and Myra's exhibition of pictorial photography in 1928 had been infused by the typically fast pace of her life. In 1926 she had accepted the chairmanship of the Division of Art, of the Washington State Federation of Women's Clubs. That same year she transformed her lecture "Trials and Triumphs of an Amateur Photographer," presented to the Yakima chapter of the American Association of University Women, into an article published in *The American Magazine of Art.*

Three of Myra's poems appeared in Frank Bellemin's book, *Our Present Day Poets: Their Lives and Works.* "All three Arts, Painting, Music, and Poetry are much alike," wrote Wiggins for Bellemin, "and each may be used to illustrate the other. All are music and should be ever uplifting and inspiring." By 1930, in fact, she had crossed the country on thirty occasions and each time when in New York had tried to take voice lessons. Singing, she said, allowed her to "express the love of music" within her and benefited her health at the same time. Yet, Myra still classified herself as a photographer.

In 1929, Wiggins made three more Dutch photographs—"Waiting for the Sandman," "Broken Threads" (or "The Tangle"), and "Sleepytime." The little girl in "Sleepytime," Lorna Robertson, recalled how tired she felt when posing for a lengthy time while Wiggins prepared the picture. The wooden shoes were placed next to Lorna because they were too small for her feet.

During this decade, Wiggins frequently was engaged as a lecturer. Besides her lantern slide talk detailing her trip abroad in 1904 and a lively lecture about her days as an amateur photographer, Wiggins spoke about William Merritt Chase "with

DETHRONED
1924, gelatin silver print
7" x 8¾"
Portland Art Museum

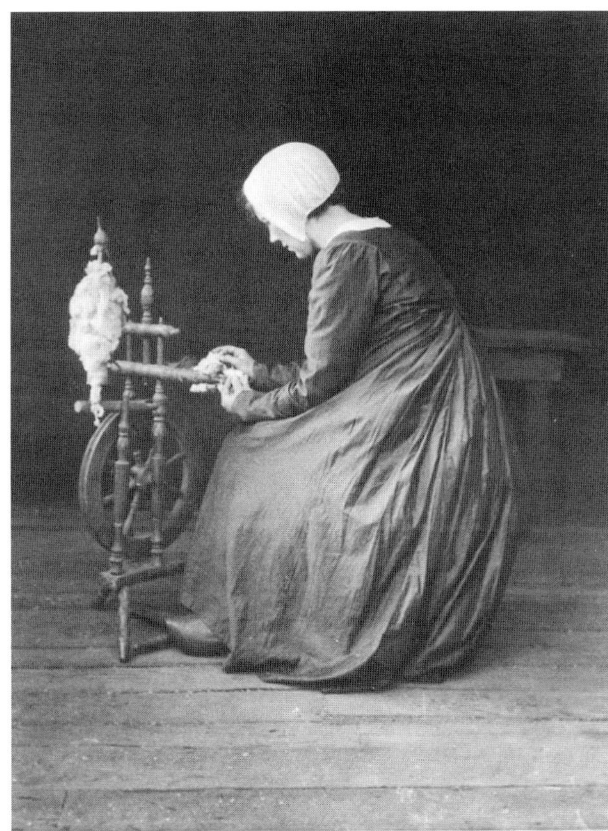

BROKEN THREADS (THE TANGLE)
1929, gelatin silver print
4¾" x 5¾"
Portland Art Museum

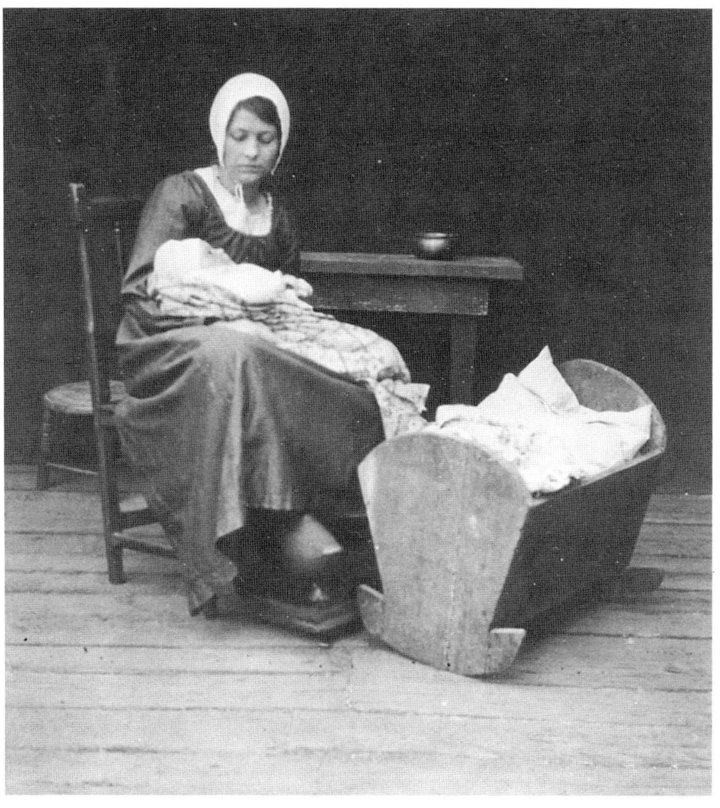

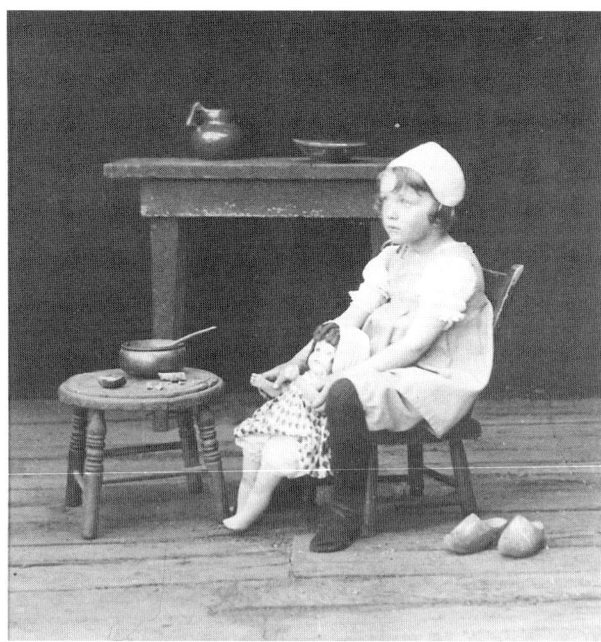

Waiting for the Sand man
1929, gelatin silver print
5⅛" x 6½"
Portland Art Museum

Sleepytime
1929, gelatin silver print
6" x 8"
Portland Art Museum

personal reminiscences," "Art and Music in the Home," and "Practical Art Talk." Her lectures outlined her world views and conveyed strong personal opinions and prejudices.

In "Art and Music in the Home," Wiggins insisted, "Anything that aids in holding the interest and raising the standards of living in the home is the worthwhile ambition of true womanhood the world over and Good *art* in the home is one factor which will tend to accomplish this end and should be seriously considered by all homemakers . . . When speaking of modern work, I am not referring by any means to the *ultra*-modern in Art—though we have learned valuable lessons from it, it is slowly but surely waning, we hope and believe. However, it seems to have just reached the far West." She also discussed the types of pictures to hang in the home, how they should be arranged, and the importance of color.

Regarding music, Wiggins stressed the positive influence of radio in the home to "train young people and in fact everyone, in the appreciation of good music" by listening to nationally broadcast symphony concerts. Good music in the home, she asserted, was just as important as good art, but "perhaps more difficult to control. The young people will have some jazz and there is even some good jazz music—but as a vocal instructor I wish to warn parents of the evils of jazz in the voice. Once in, it is very difficult to eradicate—especially that flattened out quality so if your children have promising voices by all means get rid of the jazz songs on the piano." She maintained that "with good art, music and literature in the home, the occupants of that dwelling are well fortified to resist whatever of evil may try to force itself in from outside influences."

In "Practical Art Talk," Wiggins emphasized the use of classical traditions to select art and color rather than ultra modern or jazz compositions that may not "survive the present generation." In her William Merritt Chase lecture she unsurprisingly suggested, "Perhaps no other man of his time exerted so great an influence on the development of taste and art appreciation in America."

Wiggins continued in her own traditional style of painting: "I am looking only for the beautiful . . . Beauty comforts and distills the spirit. It makes a difference what we create and live with, externally as well as internally. I have been little tempted by the new extreme because I have never felt confused in my definition of art. To me, Art is Beauty. Its purpose is to inspire us, to make us happier, saner, calmer, and kinder. I may be old fashioned, but my spirit is best fed by that definition and that aim." In later years she confessed that she was "too old to go modern" although she thought it "exciting." Wiggins did not grapple too much with philosophies or manifestos, but instead created what gave her comfort and inner peace.

Oil paintings—landscapes, still lifes of vases brimming with flowers, and studies of copper and brass—now became Myra's trademark. She recalled as a child playing with household kettles and enjoying their gleam and clanking noises. From her trips overseas she had acquired exotic jugs, bowls, rugs, and vases that became subjects on her canvases. She once admitted to being a "crank on textures" and attributed some of her success to the attention she gave to details. If the background drapery was not quite the right color, she dyed it herself. If grapes in a still life lacked the natural look she wanted, she pinned a few real ones on the canvas to find the desired effect before retouching it.

Sometimes her photographs inspired her paintings, as in the case of "Morning Blessing," painted in 1899 and based on a photograph of Mildred posed as a Dutch girl. Myra's early training under William Merritt Chase, who was known for his studies of brass and metals, still defined much of her vision, although she never had painted flowers while under his tutelage. Myra always reminded people that she had studied under Chase.

Even her studio became subject matter as she deftly arranged furniture, objects, and fabrics to her compositional satisfaction. In "A Corner of My Studio - No. 1," painted in Toppenish, she crammed an alcove below a paned window with her melodeon, a small spinning wheel, vases, jugs, and rugs, and hung framed paintings in the corner. She placed a china cabinet to the right, and a long slender wall hanging of Japanese symbols to the left. Overhead, a light fixture projected from the ceiling. When finished, she mounted the painting in an ornate frame.

In "A Corner of My Studio - No. 2," another view of the same alcove, Wiggins removed the melodeon, replacing it with a child-sized bed and setting tiny Dutch wooden shoes next to it. She also rearranged the large antique spinning wheel, basket, Japanese wall hanging, and curios.

Myra still took art classes whenever possible, even though a grandmother and art instructor herself. In 1930 she attended a portrait class given by Frederick Varley at the Henry Home on Harvard Avenue North. Two years earlier, Seattle collector and philanthropist Horace Henry had donated his Capitol Hill home for art exhibitions and classes sponsored by the Seattle Art Institute. This organization soon was absorbed by the Seattle Art Museum, which opened in 1933 in Volunteer Park on Capitol Hill.

Varley's portrait class united a group who agreed, as women artists, that they lacked exhibition opportunities and received scant professional support and encouragement. As a consequence of their discussions, Elizabeth Warhanik (1880-1968), Lily Norling Hardwick (1890-1944), Anna Belle Stone (1874-1948), Dorothy Dolph Jensen (1895-1977), Wiggins, and administrator Helen Bebb founded Women Artists of Washington, a name later changed to Women Painters of Washington.

The club made its debut on October 6, 1930, with 25 charter members in addition to the six founders. As set forth in its constitution, the club's goals included promotion of "fellowship and goodwill among the members," stimulation of each member "to an ever advancing standard of artistic achievement," and the fostering of "art appreciation in the community by lectures, exhibitions, and traveling portfolios, in connection with the work of the members."

The group set high standards for membership and for the work exhibited by members. Monthly meetings, which were held at the Seattle Art Museum after it opened on Capitol Hill in 1933, focused on organizational business, guest speakers, and art clinics. The strength of the group is evident; Women Painters of Washington continues to exist today with over 100 members.

Although Myra's paintings appeared in shows featuring works by both men and women, a considerable part of her continuing success was due to women's organizations that offered opportunities to exhibit and to participate in leadership positions. Women Painters of Washington filled a void for those women artists whose work met high standards of excellence, yet found few venues to exhibit. It also drew women together as colleagues in a professional atmosphere.

Circumstances far beyond their control ended the Wigginses' years in Toppenish. In 1929 the stock market crashed and, not long after, a freeze damaged the nursery. In the fall of 1932, as the nation was immersed in the depression, Fred and Myra moved to Seattle to live at 711 Broadway in the Lovelace Studio Building, on Capitol Hill.

Capitol Hill was a bustling neighborhood with shops and fine homes, and a good location for Myra—she was just a few blocks from the soon to be opened Seattle Art Museum and near public transportation. Fred became a master at using bus transfers, sometimes hopping off the bus for a quick bite at home and then off to catch his connection across town.

After moving to Seattle, Myra painted "My Studio" in 1932. She had broken her right wrist, but "taught" her left hand to paint, creating the study of her studio mostly by using a palette knife. Here, the melodeon is placed to the left and only the right half appears. A vase of flowers on the melodeon holds some draped fabric in place. A basket, rug, jugs, paintings, and small objects draw the eye to the paned window looking out on foliage and a neighboring building.

Living in Seattle brought Wiggins in closer contact to the activities she loved. At this stage in her life she sought women's arts organizations to fulfill her interests. In 1932, she was offered membership in the Seattle branch of the National League of American Pen Women. She had recently presided over the Art Division of the Washington Federation of Women's Clubs and, of course, helped found the new club, Women Artists of Washington. With her insights from years of experience in the arts, energy, and flair for leadership, Wiggins carved a niche for her talents.

In 1934, at an age when most people contemplate retirement, Myra announced the opening of her art studio in their tiny apartment. Her studio brochure proclaimed her achievements and advertised her availability for lectures and classes. Her winter classes were scheduled to begin December 1, and she announced she would accept commissions for painting flowers, interiors, gardens, still lifes, heirlooms, and portraits. By this time she had been included in "Who's Who in Art," "Women of the West," and "Women of Today." Her painting "Old Metals with Fruit" received a first prize at the seventh Annual Art Exhibition of the National League of American Pen Women in Chicago, and "Marigolds in the Window" had hung at the Seattle Art Museum in the Twentieth Northwest Annual Exhibition.

For a fee, Wiggins offered lectures and slide shows about art and her travels. However, she lectured on Palestine, Egypt, Athens, Italy, and the Mediterranean without charge to churches and charitable organizations. In October, she spoke on the topic "American Art" at the opening of the fall program of the Rainier Chapter of the Daughters of the American Revolution.

When most people their age were slowing down, the Wigginses had no choice but to continue working. Necessity and creativeness had sustained Myra's enterprising lifestyle and, at age 64, her energy and lively disposition continued to serve her well. She enjoyed reminding people that she had received most of her painting awards after becoming a grandmother.

Fred, meanwhile, became a traveling salesman for the Pacific Northwest Floral Company. His income depended on commissions from rhododendron, holly, and bulb sales, which meant absences of months at a time as he crossed the country serving East Coast customers. On January 1, 1938, for example, Myra held a reception and tea honoring Fred's return home after seven months on the road. A week later, Fred told Myra he would be leaving again in a few days for Chicago.

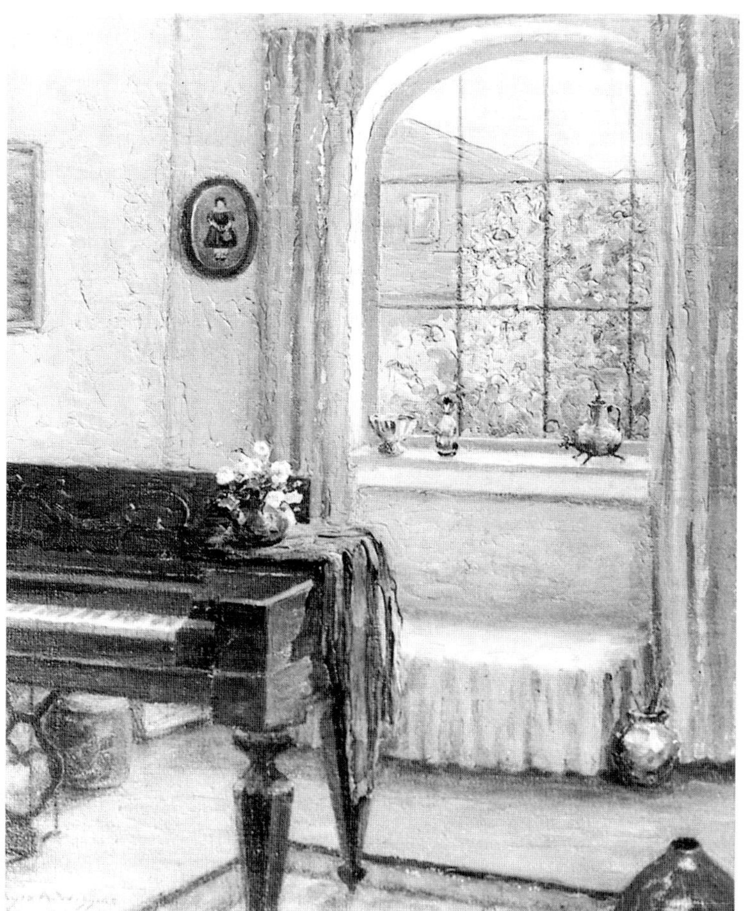

My Studio
1932, oil on canvas

Meanwhile, Myra called prospective pupils, hoping to fill her classes—probably a challenging task in the midst of the depression. She attended a myriad of club gatherings to enrich and support her creative and professional life, including regular meetings with Verse Writers, Pen Women, and a book review group. At Verse Writers, she submitted her poems for critique and club members voted for the best poems.

On Sundays after church, Wiggins often visited city or county jails and met with inmates to talk about Christianity. To one group of delinquent girls she told of her "surrender at age 14" to her faith. To groups of men, she spoke about the Bible and of beauty in nature. She attempted to provide inspiration by singing church hymns and reading her poems.

From there, Wiggins moved on to whatever club or museum activities occupied that day's calendar—receptions, meetings, or teas—or returned home to write letters, work on poems, or straighten up her studio. Besides her memberships in the Seattle Poetry Club and Verse Writers, she contributed to the Puget Sound Poets column in the *Seattle Post-Intelligencer.*

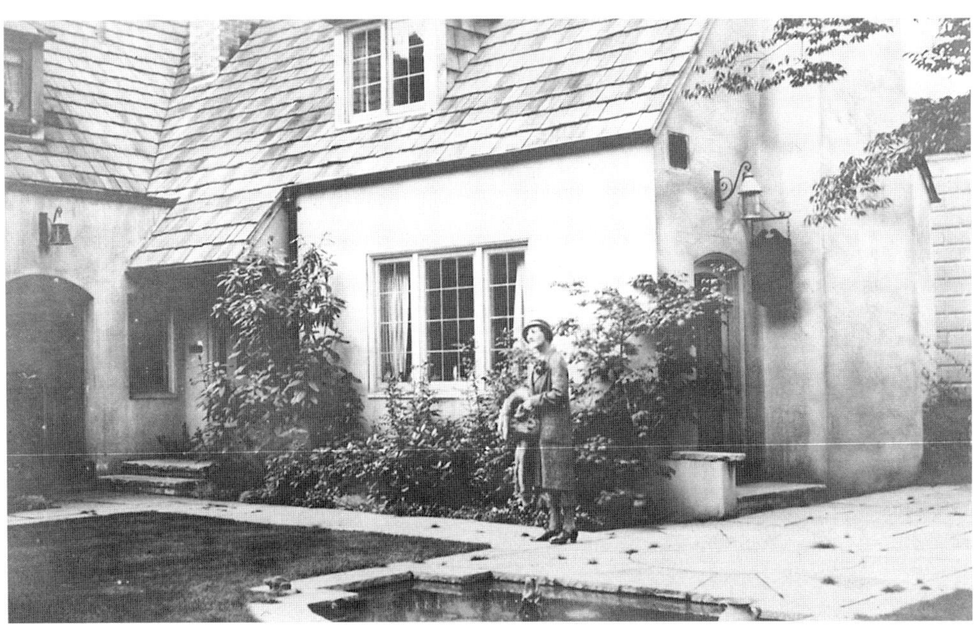

Lovelace Studio Building,
Myra's Studio
post 1932
photographer unknown
Robert and Shirley Benz Collection

In early November, 1938, Wiggins held her fourth annual "At Home," inviting the public into her studio. Between 200 and 250 people crammed into Wiggins' studio between three and eight o'clock, viewed her paintings and her students' work, ate small sandwiches and cakes, and drank apple cider. Three days later she met with patrons who were considering purchasing one of her paintings—one that she was reluctant to part with for sentimental reasons. She spent the evening fixing the heels and patching the soles on eight pairs of shoes.

Wiggins constantly fussed with her hair and clothes. She made frequent repairs and alterations to her dresses and coats because there was little money to buy new ones. She managed, however, to maintain appearances while hobnobbing with art patrons and museum supporters, whether in Seattle or during trips east.

Two days before the Northwest Annual Preview at the Seattle Art Museum, Wiggins sewed, mended, and fitted a new jacket to her old rust colored dress. The next day she arranged to have mounts cut for pictures she needed that night: "ran to Liggetts to get hair waves combed out, then caught car home—same transfer—about 6. got some supper (cold) and turned to dress—was about 10 minutes late when Claire came for me at 8:05—we then called for Daisy for Preview—a fine modern show. My 'Copper Bucket with Still Life' hung and downstairs in our WPW [Women Painters of Washington] still life show, my 'Copper Cup with Fruit' received first honorable mention . . . Bed, 5:45."

Wiggins knew the value of publicity and made a point of getting her achievements and studio announcements into the newspapers. By the end of the decade, her list of accomplishments included the selling of paintings to the state and public libraries in Olympia and to the Yakima YMCA and YWCA. One of her paintings also received a first prize at the national exhibition of Pen Women artists held in San Francisco. In 1935, Myra's paintings "Old Metals with Fruit" and "Still-Life with Flowers" were selected by the jury of the Fourth Annual Exhibition at the Portland Art Museum.

"A red letter day" in her life, as Wiggins described it, occurred in the summer of 1938 when she accompanied her son-in-law Reuben to a Washington apple promotional event. Much to her surprise, the trip included an airplane ride. As she explained, "The big thing pulled up, the steps were wheeled into place, and the cameraman appeared and took our pictures outside the plane with the hostess kneeling in front with a great basket of Washington red apples; seated inside the plane, the stewardess disposed of our wraps, then passed red apples to everyone . . . Unfortunately the atmosphere was very smoky [hazy] when we were up over the city and the Sound, so we could not see anything very distinctly, but recognized many places . . . we were up nearly an hour . . . That airplane has given me a taste for more."

In December, 1938, Wiggins printed a woodcut depicting her studio doorway along with one of her poems, "Noel," on 100 Christmas cards. Over the years she designed many such cards by combining one of her paintings or photographs with a poem. Beginning around this time, she inserted lengthy newsletters in the Christmas cards describing family activities, travels, and achievements, and attendance at museums, galleries, and events. Myra and Fred also were not shy about mentioning the names of ministers, painters, sculptors, singers, and writers they had interacted with during the year.

During trips east, Myra set up a studio in the Hotel Grand or the Milner Hotel in New York for several months while Fred traveled about taking orders from nurseries, greenhouses, and florists. On one trip east, Myra visited the New York World's Fair. She also viewed countless exhibits in museums and galleries, returning to them every few weeks as the shows changed, and sometimes met with educational directors at the museums to whom she "never lost an opportunity of praising in deserved superlatives, our outstanding museum and generous donors [at the Seattle Art Museum]."

Myra saw operas at the Metropolitan Opera and attended weekly talks by contemporary authors at the National Arts Club. Returning to her family's historical roots, she visited the site of the "old Methodist church" where 100 years earlier a farewell meeting paid homage to Almira Phelps' missionary group. Included in her planned itinerary were stops at such places as Old Williamsburg (Virginia), New Orleans, Los Angeles, Laguna Beach (California), San Francisco, and Salem (Oregon). Myra frequently traveled without Fred, meeting him in New York after taking detours around the country.

In spite of her many activities, Wiggins found time to paint. At ten year intervals—1930, 1940, and 1950—she painted portraits of herself, with each detailing her inherent dignity as she aged. "Bouquet," painted around 1945, assumed a certain significance in her career. The painting depicted a simple vase, over 100 years old, "handed down" from her maternal grandmother. Overflowing with flowers, it sits on a plain surface directly in front of shiny, draped fabric. "Bouquet" hung in

MORNING BLESSING
1899, oil on canvas
Robert and Shirley Benz Collection

the annual exhibition of the National Association of Women Artists at the National Academy in New York, and also appeared by invitation in the show "My Best" at the Downtown Gallery in Seattle. It also led to her acceptance into the National Association of Women Artists of the American Artists group in New York in 1945. This organization annually published the work of contemporary American artists on Christmas cards. They used at least four of Wiggins' subjects, one of which set a "near record sale" of 62,000 cards, providing her with substantial royalties. This heirloom vase appeared again in "Petunias and Taffeta," in which she filled it with flowers ranging in color from white, to lavender, to deep purple, with periwinkle blue flowers in clusters.

During the 1940s, Wiggins' paintings hung in annual juried shows at the Seattle Art Museum, the Pacific Coast Painters and Sculptors exhibitions, the annual Pacific Northwest art exhibitions in Spokane, Washington, and the Women Painters of Washington exhibitions. She was one of the first women jurors for the Northwest Annual art show and appeared in this exhibit twenty-nine times. Wiggins exhibited in Vancouver (British Columbia), New Orleans, Chicago, and California. What probably raised the most excitement, however, was her exhibition of seventeen paintings at the Argent Gallery on West 57th Street in New York, September 30-October 12, 1946, which was announced in *The New York Times* and *Art Digest*.

Fred and Myra traveled to New York for the Argent reception, which was described as "filled to overflowing." Two other artists shared the show. Lily Converse's lithographs and drawings were "strong, often moody interpretations of landscapes in Europe, America and Africa." Her art was considered "decorative work of considerable ability." Viola Barloga's work included "darkly painted landscapes and interiors." She "contrived credible freshness in her academic flower paintings and still lifes." Wiggins was described by *The New York Times* as a busy great grandmother who had studied at the Art Students League fifty years earlier and put aside painting for forty years to be an "art photographer encouraged by Alfred Stieglitz." Since then, the reviewer said, she had returned to painting. The writer concluded: "well-fashioned still life and florals, with emphasis on textures, formed her Argent Exhibition."

One of her paintings in the show, "Fish with Metals," had been the result of an industrious week. "I finally found him, an admirable red snapper," she said. "I kept him in the refrigerator four days until I could work at the picture. Then I had to spray him with fly spray, and keep all the windows open and work at night. But I painted my fish!"

This painting evoked memories of her art student days: "I can see Mr. Chase even yet. He'd shake his head and say 'I suppose I'll always be known as a painter of fish!' But he was also a great portraitist."

Also shown were "Still Life with Apples" and "Textures," a study of glass, ceramic, and copper objects surrounding a white sculpture made by Wiggins. Two other of her paintings in the Argent show, "Flowers in Brass" and "Old Brass with Pottery," had hung in the Northwest Annual exhibitions at the Seattle Art Museum. Fred, who was bursting with pride, quipped that for the duration of the show he was "just Mr. Myra Wiggins."

Around the time of Wiggins' Argent Gallery show, Knox Manning, a Hollywood, California, radio broadcaster, devoted four minutes in one of his afternoon programs to highlight Wiggins. He portrayed her as the "famous Great Grandmother artist of the Pacific Coast" and told " funny incidents of her life and career." The "Dorothy and Dick Show" on WOR Broadcasting in New York also aired a story on Wiggins' photography. Myra Wiggins had become a national celebrity.

Alfred Stieglitz died on July 13, 1946. At his request, there was no ceremony, eulogy, or music before his cremation. His ashes were buried among the roots of an aged tree near Lake George, New York, a favored location where he had spent considerable time. If Wiggins had contacted Stieglitz during her trips to New York, she never mentioned it, but she did write his address and phone number on the back of a print of "Dethroned." Also written next to Stieglitz's name were the New York addresses for Frances Benjamin Johnston and Mrs. Theodore Toedt.

Beginning in 1946 with the Argent Gallery show, Wiggins' career started to come full circle, achieving acclaim akin to her days as a pictorial photographer forty years earlier. In April, 1947, at the Matrix Table of Theta Sigma Phi, a journalism honorary organization, she was one of eight Pacific Northwest women honored for outstanding achievement and was called the "Dean of Women Painters of the Pacific Northwest." In July, the Seattle Branch of the National League of American Pen Women conferred on Wiggins the Kara Aesdale Dickenson Award for "achievement of the year." Phi Delta Nu, an honorary authors' and creative artists' fraternity, awarded Wiggins a lifetime membership.

Her painting "Flowers in Brass" hung in the Fifty-fifth Annual Exhibition of the National

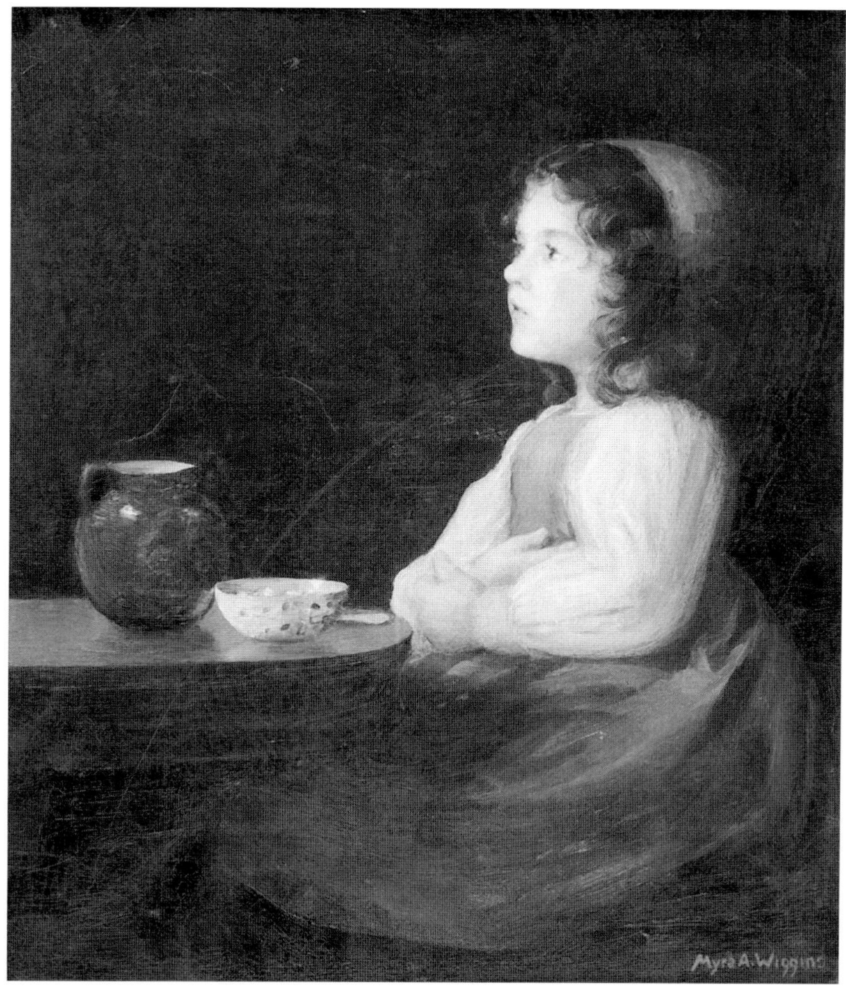

Association of Women Artists at the National Academy in New York. A reviewer in *Art Digest* praised the show, considered the work of superior quality, stimulating and varied, and added that it put to shame "many of its big-brother national exhibitions seen recently, particularly the lately reviewed Corcoran Biennial." Two of her woodcuts were used on the cover of *In Valiant Quest*, a collection of poems by Washington poets. Meanwhile,

Dr. E.O. Holland, President Emeritus of Washington State College, purchased her oil "Metals with Glass" for the college's Orton Collection, where it was included with works by the nationally noted painters Robert Henri, Maurice Prendergast, and William Glackens.

Despite his own hectic schedule, Fred assisted his wife in any way he could, usually by packing and shipping her paintings to galleries. He proudly saved newspaper clippings regarding her career. "As I look at things from time to time I try to think in the abstract, as to 'who anyway is this person,'" he wrote her, "and then I realize again that you are just you, as you always have been and always will be, a truly fine and remarkable character, who as is all too frequently true, is not fully understood and appreciated for what you are. Anyway, mother dear, honors are coming from time to time, and for many of these belated tributes, we owe more than we can express to our fine boy Reuben and to Mildred, whose love and loyalty means everything to us."

In 1948, Myra received an Art Achievement award at the biennial meeting of the National League of American Pen Women in Washington, D.C. Awards were disbursed in three areas: art, music, and letters. Recipients were determined by a panel of three judges who examined portfolios containing a summation of each candidate's life work. It pleased Myra when one of the judges, Horace Jayne, Vice Director of the Metropolitan Museum of Art, told her the award was "very deserved." Fred, meanwhile, completed his 99th trek across the country. A few months later, in mid January, 1949, when he reached Seattle after yet another crossing, he marked his 100th trip since November 27, 1888, when he had left Kansas for Salem, Oregon.

Myra's health began to deteriorate. She had long suffered from asthma, allergies, and back pain. At times over the years she had been unable to work, but her energy and positive attitude helped her overcome these phases. In the fall of 1948, nearing 80 years old, she became ill, went into the hospital, and later suffered from shingles. This occurred after the Wigginses had completed a three-month trip to Washington, D.C., with stops in Portland, Boise, Denver, Kansas, Dallas, New Orleans, Chicago, New York, and Boston. After the Wigginses' visit to Washington, D.C., to accept Myra's aforementioned Pen Women award, they had settled into a room in the Wolcott Hotel in New York and hung about a dozen of her paintings on the walls, thereby creating a "gallery" of her work. While Fred sold nursery products, Myra lunched with friends in Greenwich Village and visited the galleries on West 57th Street. At the Metropolitan Museum of Art, the Wigginses saw German paintings—hidden during the Second World War in salt mines and recently found by the American Army—and they attended concerts in the evening. She visited the Whitney Galleries, the National Academy, the Museum of Modern Art, and the old William Merritt Chase studio on 10th Street.

The Wigginses attended services in the historic Marble Collegiate Church where Myra had worshipped during the years she studied at the Art Students League. In Washington, D.C., they went to the Corcoran Gallery, the National Gallery of Art, and also viewed the Pen Women exhibition in the National Museum foyer that included two of Wiggins' oils. Myra's and Fred's pace was impressive. For example, the previous year during their train trip they had spent their time writing and preparing cards and letters. Their fellow

---

A BLESSING

THANK YOU GOD, FOR
EACH GLAD MORNING

AND THE BLESSINGS
OF THE DAY—

FOOD AND SHELTER,
FRIENDS AND DEAR ONES

AND THE TIME FOR
WORK AND PLAY.

—Myra Albert Wiggins, 1953

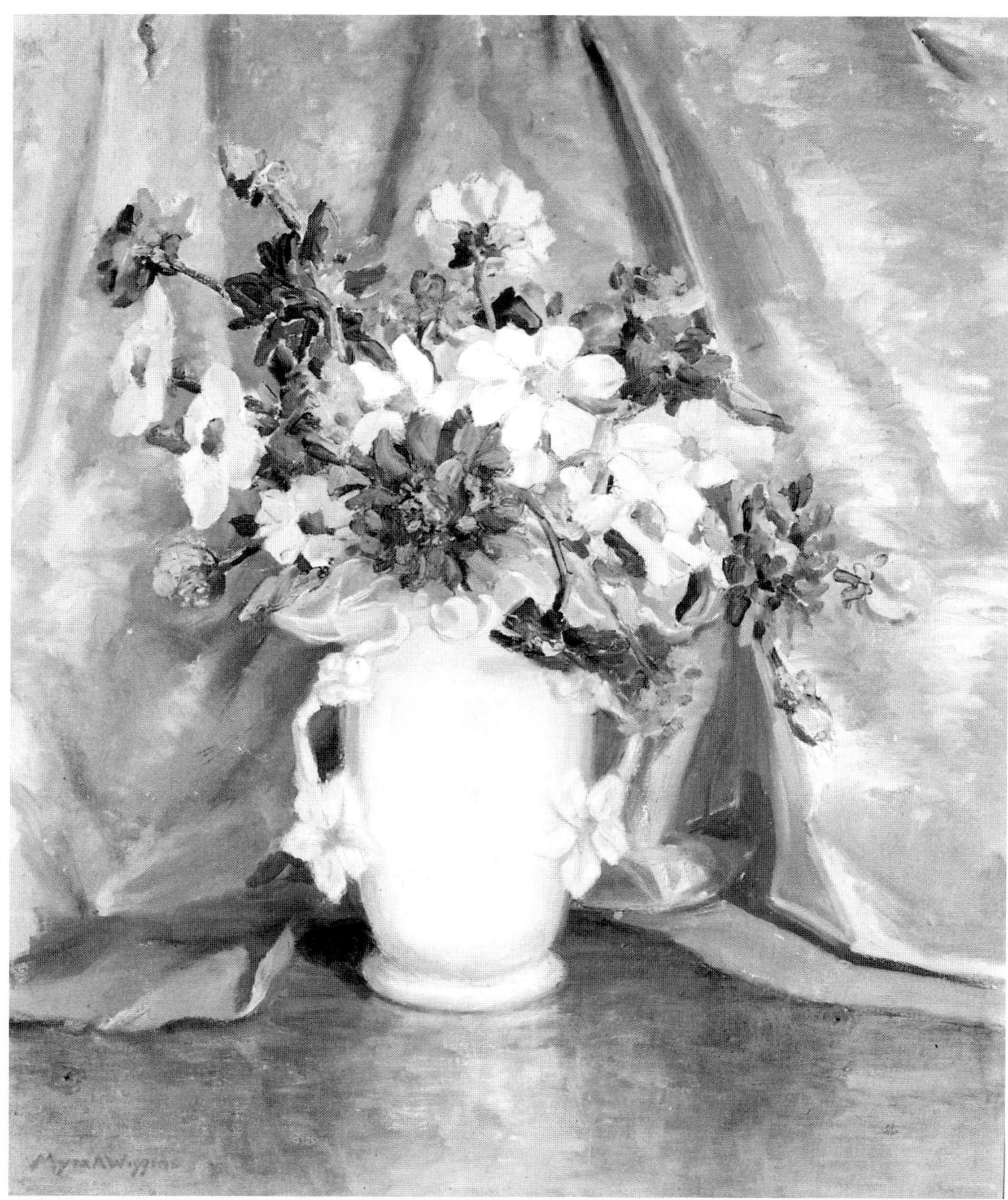

Bouquet
c. 1945, oil on canvas

passengers called them "the workingest" passengers on the train.

In May, 1949, Fred and Myra left Seattle on their spring trip, making stops in southern Oregon, San Francisco, Los Angeles, Houston, and New Orleans. She continued on to Washington and New York while Fred, now 80, wound his way through the Midwest on business. In San Francisco and Houston, Myra visited art museums, while noting how much she enjoyed viewing work by Seattle painter Kenneth Callahan as well as some portraits by George DeForest Brush, her instructor years ago. Brush's work reminded her of his "oft repeated admonition" in her life drawing class: "'Delicate as a rosepetal'—meaning the flesh, leaving accessories to furnish the darks of the picture." In Santa Barbara, Wiggins had used her new Kodak Flash Bantam camera with color film, which she carried in a small handbag fashionably chosen to match her dress.

HUNGER IST DER BESTE KOCH
(HUNGER IS THE BEST COOK)
1898, platinum print
6½" x 4½"
Portland Art Museum

In New York, Wiggins settled in at the Wolcott Hotel. Publicly, she maintained the image of a person of comfortable means flitting from one gallery or museum to another. Privately, she sometimes was desperate for money just to eat. "I have paid for a lot of my food from my purses and pockets," she wrote Fred in June, "— had a $1 bill in coat you sent which I am wearing around in my room for warmth. To take out I buy one pint milk every day and one banana a day . . . It seems like every time I leave Hotel I have to spend $1 for food—but I can't get the food I need . . . Each day only one meal out. Hotel has put bill in box—due in morning."

After disputing the hotel bill over one day's charge, she was unable to pay. Five days later in a letter to Fred she expressed her fear of not receiving money by the next day: "I have used up two $5.00 bills of mine which I pinned in purses and plenty more—phones—street car fare and incidentals—and train men, Hotel men and red caps and taxis since new Orleans and a *few* meals on train have used up the house money you gave me long ago."

With Fred's income so sporadic and unpredictable, Myra had begun stashing money here and there, pinning it in her clothes or purse, and referring to it as "her" money, as she had in the past defined the cash she earned. She wished Fred had some way of forcing his commissions from nurserymen who owed him, but avoided paying when asked. He was afraid to say anything, fearing the nurserymen might refuse his services. Moreover, Myra's health had prevented her from doing much studio work; she had painted only two pictures in over a year.

Myra made an appointment to show her photographs to Edward Steichen, by then head of the photography department at the Museum of Modern Art. In the hotel room, she spent three days mounting her pictorial photographs, working "night and day (sleeping a few hours in the afternoon)," and feeling ashamed of her work displayed at previous exhibits "because they were not properly mounted." She placed the three prints that had hung in the 1910 Albright Gallery exhibit on top so "he won't need to see the rest unless he cares to." The next day Wiggins arrived at the museum for her appointment, but Steichen was ill at his country home and not expected for at least another week. Myra never had another chance to see Steichen.

Somehow, in spite of their hardships, the Wigginses managed to continue their cross country travels. Fred, out of necessity, completed his 107th crossing of the continent, while Myra met up with

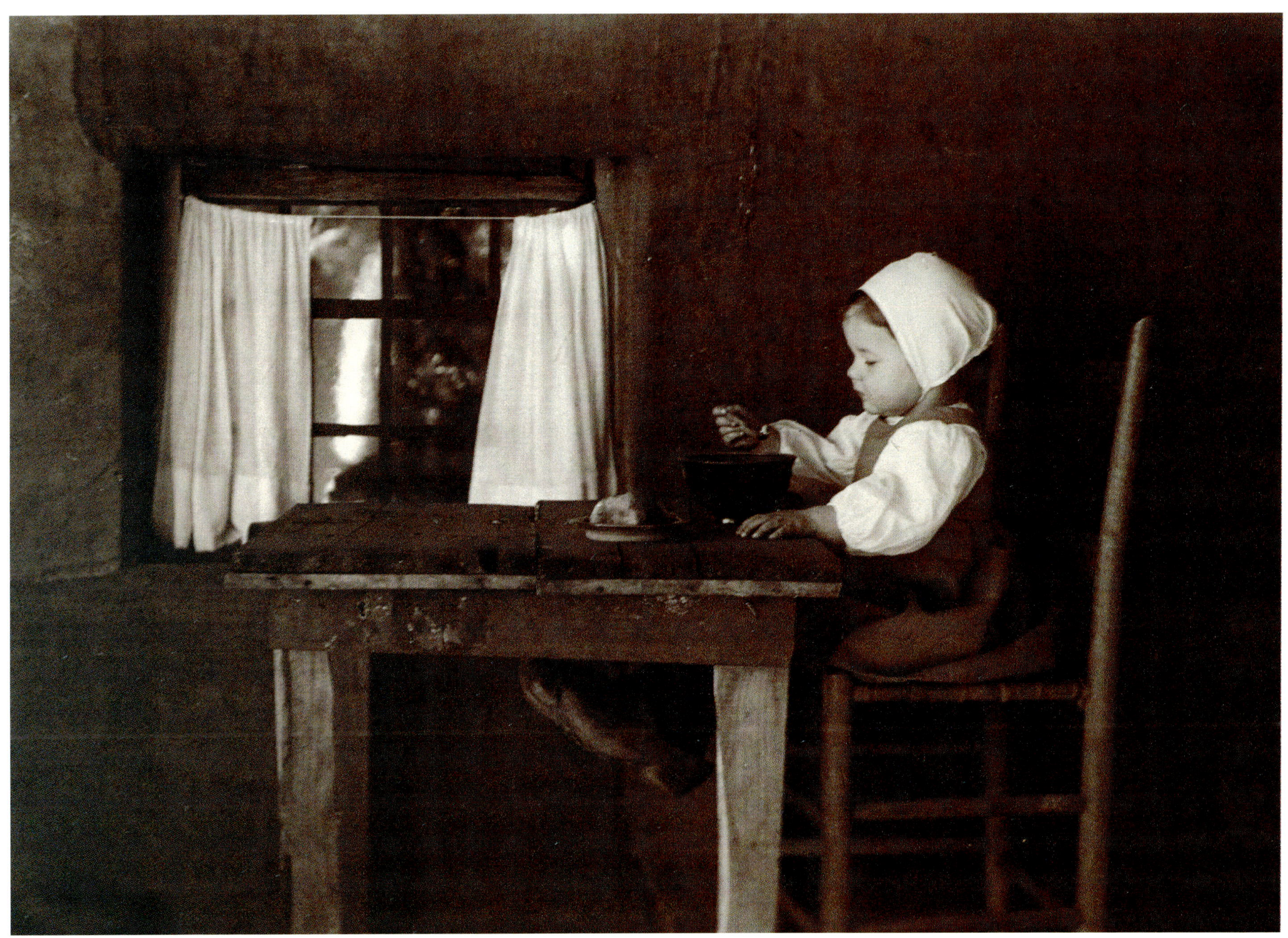

THREE GIRLS FLAT
c. 1892-93, cyanotype
Portland Art Museum

MYRA AND LENA'S
STUDIO EXHIBITION
c. 1899, cyanotype
8" x 6⅛"
Robert and Shirley Benz Collection
Myra's first studio exhibition.

POLISHING BRASS
1903, platinum print
6" x 7⅜"
Portland Art Museum

TWO PILGRIMS
1904, Middle East
Portland Art Museum
Mrs. Park (left); Myra (right); tipped in photograph from Myra's book, "Letters from a Pilgrim."

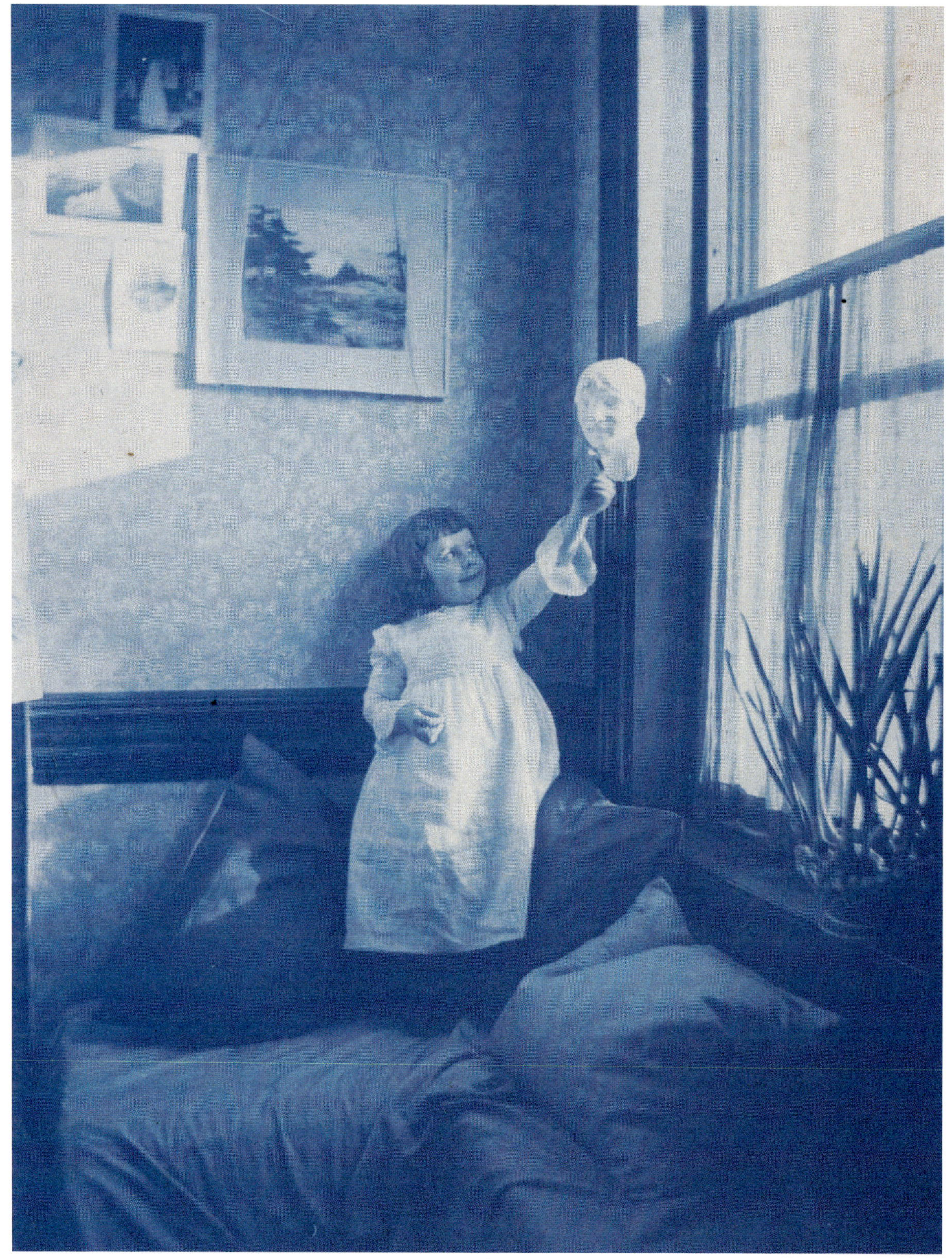

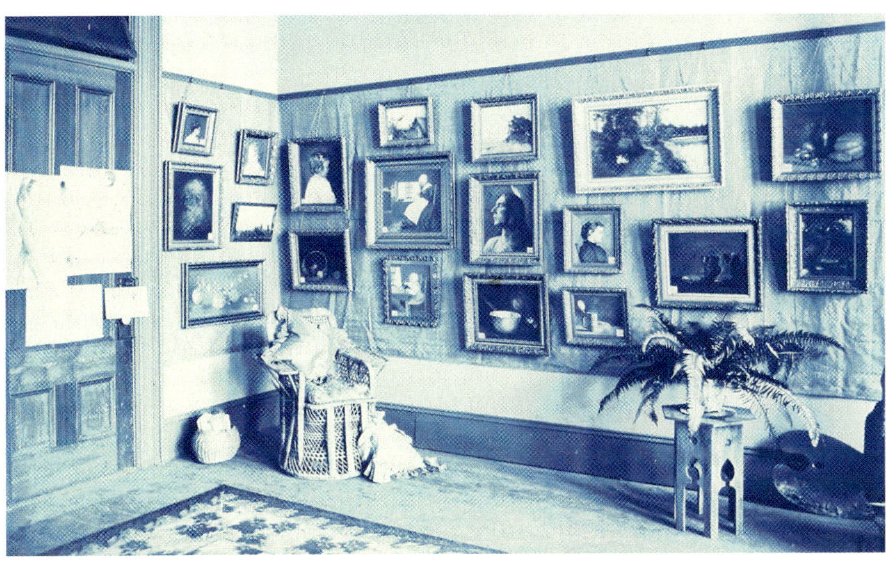

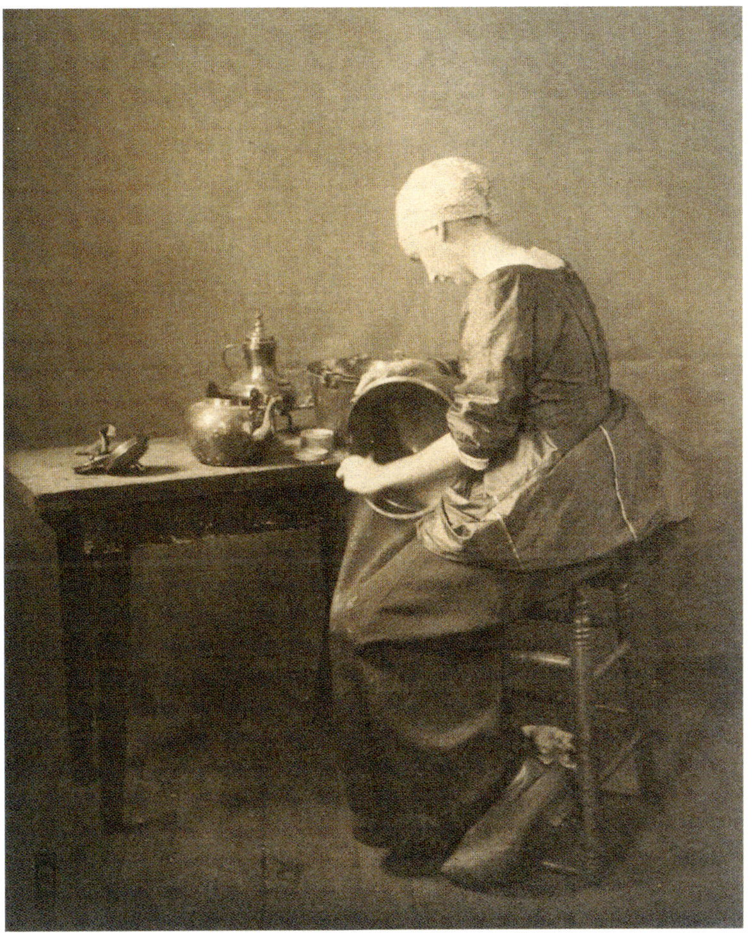

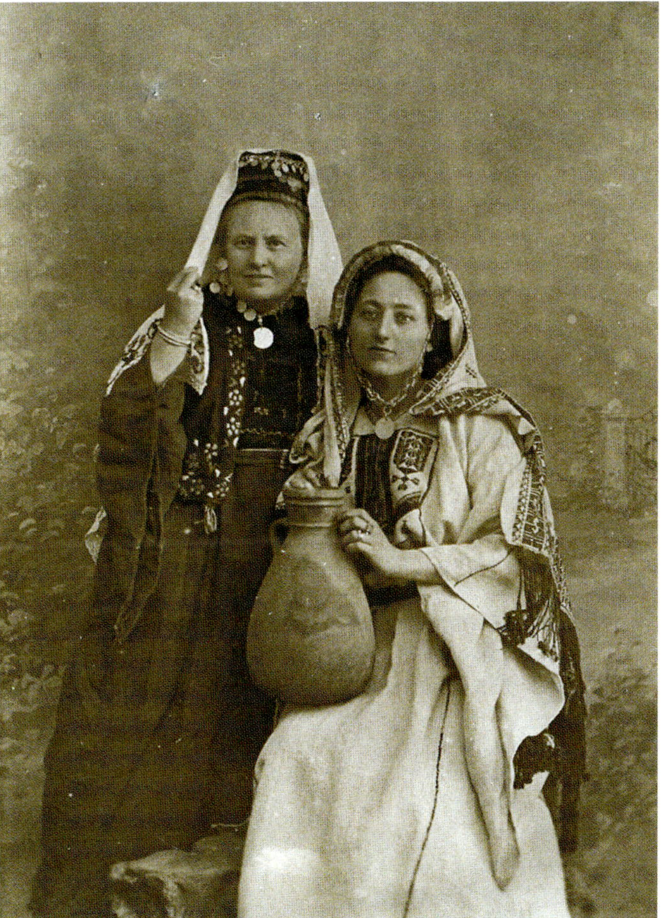

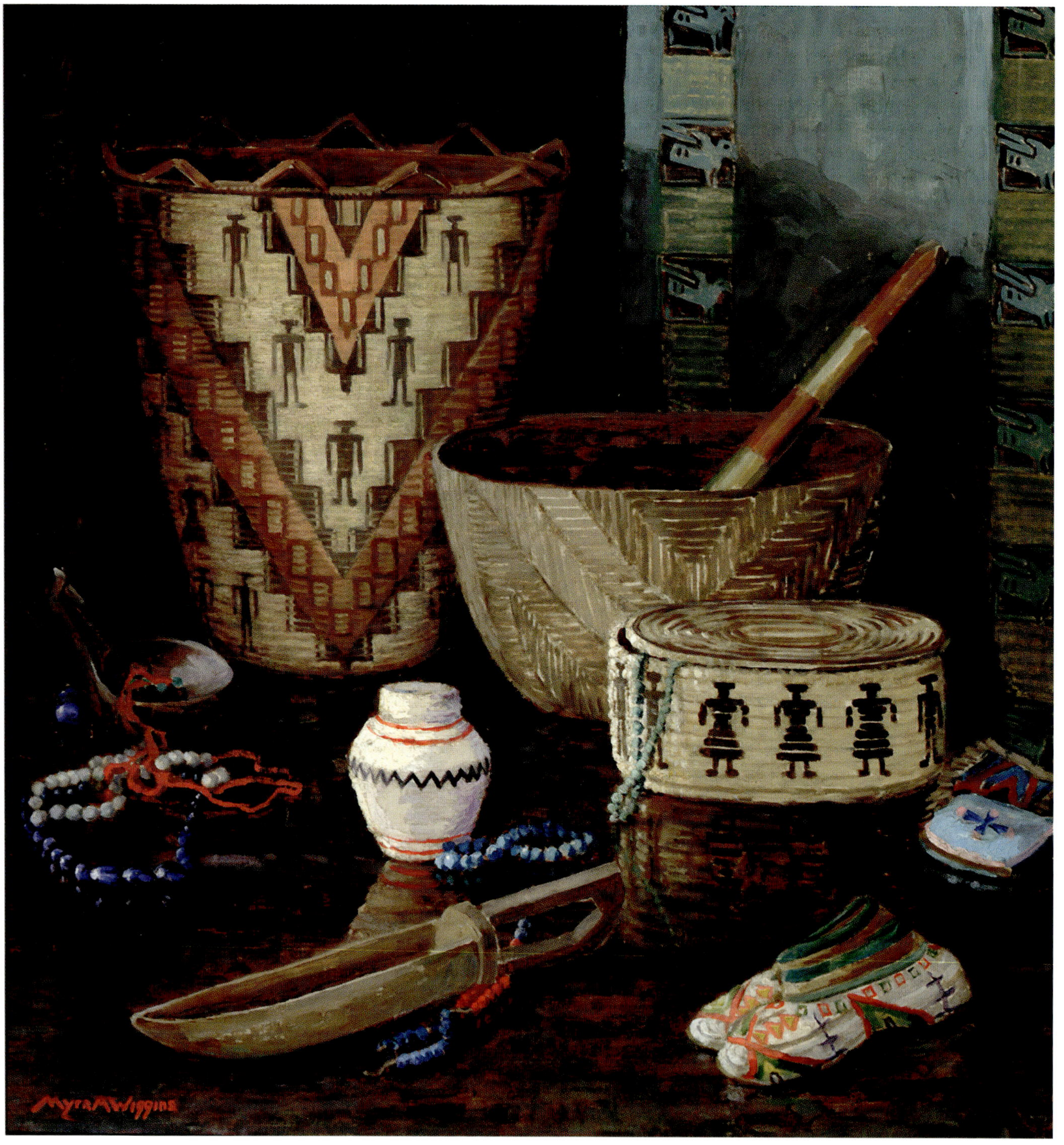

Indian Baskets and Still Life
oil on canvas
32" x 35"
courtesy of Martin-Zambito Fine Art, Seattle

Boy Twins of New York
c. 1892, cyanotype
5⅝" x 7½"
Portland Art Museum

A Corner of My Studio - No. 2
c. 1930, oil on canvas
12½" x 13¼"
Robert and Shirley Benz Collection

Mountain Rescue
watercolor
30" x 25"
Robert and Shirley Benz Collection

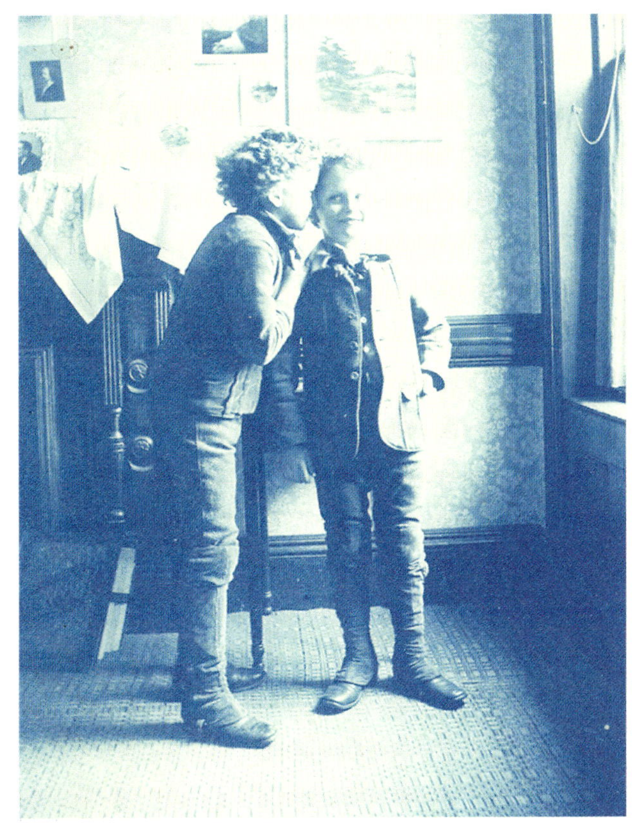

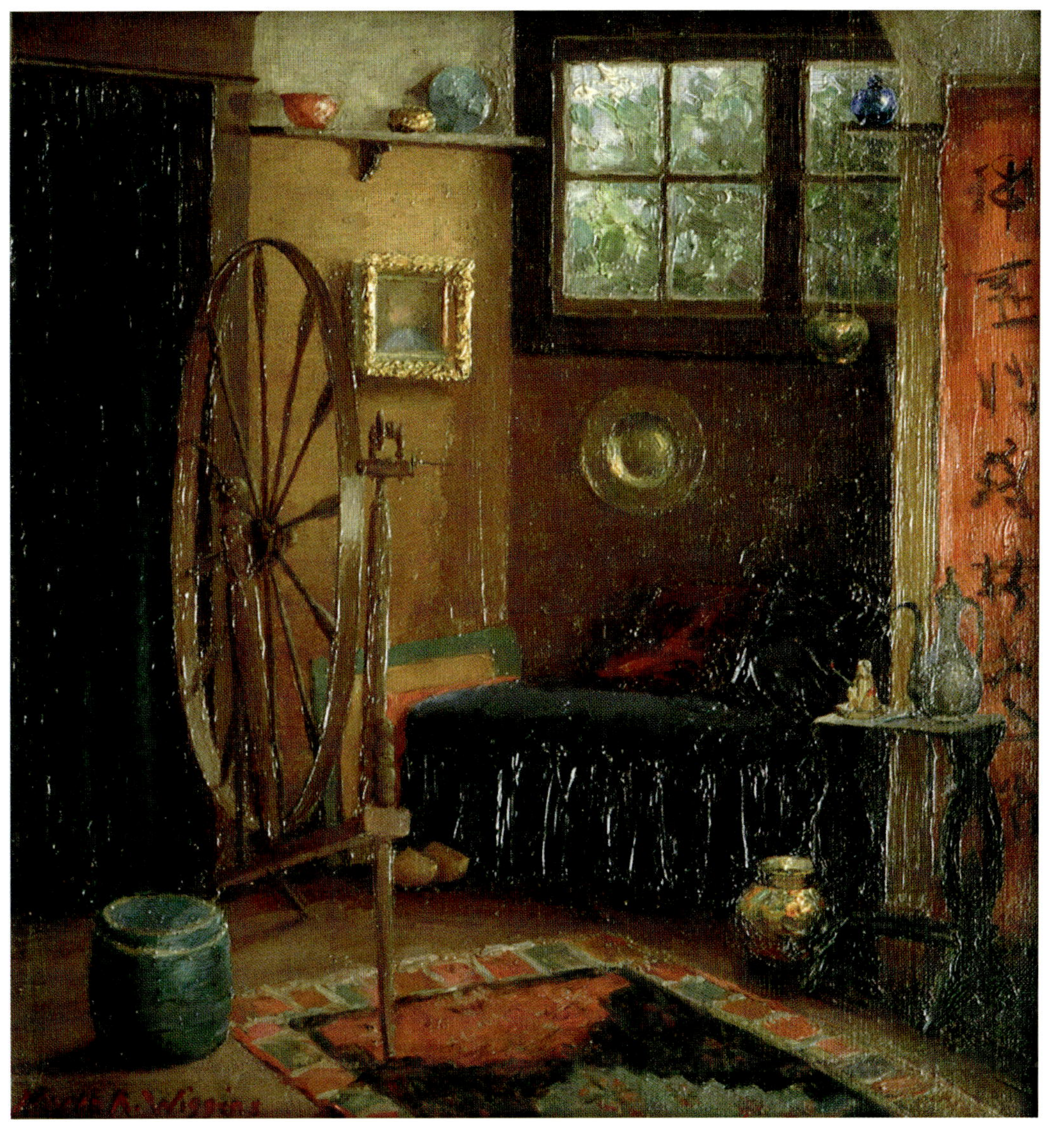

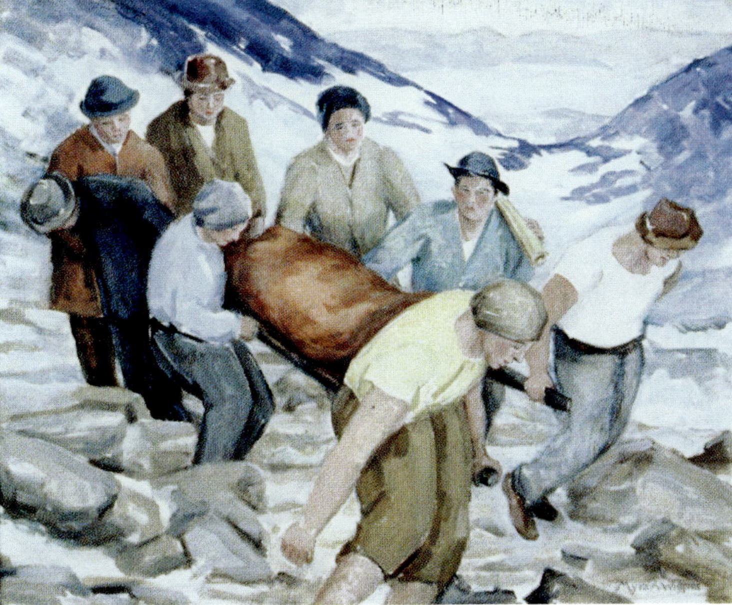

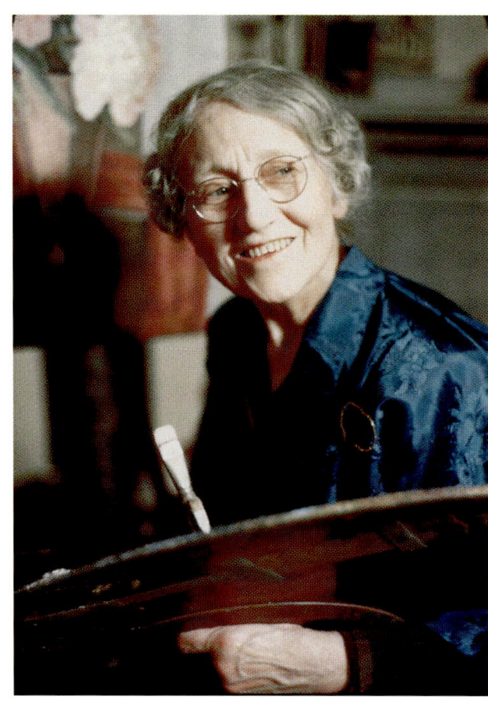

Portrait of Myra Wiggins
c. 1945
Robert and Shirley Benz Collection

Self Portrait at 60
1930, oil on board
17¾" x 23½"
Robert and Shirley Benz Collection

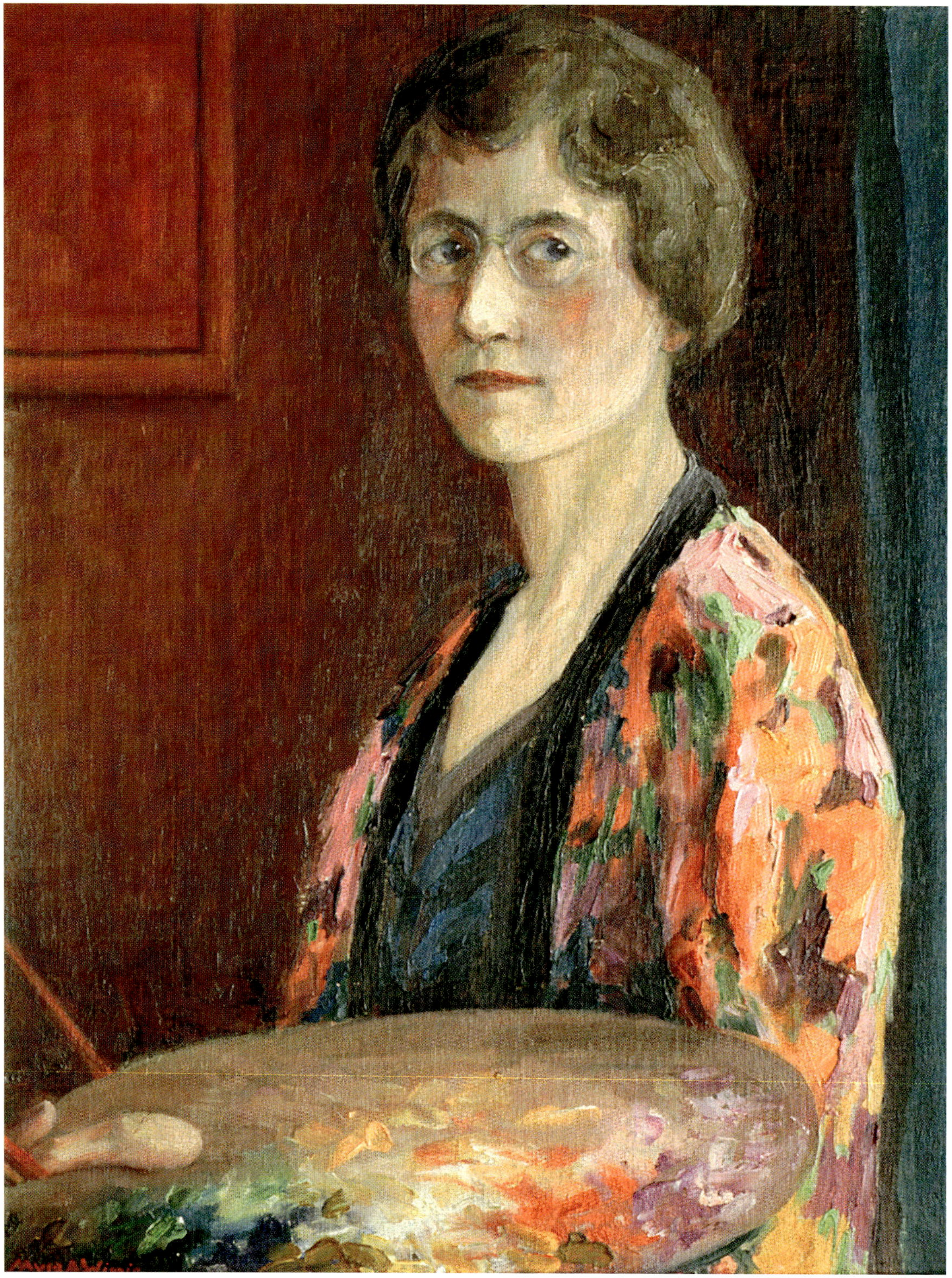

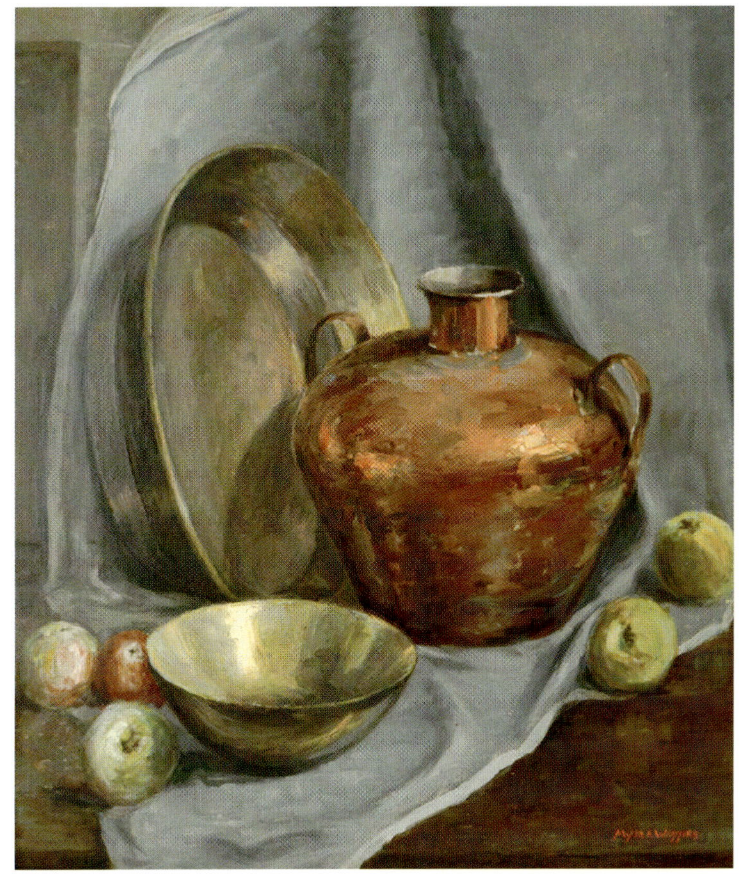

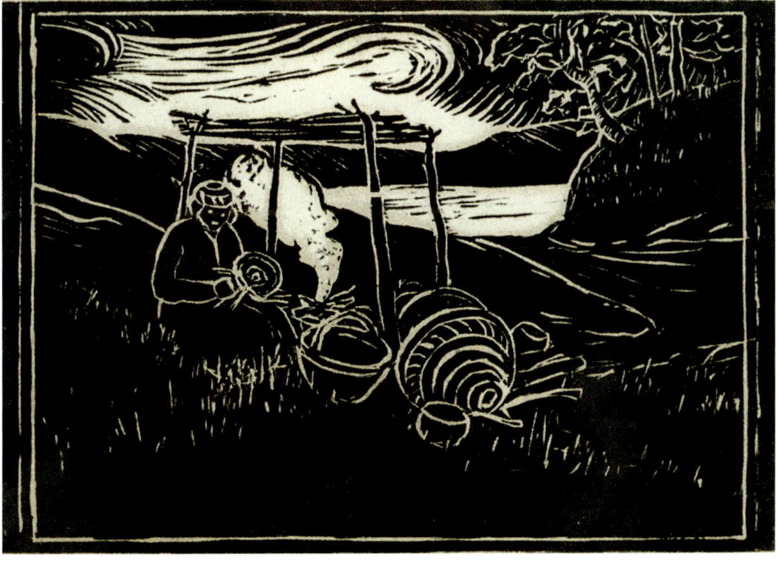

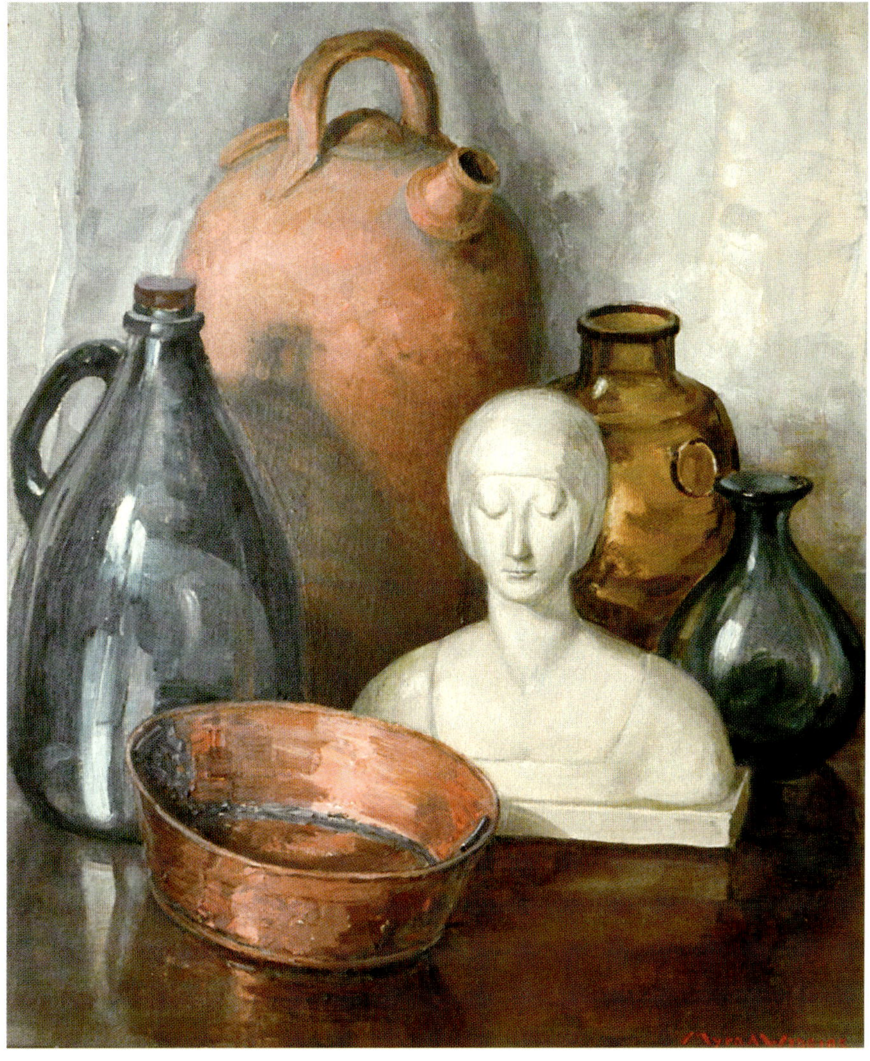

STILL LIFE WITH APPLES
no date, oil on canvas
24½" x 29½"
Robert and Shirley Benz Collection

YAQUINA BASKET MAKER
no date, woodcut
7" x 4¾"
Robert and Shirley Benz Collection

TEXTURES
c. 1944, oil on canvas
21½" x 25⅝"
Robert and Shirley Benz Collection

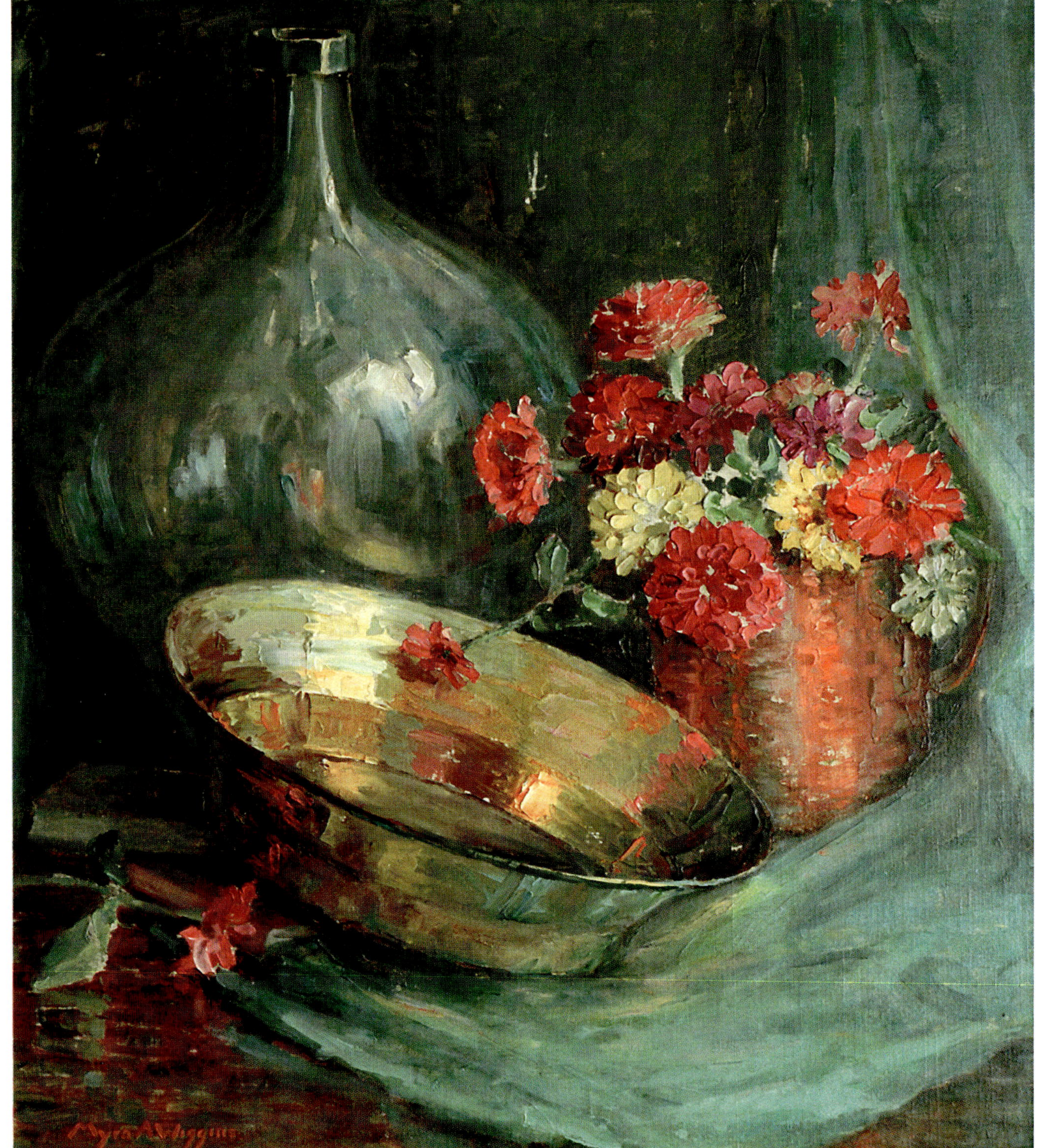

Zinnias, Glass, and Brass
1935, oil on canvas
24½" x 27½"
Robert and Shirley Benz Collection

him at various points during her six months away from Seattle. In Washington, D.C., she was a delegate at the Biennial Meeting of the National League of Pen Women. She previously had packed and shipped three paintings to submit to the Biennial Art Exhibit. These paintings hung in the "New Museum" branch of the Smithsonian during April.

As the Art Students League prepared to celebrate its 75th jubilee year, a jubilee history catalogue was illustrated with Myra's photographs of Chase's painting class and Augustus St. Gauden's modeling class made 57 years earlier on glass plates. *Art Digest* also reproduced these photographs, igniting in Myra memories of her first year of classes in the old stables before the League moved to a new building on 57th Street. For the first time, Wiggins visited the Eastman Kodak Company in Rochester, New York, where the staff members, after hearing a bit of her history, feted and later featured her in their house magazine *Kodakery*.

After returning to Seattle in the fall, the Wigginses traveled to western Oregon where the Salem Art Association honored Myra with a sixty-year retrospective of her paintings at the Elfstrom Galleries. The show of thirty paintings ranged from her earlier painted work "Thunder Cloud" (1893), to "Baby Mildred" (1897), to her self-portraits painted at ages 60, 70, and 80. The familiar "Fish with Metals," "My Studio," "Copper Kettle with Still Life," and "Bouquet" highlighted this sampling of her life's work.

In April at the Pen Women's Annual Tea and Exhibition in Seattle, a jury that included Walter Isaacs, head of the University of Washington Art School, awarded her painting "Peruvian Lillies" the first prize for oils. In May, Fred and Myra prepared for their usual summer trip to San Francisco and Los Angeles.

While in San Francisco, Myra's tenacity and belief in her work paid off. When she visited the Rotunda Art Gallery, directed by Beatrice Judd Ryan, Myra inquired if Ryan "knew of any gallery or museum that would be interested in pictorial photography of the past sixty years." Ryan referred Wiggins to Ninfa Valvo, curator of the De Young Museum in Golden Gate Park.

The next day, and Myra's last in San Francisco, she phoned Ninfa Valvo's secretary for an appointment, but Valvo had no openings. When Myra persisted, asking if Miss Valvo could give her just five minutes, the secretary relented. According to Wiggins, when Valvo first saw the mounted photographs she thought they were photos of paintings. Wiggins explained that for fifty years she had known Alfred Stieglitz, who had "encouraged" her work, and that the prints in her portfolio won more than fifty awards and honors and had hung in the salons of Europe and America, even though Myra never had a darkroom. Myra claimed, "I always tell everyone that my photographs are better than my paintings, but most people like color best." Valvo enthusiastically agreed to show Wiggins' work, but it would be several years before the show would come to pass.

In the fall of 1951, the Larson Museum in Yakima paid homage to Myra with a sixty year retrospective. Seventeen of the fifty paintings shown were loaned by local owners. In three weeks, over 2,000 people viewed her paintings. She laughed when one visitor, who after closely studying the self-portraits, asked Myra if all her teeth were her own.

In December, a few days before she turned 81, the Phi Delta Nu society of which Wiggins was an honorary member feted her as "Artist of the Year."

Her oil "Still Life with Limes" hung at the Henry Gallery in the "Invitational Exhibit of the Music and Art Foundation." And, despite severe asthma and allergies, Wiggins painted and sold fifteen pictures in Seattle, New York, Yakima, Portland, and Salem.

The year 1952 opened with Fred's usual business schedule and Myra involved with art and studio activities. They left Seattle at the end of March, stopping in San Francisco and Los Angeles where they parted company with Myra continuing to New Orleans and Washington, D.C. In New Orleans, she decided to fly to Washington, D.C., and, after waiting ten hours overnight at the airport, secured a seat. The plane dropped and jerked its way through air pockets before landing at the capitol.

DIFFICULT PHRASING
c. 1900, platinum print
5½" x 7½"
Portland Art Museum

Wiggins, attending the American Pen Women Biennial Meeting as a delegate, did not want to miss an invitation to tea at the White House. After rushing to register for the conference at the Statler Hotel and finally settling in at the Potomac Hotel, she found herself a little early for the tea and sat outside on a bench opposite the White House. This turned out to be a mistake since hundreds of arriving delegates created a long line. By the time Myra reached the front of the receiving line, Mrs. Truman had retired to her living quarters. Instead, Myra shook hands and conversed with Mrs. Barkley, wife of the Vice-President. Myra commented, "the food at the tea . . . was delicious and most abundant."

During the convention, paintings by delegates from 26 states were on view. Wiggins, as one of five exhibitors from Washington State, had two paintings in the exhibit: "The White Vase" and "Copper Pitcher with Chinese Tea Pot." At the Statler Hotel, she attended the Art Dinner, which was followed by music and speakers. "That," Wiggins said, "is when I raised my voice for the first time, when the Vice-Principal of the Corcoran School of Art said that Pictorial Photography was entirely mechanical and uncreative art. Many delegates had their hands up and my neighbor kept nudging me to speak, so when the very last minute allowed had arrived, up went my hand and being so near the speaker's table, I was recognized. I spoke with feeling, perhaps too much so, when I quoted the speaker of the evening as wishing to put Rembrandt and other so-called Old Masters on the shelf, and there was immediate applause which was stopped by the presiding officer, since it was against the rules. Anyway, when I sat down there was applause and the art speaker arose and attempted to explain what he meant regarding Rembrandt, (and we don't know yet)."

One evening, at seven o'clock, Wiggins returned to her room to rest before going out later. "[I] left a call for 7:30—clerk said 'in the morning?' and I said no, tonight—so I slept 15 min., then up, powdered my nose (hair was O.K. as I used the phone book for a pillow) and ran to catch a car for [the] National Gallery where a concert was being given in one of the great wings."

Myra added many concerts and art gallery visits to her itinerary in Washington, but, lurking behind her gaiety while she dashed about town, she grappled with the fact that she had little money. To make matters worse she had not heard from Fred and did not know his whereabouts. "Tell me *right away* when I can draw on our joint bank and how much . . . I asked you several times about your plans and you said each time, you'd let me know later, but didn't . . . Your last letter Father, gave me the inkling that you were not going to meet me here—I'm almost afraid to pack and start out alone—my feet are very unreliable. I do hope that you get [paid] soon, so that I can pay for the room, of course I can't leave till I do—I myself have paid for food and everything else."

On May 18, from the Milner Hotel, Myra wrote Fred again: "Father dear You did not say if I should send the $75 check (repaying what you had recently borrowed) to my bank, and what was the $50 check for—maybe latter was for expenses here (food etc) because the $25 check pays a week rent and there's only $2 and some change left for a week and of course that won't pay for food even tho I eat in my room, so I have had to use two $5.00 bills of mine lately."

On May 24, Myra again wrote Fred: "Finally found your letter. Yes, dear each report seems very wonderful but I worry because like now we use it *all* up before the next season—As soon as we can start a real savings account and not just a checking account—I will be very happy—here we are *in* our old age and *nothing* of *all* the money (and a lot of it) you have earned is yet saved—you are truly wonderful! and we must do something about it—save some of it I mean. How about that Social Security? Are we getting it—I surely need my share and I have spent and am still spending for living (eating) bills [money] I have had put away for *years* and *years*—or I could have never gone or done anything. Now I *hope* to teach again—maybe *casein* who knows—Anyway I hope to see you soon."

June 4, at the Milner Hotel: "Well we surely have been blessed in every way, and your continued good sales are helping wonderfully—I do hope we can put some of the money away."

On July 15: "Dear Father . . . Do be careful! At our age maybe it would be better if you made less and stayed home except 2 months in the East or

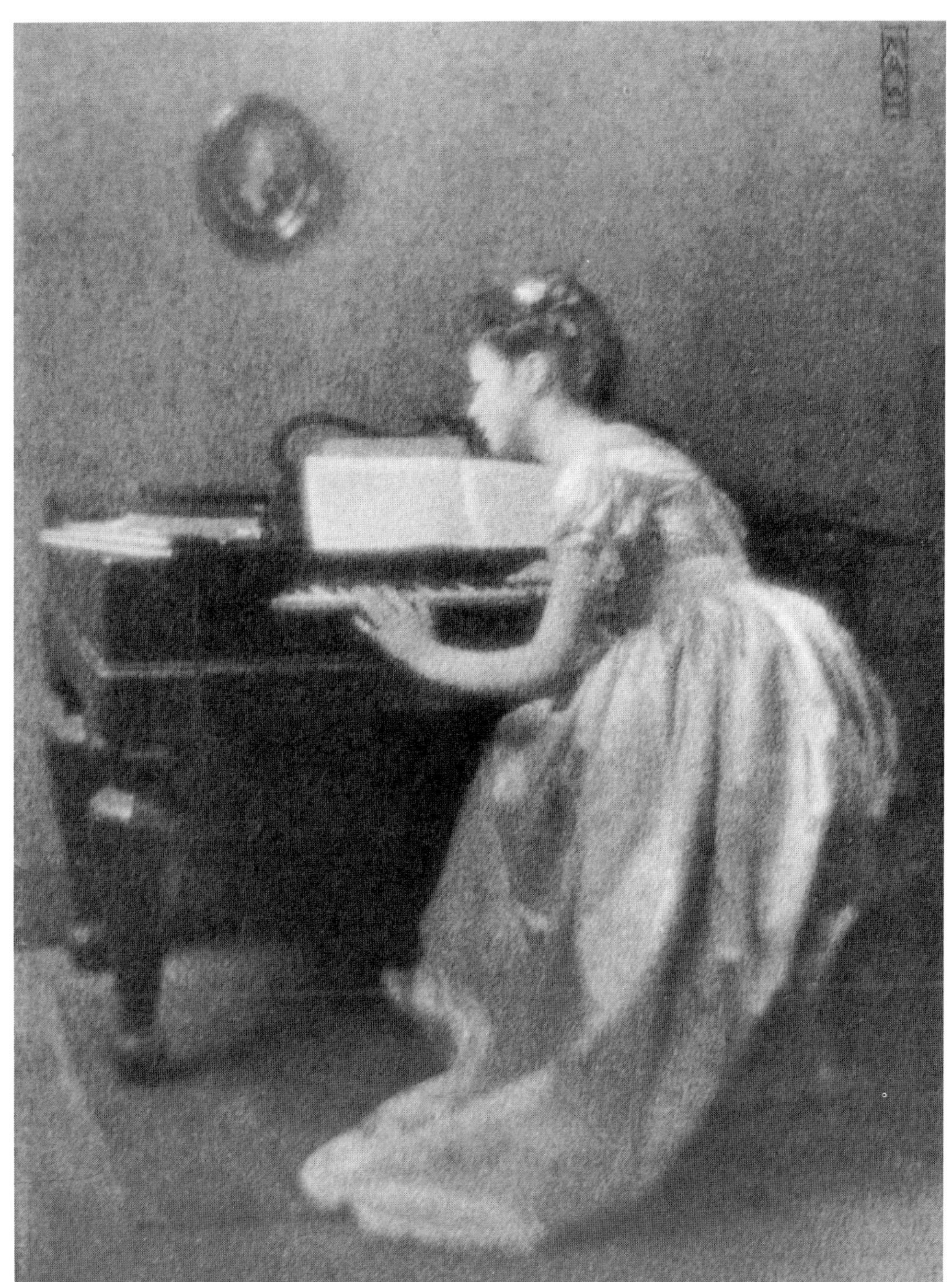

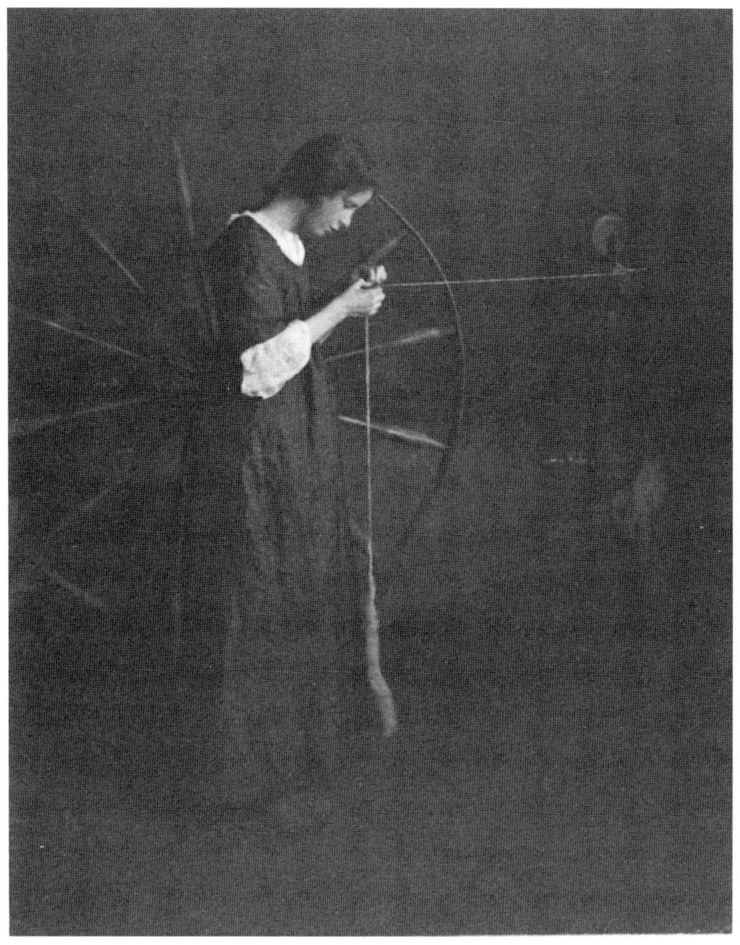

The Knot
c. 1899, platinum print
4⅞" x 6¾"
Portland Art Museum

Madonna
1908, gelatin silver print
5¼" x 7⅜"
Portland Art Museum

maybe 3 in the Spring, not summer—when we get our allowance from the Government. We should not be separated *at all.*" The Wigginses, however, disclosed no hint of these problems in their annual Christmas newsletters to friends and family.

In New York, Myra saw Helen Xavier DuMond at the DuMond Memorial Exhibit at the National Academy. Myra recalled how they had known each other for sixty years. "She [Helen] had studied composition with Mr. DuMond. I studied life drawing with him. We visited one another in our different classes and it is no wonder her instructor fell in love with her." On several occasions Wiggins visited the Art Students League where the students enjoyed hearing stories about her days as an art student.

After Myra's reunion with Fred in New York, they "rented a suite in an old hotel . . . and the front room was Mr. Wiggins' office and my studio, where I painted 5 pictures, 3 oils and 2 caseins,—also I executed a commission in Westchester County, New York, in oil, where I commuted frequently for 3 or 4 weeks."

After leaving New York, Wiggins visited the Eastman Kodak offices and stopped at the Albright Art Gallery in Buffalo where, "once more I saw the paintings of my wonderful instructors of the Art Students League, met the Director, and was shown through the great Galleries. In 1910, Mr. Stieglitz showed 3 of my Pictorial Photographs in his historical Exhibit of Photography there." She also stopped in Chicago and visited the Art Institute, talked to the director, and reminisced about her show there many years earlier.

In the summer of 1953, Wiggins' portrait "Miss New York" hung at a Henry Gallery invitational exhibit. In December, "the dream of my life," as she put it, came true. Dr. Richard E. Fuller, Director of the Seattle Art Museum, invited her to assemble a 62-year retrospective of her paintings and photographs at the museum.

The exhibit of 53 paintings and 23 photographs opened December 9, and for one month Myra reveled in the attention lavished on her by friends and the media. Among the paintings installed were "Textures," a water color titled "Mountain Rescue," "A Corner of My Studio - No. 2," "Indian Baskets and Still Life," and her "Self Portrait at 60." She described a "well-known art critic and reporter who, as he was leaving the Preview, bowed low and said: 'Mrs. Wiggins, never in my life before have I seen

Vermeer in Photography.'" Ed Thomas, Educational Director of the museum, interviewed her on television, and articles about her life and work appeared in Seattle newspapers. Writer, critic, and artist Kenneth Callahan wrote, "Not many producing artists—and to my knowledge no other Pacific Northwest artist—can look back on such a long period of experience in the arts." Thus Myra, the "Dean of Northwest Women Painters," celebrated her 62 years as an artist.

The M.H. De Young Museum in San Francisco opened Wiggins' retrospective in February, 1954. Ninfa Valvo borrowed fourteen oils from Myra's exhibit in Seattle to show along with twenty pictorial photographs. Wiggins' well-known photographs "Hunger ist der Beste Koch," "Heimweih," and "Laverne" appeared, but the show also included lesser known images such as "Difficult Phrasing," "Madonna," and "The Knot." In San Francisco, she was interviewed on television and radio, and *The San Francisco News* featured a story about her life. Myra enjoyed celebrity status in San Francisco much as she had in Seattle.

In the spring of 1954, Myra and Fred again traveled to New York where she appeared on the nationally broadcast Nancy Craig Show. So well received was this program that she was asked to appear on national television in Hollywood, California, in January, 1955, for the 100th anniversary of the founding of the YMCA. "But," Myra said, "that may not come to pass." In May, "Miss New York" hung in the annual show of the National Association of Women Artists of New York at the Academy Galleries. *The New York World Telegram* carried a story about Wiggins, showed her with her 65-year-old camera, and reproduced the wedding picture she took in 1894. *The Christian Science Monitor*, published in Boston, ran a lengthy biographical article with her photograph of Chase's art class and a reproduction of "Morning Blessing."

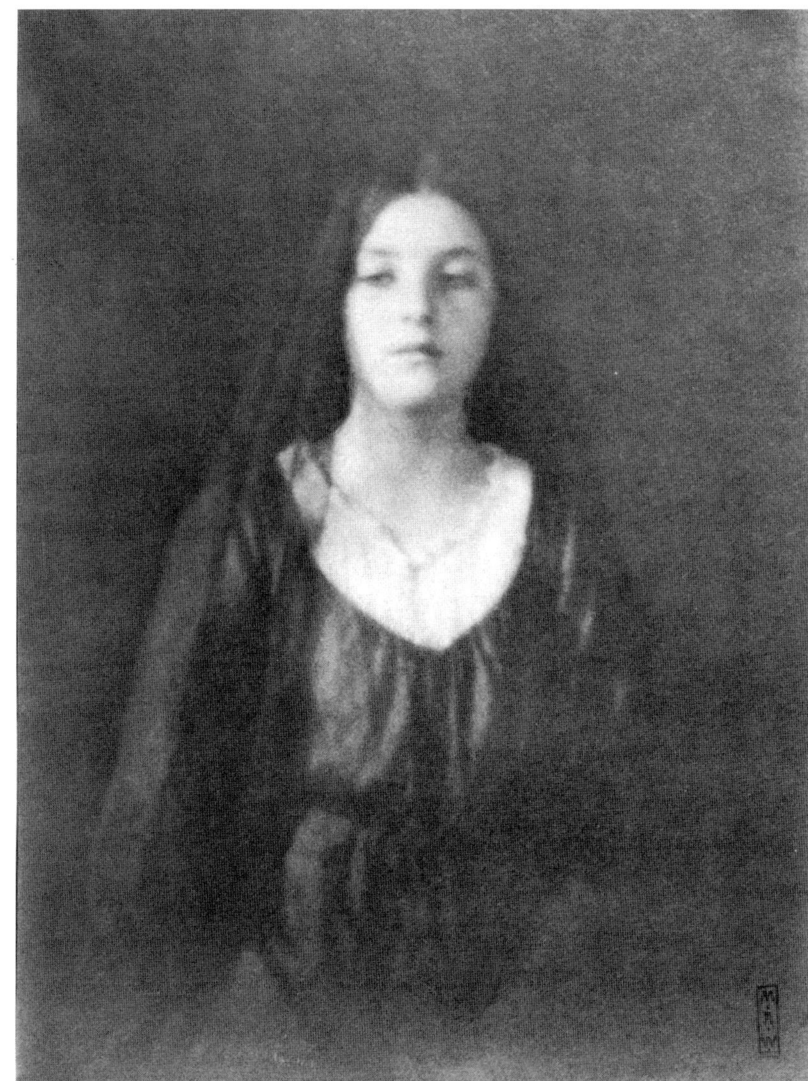

On their way back to Portland in July, Myra and Fred stopped in Rochester to visit Beaumont Newhall, the curator at the George Eastman House. When Myra showed him her portfolio of photographs, Newhall recalled that "The Forge" had hung in George Eastman's office.

Fred and Myra Wiggins' 60th Wedding Anniversary
1954
photographer unknown
Robert and Shirley Benz Collection

On November 21, 1954, friends and family gathered at the Women's Century Club on Capitol Hill in Seattle to celebrate Myra and Fred Wiggins' 60th wedding anniversary. She wore her original wedding gown with bustle, mammoth sleeves, and short train, and long, pointed shoes with "fancy little curved heels." Newspapers in Seattle, Yakima, Portland, and Salem announced the event and people inundated the Wigginses with letters, phone calls, telegrams, and flowers. Fred's secret for a long and happy marriage: "Maintain an active interest in worthwhile activities. And check regularly on your great-grandchildren." One relative commented, "Myra has done everything in her lifetime but jump off the Eiffel tower, and she could probably do that safely if she wanted to."

In spite of their full lives, Fred and Myra instinctively knew time was short. In October, 1955, Fred wrote Myra from the Milner Hotel in New York: "I do trust that you finally got the various pictures to the museums where they belonged, in time. I felt terribly sorry for you when you told me of the [list] of things you had to do and lack of time to accomplish all that your busy mind has scheduled ahead. However it was always thus and always will be, with a conscientious soul like you who never knows an idle minute. I only hope that St. Peter or Paul or Gabriel or some of the other members of the welcoming committee will get you to take a few hours rest before you call for easel and brushes and canvas. However there will be plenty of time ahead and I am sure they have provision[s] made for such as you and the other 'immortals' who have so much unfinished work to do."

That November, 1955, a deadly freeze settled on the Pacific Northwest. Rhododendrons, azaleas, roses, holly, strawberries, and flowering trees died or suffered damage that prevented shipment to Eastern dealers. Fred had witnessed nothing like this in his 67 years in the Pacific Northwest and he suffered losses in canceled commissions. "But," he said, "I'm truly thankful to be alive and well and able to carry on as usual."

By the time Myra turned 86 on December 15, 1955, she had completed over 114 paintings. Fred planned his usual mid-winter Eastern business trip; Myra would join him in Chicago in February. Barely a month later, on January 13 as Myra worked in her studio, she collapsed. An ambulance sped her to a hospital where, after half an hour of intense suffering, she dropped into a deep coma until she died at eleven o'clock the next morning, January 14, 1956. A stroke had claimed her life quickly, without prolonged suffering, as she had wished.

Kenneth Callahan wrote: "Probably no individual in the art life of Seattle was more familiar than the tiny, energetic Mrs. Wiggins with her smiling face, rushing from place to place carrying large, wet canvasses with enormous heavy frames in and out of galleries. She was never in too much of a hurry, however, to stop and offer warm congratulations to any and all of her contemporaries who had received even minor good fortune in the art world of the community."

Fred had known Myra 67 years. To carry on without her required courage. In May, he traveled east on his annual business trip. While in New York, as he crossed a street, perhaps thinking about the years he had shared with Myra, a car struck him. Fred Wiggins died just four months after Myra Albert.

They were gone, but Myra's magic and Fred's dedication to it lives on forever in her photographs, paintings, and poems.

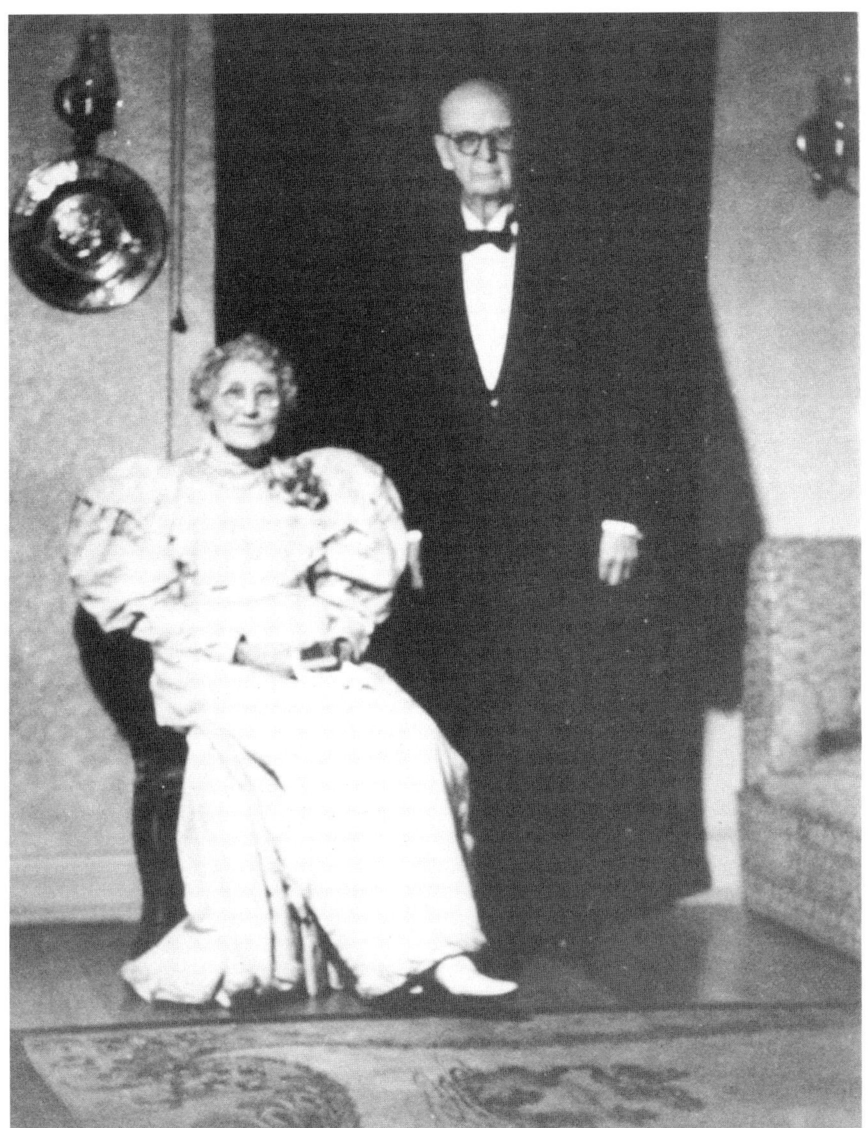

SETTING SAIL

As I set sail for another New Year,
May the winds be gentle, the weather clear-
And touching each Port, as I bear to the West
May I barter for Pearls, and give of my best.

Should storms lash the sail and waves sweep the deck,
May I trust the Wise Pilot through threatening wreck-
And should I debark, leaving cargoed regrets,
May I reach the last Port as the evening Star sets.

—Myra Albert Wiggins

References

List of Abbreviations

ASA .... **Alfred Stieglitz Archive.** Yale Collection of American Literature, Beinecke Rare Book and Manuscript Library, Yale University, New Haven, Connecticut.

JAS .... **Josephine Albert Spaulding** interviews. Author's interviews with Myra Wiggins' niece, Josephine Albert Spaulding (1989-91).

LC .... **Library of Congress,** Washington, D.C.

LIST OF PRIZES .... **"List of Prizes,** Articles, and Mentions on the Pictorial Photographs of Myra Albert Wiggins." Compiled by Myra Wiggins (1939).

MAW .... **Myra Albert Wiggins** recollections. Typescript presentation prepared for the American Association of University Women, Yakima; later edited and published as, "Trials and Triumphs of an Amateur Photographer," *American Magazine of Art* 17 (September 1926).

MWB ....,............ **Mildred Wiggins Benz** interviews. Author's interviews with Myra Wiggins' daughter, Mildred Wiggins Benz (1989-90).

NEWSLETTER ...... **Newsletter,** prepared and typed by Myra and Fred Wiggins for sending to friends and family during the end-of-year holiday season. Beginning in the late 1930s, the Wigginses sent out annual newsletters highlighting their activities and accomplishments of the previous year.

OHSL...................... **Oregon Historical Society Library,** Portland, Oregon.

OSL .... **Oregon State Library,** Salem, Oregon.

RB .... **Robert Benz** interviews. Author's interviews with Myra Wiggins' grandson, Robert Benz (1991).

RSBC .... **Robert and Shirley Benz collection.**

SAML .... **Seattle Art Museum Library,** Seattle, Washington.

WCPAM .... **Wiggins Collection, Portland Art Museum,** Portland, Oregon.

Part One, 1869-1890 (pp. 1 - 13)

little steps .... Jack McLauchlin, telephone interview with author, 11/1/1991; Myra Wiggins diary, 8/16/1942.

Almira Phelps .... *The Phelps Family of America and Their English Ancestors,* compiled by Judge Oliver Seymor Phelps of Portland, Oregon, and Andrew T. Servin of Lennox, Massachusetts (Pittsfield, Massachusetts: Eagle, 1899), RSBC.

Lausanne .... Henry Bridgeman Brewer, "Log of the Lausanne as Kept by Mr. Brewer," *Oregon Historical Quarterly* 29 (June 1928) [p. 191].

Jason Lee .... John B. Horner, *Days and Deeds in the Oregon Country* (Portland: J.K. Gill, 1928) [p. 94].

Joseph Holman .... "Short Biography of Joseph Holman," *Oregon Historical Quarterly* 4 (December 1903) [p. 392]. Holman dictated this account to his wife in 1880.

oath .... Philip H. Parrish, *Historic Oregon* (New York: MacMillan, 1943) [p. 127].

Peoria Party .... Randol Beryle Fletcher, "The Peoria Party," self-published, 1978 [pp. 1-4], OHSL; see also, S.A. Clarke, *Pioneer Days of Oregon History,* Vol. 2 (Portland: J.K. Gill, 1905) [pp. 142-46]. Clarke claims he knew Holman well, and took notes from him in 1880.

Lausanne .... Brewer [p. 358].

"That's the girl" .... Verso of season's greetings card with reproduction of oil painting "Blue and Coral," by Myra Wiggins, n.d.

married .... "Short Biography of Joseph Holman" [p. 394].

gave birth .... Ibid.

debate .... Peter H. D'Arcy, "Historical Review, Champoeg, The Plymouth Rock of the Northwest," *Oregon Historical Quarterly* 29 (September 1928) [p. 221].

"cut the first" .... "Short Biography of Joseph Holman" [p. 394].

art teacher .... Form completed by Myra Wiggins for the Seattle Fine Arts Society, citing early influences, SAML.

John Albert .... "The Albert Family in America from 1748 to Date, 1928," RSBC; Marion County Marriage Records, 1849-71, OSL; partial newspaper clipping, 7/25/27.

By 1869 .... Alan Gustafson, "Salem Started with Wilson Plat," *Statesman-Journal* (Salem), 9/15/1985; Ben Maxwell, "Pleasant and Unpleasant Things in the History of Salem," Parts I, II, III, *Capital Journal* (Salem), 11/21/1950, 11/22/1950, 11/23/1950; "70 Years, Ladd & Bush Bankers," Salem, March 1939 [p. 5], RSBC.

December 15, 1869 ... *Oregonian* (Portland), 12/15/1869.

John Albert .... "70 Years, Ladd & Bush Bankers" [p. 4]; Myra Wiggins, handwritten manuscript, n.d., RSBC.

Joseph Albert .... Partial newspaper clipping, 7/25/1927, RSBC.

"no boy or man" .... Myra Wiggins diary, 8/16/1942.

her childhood .... Goldie Robertson Funk, "Mrs. Wiggins of Toppenish Wash—One of the State's Most Remarkable Women," *Seattle Times,* 3/9/1930.

Oregon state fair .... I am grateful to Jack Cleaver at the Oregon History Center for researching and providing information about the awards won by Myra Wiggins and Helen Gatch at the Oregon State fairs.

Clyde Cook .... Unpublished autobiographical typescript by Myra Wiggins, n.d.; "Sixty-two Year Retrospective Invitational Exhibition" brochure, Seattle Art Museum, 1953.

Frederick Wiggins ..... NEWSLETTER, 1952.

Thomas Holverson ... Ben Maxwell, "Wiggins Who Sold First Car Here Still Active at age 81," *Capital Journal* (Salem), 6/14/1950.

bicycle .... NEWSLETTER, 1949.

"Wiggins Bazaar" ...... Advertisement, *Oregon-Statesman* (Salem), 7/1/1899.

could sell .... JAS to author, 11/7/1991.

club mania .... Winifred H. Cooley, "The Future of the Women's Club," *Arena* 27 (April 1902) [pp. 367-80].

Outing magazine .... *Outing* magazines for 1890.

Shared interests .... JAS to author, 9/26/1989; RB to author, 8/1991.

were members .... MWB to author, 4/11/1990.

Nestucca .... "Nestucca," *Oregon-Statesman* (Salem), 8/16/1888; "Fun at Little Nestucca," *Oregon-Statesman,* 7/30/1889; "At Nestucca," *Oregon-Statesman,* 8/2/1889.

first camera .... MAW.

"the country people" ... Ibid.

yielded "more" .... Myra Albert, "Amateur Photography through Women's Eyes," *Photo-American* (March 1894) [p. 134].

pack train .... MAW.

Helen Gatch .... MAW; Roger Hull maintains that Myra Wiggins and Helen Gatch were rivals rather than colleagues, see "Myra Wiggins and Helen Gatch: Conflicts in American Pictorialism," *History of Photography* 16 (Summer 1992).

George Eastman .... Douglas Collins, *The Story of Kodak* (New York: Harry N. Abrams, 1990) [pp. 46-60].

coined the phrase ...... Frank Presbrey, *The History and Development of Advertising* (Garden City, New York: Doubleday, Doran, 1929) [p. 401].

By 1886 .... C. Jane Gover, *The Positive Image* (Albany: State University of New York Press, 1988) [p. 14].
"endeavored to" .... Letter, Myra Wiggins to Frances Benjamin Johnston, 6/25/1900, LC.
"Miss Albert" .... Letter, to Myra Albert from F.N. Owen & Co., Mercantile Photographers, 4 East 20th St., New York, 7/17/1893, RSBC.
first prize .... "The Photographic Contest," *West Shore* (October 4, 1890) [pp. 115, 124].
"Women with" .... Margaret Bisland, "Women and their Cameras," *Outing* 17 (October 1890) [pp. 37-38].

PART TWO, 1891-1896 (PP. 14 - 23)

concerns raised .... For example, these concerns were discussed by "An American Mother" in an article titled "What of the Woman Herself," *Ladies Home Journal* 18 (June 1901) [p. 10].
Myra chose .... Unpublished autobiographical typescript by Myra Wiggins, n.d.
her palette .... Queena Davison Miller, "Half a Century an Artist," *Seattle Times,* 11/24/1946.
first poems .... Frank James Bellemin, *Our Present Day Poets: Their Lives and Works,* Vol. 1 (Amity, Oregon: Beaver Engraving, Standard Press, 1926) [p. 128].
"Home Sweet Home" ... RSBC.
four or five tents .... Myra Wiggins diary, 7/5/1942; letter, from Ah Sin to Mrs. J.H. Albert from Slab Creek, 7/17/1892; letter, from Ah Sin to Miss Blanche Albert from Slab Creek, 7/20/1892, RSBC.
"My Dear Myra" .... Partial letter, from Portland, Oregon, to Myra Albert, sender unknown, 9/19/1892, RSBC.
N.Y. Camera Club .... NEWSLETTER, 1950; SAML.
Joseph Keiley .... Handwritten note by Myra Wiggins next to Keiley's picture "Indian Girl" in her copy of *Photographic Times* (February 1900) [p. 78], WCPAM.
Myra photographed ... "Art Students League Jubilee Catalogue" (1950/1951). Myra Wiggins' photographs of St. Gauden's sculpture class and Chase's painting class appear on pages 94 and 97; NEWSLETTER, 1950; SAML.
The Kodak Girl .... Gover [p. 15].
"at Chatauqua" .... *Photographic Times* 21 (October 16, 1891) [p. 518]. I wish to thank Becky Simmons at the International Museum of Photography, George Eastman House, for bringing this item to my attention.
American progress .... Thomas J. Schlereth, *Victorian America* (New York: Harper Collins 1991) [pp. 169-75].
Fine Arts Palace .... Barbara Michaels, *Gertrude Käsebier* (New York: Harry N. Abrams, 1992) [p. 18].
First Annual .... "Annual Exhibition of the New York Camera Club - First Annual Members Exhibition of the Society of Amateur Photographers of New York," *American Amateur Photographer* 5 (April 1893) [pp. 168-73].
Joint Exhibition .... Alfred Stieglitz, "The Joint Exhibition at Philadelphia," *American Amateur Photographer* 5 (May 1893) [pp. 201-02]; Sprange's annual *The Blue Book of Amateur Photographers* lists Myra Albert as an exhibitor in the society's exhibition and gives her address as 49 West Sixty-third Street, New York. *The Blue Book of Amateur Photographers* (Beach Bluff, Massachusetts, 1893) [p. 225].
"We know" .... Albert [p. 134].
New York Herald .... *New York Herald,* 4/15/1894.
Camera Mosaics .... *Camera Mosaics,* Camera Series No. 8 (May 5, 1894) [pp. 50, 63, 132, 165], WCPAM.
the wedding .... Charlotte Widrig, "Dean of Northwest Painters," *Seattle Times,* 12/13/1953; Sixtieth Wedding Anniversary brochure, RSBC.
Fred Wiggins .... *Salem City Directory,* 1896, OSL.
in a hospital .... Gillian Marrah, "Photographers in Seattle: The Extraordinary in the Ordinary Woman," Women's Studies Senior Thesis, University of Washington, 1981.
"Dutchy" Mildred .... MWB to author, 4/11/1990.

PART THREE, 1897-1899 (PP. 24 - 37)

"The Forge" .... "Kodak's Marvels," *Mail and Express* (New York), 1/1/1898; Marmaduke Humphrey, "Triumphs in Amateur Photography," *Godey's Magazine* (March 1898) [pp. 257-65]; "Catalogue Eastman Photographic Exhibition," National Academy of Design, New York, 1898, and *Bits from the Kodak Exhibitions,* Catalogue of Eastman Kodak Exhibition, National Academy of Design, New York, January 1-15, 1898; verso, "The Forge," WCPAM; didactic label, International Museum of Photography at George Eastman House.
Eastman Kodak .... "Two Kodak Exhibitions," *Camera Notes* (April 1898) [p. 99].
first Eastman Prize .... "Bedtime Stories Told by the Light of the Moon," *Oregon-Statesman* (Salem), 6/6/1897.
Arts and Crafts .... Christian Peterson, "American Arts and Crafts, The Photograph Beautiful 1895-1915," *History of Photography* 3 (Autumn 1992) [pp. 189-232]; Frederic Flagler Helmer, "A Monograph on Monograms, with Examples by the Author," *Craftsman* 8 (April-September 1905) [pp. 349-56]; Eva Watson Schutze, "Signatures," *Camera Work* 1 (January 1903) [p. 36].
fall of 1898 .... "Catalogue of Prints, The Photographic Section, American Institute, National Academy of Design," New York, 1898, WCPAM.
Dutch pictures .... MAW [pp. 6-8].
Stieglitz used .... "Members Exhibition of Prints," *Camera Notes* 3 (October 1899) [p. 79].
consequently .... "Photography Outdoors Edition," *Photo-Miniature* 1 (July 1899) [p. 167]; "The Philadelphia Salon," *Photo-Era* (Christmas 1899) [p. 526].
London Graphic .... "Salem Amateur Artist," clipped newspaper article in album of memorabilia, WCPAM.
"The Lacemaker" ...... Youth's Companion Certificate of Award, WCPAM; brochure, *Youth's Companion 4th Annual Exhibition of Amateur Photographs,* 1899; *Photographic Times* 32 (February 1900) [pp. 68 and 90]; MAW.
"The Gathering Mist" Brochure, "The Heinn Specialty Company's Contest," 1899, WCPAM; LIST OF PRIZES.
"The First Snow" ...... Verso, "The First Snow," WCPAM; "Award Certificate from the American Institute of the City of New York," 1899, WCPAM; LIST OF PRIZES.
to Alaska .... "Personals," *Oregon-Statesman* (Salem), 8/3/1899; Eliza Ruhamah Scidmore, "The Northwest Passes to the Yukon," *National Geographic* 9 (April 1898) [pp. 105-12], and "The Stikine River in 1898," *National Geographic* 10 (January 1899); "Explorations in Alaska," *National Geographic* 10 (July 1899) [pp. 269-71].
"Alaska outfits" .... Archie Binns, "Gateway to Gold," in W. Storrs Lee, ed., *Washington State: A Literary Chronicle* (New York: Doubleday, 1941 [1969]) [pp. 390-94].
Travelers observed ..... Daniel L. Pratt, "Through the Wonderland of Alaska," *Pacific Monthly* 14 (August 1905) [p. 190].
photographs .... Verso, photographs of Alaskan scenes by Myra Wiggins, WCPAM and RSBC.
Wigginses returned ... "Personals," *Oregon-Statesman* (Salem), 8/17/1899.
studio exhibition ...... Verso, "Myra and Lena's Studio," RSBC; "Catalogue, Myra A. Wiggins and Wilena M. Knight," c. 1899. I am indebted to Sharon Baerny for bringing this catalogue to my attention.

"How do you" .... Letter, Frances Freiot Gilbert to Myra Wiggins, 2/18/1900, RSBC.
"in all my work" .... Myra Albert Wiggins, "Trials and Triumphs of an Amateur Photographer," *American Magazine of Art* 17 (September 1926) [p. 484]; Janet Henderson, "Took Her Own Wedding Photo," *San Francisco News,* 1/1954.
broke her nose .... RB to author, 8/1991.
niece recalled .... JAS to author, 9/26/1989.
a flashlight .... Muriel Thurber Clark, "Art Museum Notes," *Capital Hill Times* (Seattle), 12/19/1953; Bellemin [p. 129].
Time .... Jack McLauchlin.

PART FOUR, 1900 (PP. 38 - 47)

The Witchery of... ...... *Western Camera Notes* 1 (May 1900) [p. 96]; *The Witchery of Kodakery,* Eastman Kodak Company, 1899; letter, from Mr. Donald D. Yokel, Eastman Kodak Company, 10/13/1992.
100,000 cameras ...... Gover [p. 14].
"etiquette of" .... "Kodak Manners," *Ladies Home Journal* 17 (February 1900) [p. 16].
To offset the idea ...... Collins [p. 84].
the closure of .... Advertisement for Wiggins Bazaar, *Oregon-Statesman* (Salem), 1/12/1900.
a free trip .... "A Fine Prize," *Oregon-Statesman* (Salem), 1/30/1900.
Paris Exposition .... Jean-Louis Ferrier and Yann Le Pichon, *Art of Our Century* (New York: Prentice Hall, 1989) [pp. 16-17].
moving sidewalk .... *Scientific American,* 5/19/1900 [p. 310], 7/21/1900 [p. 35], and 8/11/1900 [pp. 81, 87].
defined rules .... "Hand Held Cameras at the Paris Exposition," *Western Camera Notes* 1 (May 1900) [p. 95].
Johnston inviting ...... Correspondence, Johnston and Wiggins, in Frances Benjamin Johnston Collection, LC; letter, Alfred Stieglitz to Johnston, 6/1900, Frances Benjamin Johnston Collection, LC; Toby Quitslund, *Her Feminine Colleagues* (Baltimore: University of Maryland and the Women's Caucus for Art, 1979) [pp. 97-98]; Johnston also sent her list of names to Juan C. Abel, the editor of *Photographic Times.* Abel suggested in a letter, 6/27/1900, that Johnston "add the name of Mrs. Claude Gatch of Salem, Oregon, a personal friend of Mrs. Wiggins, and one who is doing very good work." However, Johnston did not include Gatch in the exhibition.
attending classes .... "A Useful Present," *Oregon-Statesman* (Salem), 4/19/1900.
Gertrude Käsebier .... Letters, Myra Wiggins' first trip to Europe, privately printed in untitled book bound with string by Fred Wiggins, 9/1900, RSBC.
Kodak camera .... "A Useful Present."
felt so unwelcome ..... Myra Albert Wiggins, "Alone in Holland," *American Annual of Photography and Photographic Times Almanac* (New York, 1903) [pp. 227-31].
"I was sorry" .... Frances Benjamin Johnston Collection, LC.
Barnes .... Peter Palmquist, *Catharine Weed Barnes Ward: Pioneer Advocate for Women in Photography* (Arcata, California: Peter Palmquist, 1992); notes tracing a possible connection between the Wiggins and Weed families were handwritten by Myra Wiggins on the verso of "Nymphaea," WCPAM.
Chauncey Depew ..... Letters, Myra Wiggins' first trip to Europe. Chauncey Depew was a United States Senator from New York, 1899 to 1911, and renowned as a public speaker, especially on festive occasions.
Chicago .... *Chicago Times Herald,* 11/11/1900; "Catalogue," First Loan Exhibit, Chicago Society of American Photographers, Art Institute, Chicago, 1900. Thirty-seven Wiggins photographs are listed, WCPAM; LIST OF PRIZES.
Ray Camera .... Advertising brochure for the Ray Camera Company, 1900, WCPAM.
Third Annual .... *Camera Notes* 4 (October 1900) [pp. 107-08].
"The Gathering Mist" Ibid.
"The Spinner" .... "Camera Art Studies that Win Express Prizes with some Others," *Buffalo Express* (New York), 12/23/1900.
"...Grand Court" ...... *Leslie's Weekly* (New York), 11/1/1900.
"making money" .... Candace Wheeler, "Art Education for Women," *Outlook* 55 (January 1897) [p. 81].

PART FIVE, 1901-1903 (PP. 48 - 63)

many hotels .... *Camera Craft* (January 1902); Sprange's Annual *The Blue Book of Amateur Photographers* (Beach Bluff, Massachusetts, 1893) lists 28 hotels with darkrooms [p. 261].
Lily White .... Notes from the book of minutes of the Oregon Camera Club, OHSL.
Member's Exhibition .. "Catalogue of the Members Exhibition, the Camera Club of New York, May-June, 1901." *Camera Notes* 5 (October 1901) [pp. 143, 145, 149].
San Francisco .... "Catalogue," First San Francisco Salon, 1901 [compliments of *Camera Craft*].
Bausch & Lomb .... *Plastigmat Art, A Souvenir,* 1901, WCPAM.
"The Mother" .... *Photo-Era* (October 1901) [p. 133]; verso, "The Mother," WCPAM. According to Myra Wiggins, the negative later was ruined when a technician at Eastman's spilled chemicals on it.
Witch of Kodakery ..... "Books and Magazines," *Western Camera Notes* 3 (September 1901) [p. 179].
"Today the woman" .. Juan C. Abel, "Women Photographers and Their Work," *Delineator* (September 1901) [pp. 406-11] and (November 1901) [p. 751].
"The Babe" .... F. Dundas Todd, Preface to "Souvenir, Chicago Photographic Salon," *Photo-Beacon* (September 1901); Carl Rau, "Impressions of the Chicago Salon," *Western Camera Notes* 3 (November 1901) [p. 209]; LIST OF PRIZES.
"Heimweih" .... Charles E. Fairman, "The Western Exhibitors at the Philadelphia Salon of 1901," *Western Camera Notes* 3 (December 1901) [p. 224]; LIST OF PRIZES.
"one narrow" .... Quoted from *American Amateur Photographer* 12 (December 1900) [p. 567], in Keith F. Davis, *An American Century of Photography: From Dry-Plate to Digital* (New York: Hallmark Cards, Harry N. Abrams, 1995) [p. 35].
Portland Carnival ..... "Photos at the Carnival," *Oregonian* (Portland), 9/26/1901; "Catalogue of Photographs," Portland Carnival, 1901, WCPAM.
"society ladies" .... "Two Amateur Artists—Mrs. Wiggins and Mrs. Gatch Win High Honors," *Oregon-Statesman* (Salem), 6/6/1901.
San Francisco Salon .. "Leading Pictures by Western Workers in the 2nd San Francisco Salon at the Mark Hopkins Institute of Art, Jan 9 to 30, 1902," *Camera Craft* (January 1902) [pp. 89, 115, 145]; "Oregon Amateurs Win in World Competition. Ten Out of 137 Awards Go to This State," *Oregonian* (Portland), 1/19/1902 [pp. 20, 24]; "The Mother," *Oregonian,* 2/2/1902 [p. 21].
"Certainly there" ...... *Western Camera Notes* 4 (April 1902) [pp. 72-73].
"out of doors" .... Helen L. Davie, "Women in Photography," *Camera Craft* (August 1902) [pp. 130-38.]
Photographic Salon .. "Catalogue of the Tenth Annual Exhibition of the Photographic Salon," Dudley Gallery, Egyptian Hall, Piccadilly, London, 1902, RSBC; LIST OF PRIZES.
Interestingly, ... *Photograms of the Year, 1902*; LIST OF PRIZES.
Fred Wiggins .... Letters, Fred Wiggins to Myra Wiggins, 12/8/1902 and 12/10/1902, RSBC.
"Family Cares" .... LIST OF PRIZES.
Implement House ..... Advertisement, *Oregon-Statesman* (Salem), 5/11/1901.
Toronto .... "Catalogue of the Toronto Camera Club,"

Eleventh Annual Exhibit, April 1-5, 1902, WCPAM; LIST OF PRIZES.

"The Babe" .... *Camera Notes* 6 (October 1902) [photograph reproduced between pp. 116-17]; "Catalogue," Print Competition by Members of the Camera Club, at the Club Rooms, Camera Club of New York, May 1-15, 1902, WCPAM.

"The Raysark" .... Sidona V. Johnson, "Houseboating in the Pacific Northwest," *Pacific Monthly* 16 (August 1906) [pp. 213-28] includes reproductions by Ladd, White, and Ainsworth.

"a lone woman" .... Lily White, "From the Log of the 'Raysark,'" *Pacific Monthly* 16 (August 1906) [pp. 160-63, photographs by Lily White]. I wish to thank Terry Toedtemeier for introducing me to the work of White, Ladd, and Ainsworth, and the research done on their lives by Melanie Pryon Tolbert.

Turin, Italy .... "Turin International Exhibition, List of Photographers Invited to Represent the United States," *Camera Notes* 6 (July 1902) [p. 50].

Stieglitz penned .... Alfred Stieglitz, "Painters on Photographic Juries," *American Amateur Photographer* 14 (July 1902) [pp. 311-14].

Stieglitz announced .. *American Amateur Photographer* 14 (September 1902) [p. 387].

"as applied" .... "The Photo-Secession," *American Amateur Photographer* 15 (January 1903) [pp. 20-21].

their election .... *Photo-Secession Supplement* 1 (1903), ASA.

The first issue .... "America at the London Salon," *Camera Work* 1 (January 1903) [pp. 26-29].

D.S. Plumb .... "Society News—Camera Club of NY—Annual Dinner Review," *American Amateur Photographer* 15 (March 1903) [p. 132].

"Indian Basket Maker" T. Thorne Baker, "Edinal, an Ideal Developer for Bromide Paper," *American Amateur Photographer* 15 (March 1903) [p. 111].

Photo-Secession .... "The Photo-Secession," *American Amateur Photographer* 15 (May 1903) [p. 213].

"eligible by" .... "The Photo-Secession," *Camera Work* 3 (July 1903).

Meanwhile, Fred .... Advertisement, *Oregon-Statesman* (Salem), 8/7/1903; *Salem and Marion County Directory,* 1902, OHSL; Maxwell, "Wiggins Who Sold First Car Here Still Active at Age 81."

About this time .... Letters, Fred Wiggins to Myra Wiggins, 4/26/1903 to 6/5/1903, RSBC.

Hamburg Jubilee ...... "Photo-Secession Notes," *Camera Work* 4 (1903) [p. 55].

Linked Ring's .... "The Two Exhibitions," *Photography* 16 (September 26, 1903) [pp. 254, 262], WCPAM.

Bausch & Lomb .... "The Bausch & Lomb Lens Souvenir," Bausch & Lomb Optical Company, Rochester, New York, 1903.

Youth's Companion .... "Announcement of Awards of the Youth's Companion's Amateur Photographic Offers for 1903," *Youth's Companion,* New England ed. (December 24, 1903) [p. 655 and cover photograph], WCPAM.

Stieglitz renamed ...... Verso, "The Edge of the Cliff," WCPAM.

technical details .... "How the Studies Were Made," *Library of Practical Photography,* Vol. 3 and 5 (1909), and Vol. 3 (1911). In Goldie Robertson Funk, "Mrs. Wiggins of Toppenish Wash—One of the State's Most Remarkable Women," *Seattle Times* [p. 5], Wiggins mentions using half of her Darlot lens: "My own discovery—for softer effects."

"Photo-secession" ..... Sadakichi Hartmann, "The Photo-Secession Exhibition at the Carnegie Art Galleries, Pittsburgh, PA," *Camera Work* 6 (April 1904) [pp. 39, 47]; *Photo-Secession Supplement* 5 (May 1904) [p. 39]; verso, "The Edge of the Cliff" and "Polishing Brass," WCPAM; LIST OF PRIZES.

PART SIX, 1904 (PP. 64 - 77)

Middle East .... Unedited letters, Myra Wiggins to Fred Wiggins, 3/9/1904 to 5/8/1904. Edited versions of the letters were published sequentially in the *Oregon-Statesman* (Salem) beginning 4/12/1904. In December 1904, the edited letters were published in book form, titled *Letters from a Pilgrim.*

Wiggins presented .... "Illustrated Lecture, Mrs. Myra A. Wiggins Gives the Second of Her Entertainment to Good Audience," *Oregon-Statesman* (Salem), 12/17/1904.

young Mildred .... MWB to author, 4/11/1990; JAS to author, 9/26/1989.

Fred .... Ibid.

Fred wryly stated ...... Margaret Marshall, "Classic Style Favored, Busy Sixty Years," *Christian Science Monitor* (Boston), 5/4/1954.

Oregon Building ...... "Mrs. Wiggins Defends Oregon's Building at St. Louis World's Fair," *Oregon-Statesman* (Salem), 7/5/1904.

Wiggins' return .... Mother and Child Number, *Photo-Era* (August 1904); *Photo-Miniature* 6 (September 1904) [pp. 313, 326-27].

German portfolio ..... *Die Kunst in Der Photographie* (Achter Fahrgang, 1904), WCPAM; Jean-Claude Lemagny and Andre Rouille, *A History of Photography: Social and Cultural Perspectives* (New York: Cambridge University Press, 1986) [p. 89].

Hague International .. "Foreign Exhibitions and the Photo-Secession Notes," *Camera Work* 7 (July 1904) [p. 40]; "Exhibition Notes," *Camera Work* 8 (October 1904) [p. 37].

a misunderstanding .. Ibid., [p. 38].

"Song of the Sea" ...... Fayette J. Clute, "The Western Workers of the United States," *Photograms of the Year, 1904* [pp. 167-68, 171].

Bell visited .... Letter, Myra Wiggins to Alfred Stieglitz, 3/26/1907, ASA.

Hartmann reviewed .. Sadakichi Hartmann, "The Salon Club and the First American Photographic Salon at New York," *American Amateur Photographer* 15 (July 1904) [pp. 296-305].

memorandum .... Memorandum, Alfred Stieglitz to Frank Eugene, 8/8/1904, ASA. Quoted in Gillian Greenhill Hannum, "Photographic Politics: The First American Photographic Salon and the Stieglitz Response," *History of Photography* 15 (Spring 1991) [p. 70].

"compelled to" .... Anonymous, "Two Points of View," *Photo-Beacon* 16 (September 1904) [p. 287], quoted in Hannum [pp. 70-71].

Gatch represented ..... Gatch's name appears on the salon committee list in the "Catalogue of the First American Photographic Salon, 1904" [Portland Art Museum Library copy].

portfolio traveled ...... "Samples of Fine Art. Work of Some of the Greatest Amateur Photographic Artists in Salem," *Oregon-Statesman* (Salem), 10/20/1904.

"she explained" .... Anon, "About Photos. Something of the Work of the Secessionists in the United States. Proposed that Lewis and Clark Exposition Secure a Collection of First Class Works of Photographic Art for that Exhibit Next Year," *Oregon-Statesman* (Salem), 10/21/1904.

"Am looking" .... Letters, Myra Wiggins to Alfred Stieglitz, 2/4/1905 and 3/26/1907, ASA.

"anyone having" .... "Some of the Pictures to Be Seen at the Photographic Exhibit this Week," *Oregonian* (Portland), 4/23/1905 [p. 40].

"What do" .... Letter, Myra Wiggins to Alfred Stieglitz, 3/26/1907, ASA.

PART SEVEN, 1905-1910 (PP. 78 - 93)

"Even out here" .... Ibid.

"A worker whose" ..... Catharine Weed Ward, "Women in Photography," *Photogram* (April 1905) [p. 122].

"Still Life" .... *Photo-Secession Supplement* 6 (February 1905) [p. 49], ASA; *Camera Work* 10 (April 1905); LIST OF PRIZES.

"Hallowe'en" .... LIST OF PRIZES.

Kodak Competition .. "Catalogue of the Kodak Exhibition" [pp. 3-7, 18]; "Notes and Comments," *Camera Craft* (March 1906) [p. 141].

Lewis and Clark .... "Official Guide to the Lewis and Clark Centennial Exposition (Portland, June 1-October 15, 1905)" [copy in the Multnomah County Library, Portland].

fine arts section .... Robert Joki, interview with author, 10/28/1992; "The Effect of the Exposition," *Pacific Monthly* 14 (July 1905) [p. 106]. This issue reproduced the second series of "Columbia River Scenery" by Sarah Ladd. The first series appeared in the January 1905 issue. Sarah Ladd's husband, Charles E. Ladd, was president of the Pacific Monthly Publishing Company, Portland; "Catalogue of the Fine Arts Exhibit," Lewis and Clark Exposition, 1905 [copy in the Multnomah County Library, Portland].

"The proportion" ..... "The Art Exhibit at the Fair, An Interview with Frank Vincent DuMond, Director of Fine Arts Section at the Lewis and Clark Exposition," *Pacific Monthly* 14 (September 1905) [p. 279].

"As we go" .... "Pictorial Photography at the Lewis and Clark Exposition," *Camera Work* 11 (July 1905) [p. 57].

Mary Albert .... "Lost Key Is Responsible, J.H. Albert's Automobile Is Overturned on Steep Hill," *Oregon-Statesman* (Salem), 7/6/1905; "Mary Albert Funeral," *Oregon-Statesman,* 7/10/1905.

"My Dear Myra" .... Letter, Agnes (surname unknown) to Myra Wiggins, Portland, Oregon, 7/12/1905, RSBC.

"Thanks for your" ..... Letter, Alfred Stieglitz to Myra Wiggins, 11/6/1905, RSBC.

"I am sending" .... Letter, Myra Wiggins to Alfred Stieglitz, 2/22/1906, ASA.

"I should like" .... Letter, Sarah Ladd to Mildred Wiggins, 3/20/1906, RSBC.

Women .... "Exhibition of Photographs, the Work of the Women Photographers of America," Catalogue, the Camera Club of Hartford, Connecticut, April 6, 7, 8, 9, 1906, WCPAM; "Photographs all Made by Women," *Hartford Daily Courant,* 4/7/1906.

"Dear Mr. Stieglitz" .. Letter, Myra Wiggins to Alfred Stieglitz, 10/21/1906, ASA.

"Edge of the Wood" .. "Catalogue of the Photo-Secession Galleries," November 10-December 30, 1906.

Fred Wiggins sold ..... Advertisements, *Oregon-Statesman* (Salem), 10/2 and 10/9/1906; Maxwell, "Wiggins Who Sold First Car Here Still Active at Age 81."

"We are moving" ...... Letter, Wiggins to Alfred Stieglitz, 3/26/1907, ASA; NEWSLETTER, 1955.

Mildred felt .... MWB to author, 7/30/1989.

"drab isolation" .... Kirk Monroe, "Eastern Washington and the Water Miracle of Yakima," *Harper's Weekly* (May 19, 1894), reprinted in W. Storrs Lee, *Washington State: A Literary Chronicle* (New York: Funk and Wagnalls, 1969 [1941]).

irrigation law .... Cecil Dryden, *Dryden's History of Washington* (Portland: Binford and Mort, 1968) [pp. 245-46]. See also: "Irrigation," *Pacific Monthly* 9 (May 1903) [p. 406]; "Big Irrigation Project," *Pacific Monthly* 10 (July 1903) [p. 56]; "Irrigation," *Pacific Monthly* 14 (July 1905) [p. 107]; "The Irrigation of Arid Lands," *Pacific Monthly* 7 (January 1902) [p. 51].

The first year .... Handwritten statement by Mildred Wiggins Benz, RSBC.

"Hallowe'en" .... *Western Camera Notes,* Eighth Year (February 1907) [p. 52].

"Shadows" .... *Photograms of the Year, 1907* [p. 28].

"A Westerner is" .... Fayette Clute, "Work in the Western States," *Photograms of the Year, 1907* [pp. 93-94, 154].

Dutch dress .... MAW [p. 7].

She advised .... Ibid., [p. 9].

were subjects .... MWB to author, 4/11/1990.

"I watched" .... MAW [p. 9].

"Nymphaea" .... *Photograms of the Year, 1908* [pp. 62, 70].

"The Lily Pond" .... "Catalogue Photo-Secession Galleries, Exhibition of Members Work, November 18-December 30, 1907."

invariably .... Annie Brigman, "The Prints at Idora," *Camera Craft* (December 1908) [p. 463].

"Enclosed please" ...... Letter, Myra Wiggins to Alfred Stieglitz, 10/6/1908, ASA.

"I may be able" .... Ibid., 6/29/1909, ASA.

Women's Building .... Karen Blair, ed., *Women in the Pacific Northwest: An Anthology* (Seattle: University of Washington Press, 1988) [p. 60].

exposition awarded ... Award Certificate, Alaska-Yukon-Pacific Exposition, 10/16/1909, WCPAM.

National Arts Club ... J. Nilsen Laurvik, *Camera Work* 26 (April 1909) [p. 42].

"Polishing Brass" .... Verso, "Polishing Brass," WCPAM.

Albright Art Gallery .. *Camera Work* 30 (April 1910) [p. 60]; *Camera Work* 33 (January 1911) [pp. 61-62]; H. Snowden Ward, "The Work of the Year," *Photograms of the Year, 1911-1912* [p. 15]; F. Austin Lidbury, "Some Important Impressions of the Buffalo Exhibition," *American Photography* 22 (December 1910), reprinted in Peter C. Bunnell, ed., *A Photographic Vision: Pictorial Photography, 1889-1923* (Salt Lake City, Utah: P. Smith, 1980); LIST OF PRIZES; "Statement of Photographs for which Money Has Been Received," in Buffalo Fine Arts Academy file, ASA. According to this list, Mr. Spencer Kellogg purchased a number of prints at the exhibition.

Stieglitz's efforts .... Joseph Keiley, "The Photo-Secession Exhibition at the Pennsylvania Academy of Fine Art: It's Place and Significance in the Progress of Pictorial Photography," *Camera Work* 16 (October 1906). Keiley noted: "Today in America the real battle for the recognition of pictorial photography is over. The chief purpose for which the Photo-Secession was established has been accomplished—the serious recognition of photography as an additional medium of pictorial expression."

Camera Work .... Paul Rosenfeld, "The Boy in the Darkroom," in *America and Alfred Stieglitz: A Collective Portrait* (New York: Literary Guild, 1934) [p. 84].

Part Eight, 1911-1956 (pp. 94 - 125)

Annual Exhibition .... *Museum Auditorium Monthly* 2 (January 1913), published by the Seattle Art Association.

wrote poems .... Bellemin [p. 128].

Mildred recalled .... Handwritten manuscript by Mildred Wiggins Benz, n.d., RSBC.

San Francisco .... Telegram, Joseph Albert to Fred Wiggins, 9/13/1915, RSBC; postcard, Myra Wiggins to Fred Wiggins, 9/15/1915, RSBC; letter, Myra Wiggins to Fred Wiggins, 9/16/1915, RSBC.

"The Pines" .... Application form, Seattle Fine Arts Society, n.d.; Wiggins' address is given as Toppenish, Washington, SAML.

Besides enjoying .... Schlereth [p. 297].

"I came to" .... Letter, Fred Wiggins to Myra Wiggins, 11/21/1917, RSBC.

Reuben Benz .... RB to author, 8/1991; NEWSLETTER, 1955.

"After several years" ... MAW.

"Dethroned" .... "Rotogravure Pictorial Section," *Seattle Daily Times* (10/ 9/1924).

Seattle Fine Arts .... Brochure, "Exhibition of Pictorial Photography by Myra Albert Wiggins," December 1928.

personal favorites ...... MAW.

Four years .... Funk [p. 5]; Myra Wiggins, "Trials and Triumphs of an Amateur Photographer" [pp. 481-85]; Bellemin [pp. 128-29].

Yet, Myra .... "Roll of Artists of the Pacific Northwest," compiled by Mrs. Harry Paul Pierce, Chairman, Department of Fine Arts,

Washington State Federation of Women's Clubs, 1924-26 (published 1926).

"Sleepytime" ... Lorna Robertson, interview with author, Yakima, Washington.

Her lectures ... Myra Wiggins, handwritten unpublished manuscripts of her lectures, RSBC.

traditional style ... Funk [p. 5].

gave to details ... Charlotte Widrig, "Dean of Northwest Women Painters," *Seattle Times,* 12/13/1953.

Henry Home ... I wish to thank David Martin for his information regarding Seattle arts organizations from 1900 to 1935.

Women Artists ... "Women Painters of Washington Yearbook," 1947-48, and 1952-53.

"My Studio" ... Handwritten note on verso of black and white press print of "My Studio."

her art studio ... Brochure, "Myra A. Wiggins Art Studio," printed 11/1934, SAML.

January 1, 1938 ... Myra Wiggins diary, 1/1/1938, 2/6/1938, 10/3/1938, 10/4/1938, 10/5/1938, 11/5/1938, 11/18/1938, 11/20/1938, 12/4/1938.

accomplishments ... Brochure, "Myra A. Wiggins Art Studio," Wiggins penciled in the 1939 updates.

Fourth Annual ... Catalogue, "Portland Art Museum Fourth Annual," November 6-December 1, 1935 [Portland Art Museum Library copy].

"A red letter day" ... Letter, Myra Wiggins to her family, dictated to Marjorie Little (stenographer), 7/24/1938.

Christmas cards ... Myra Wiggins diary, 12/1/1938.

She also viewed ... Typed rough draft of 1939 NEWSLETTER, 12/19/1939, from the Hotel Grand, Broadway Avenue and 31st Street, New York.

"Bouquet" ... Verso of press print of "Bouquet," dating from Wiggins retrospective at the M.H. De Young Memorial Museum in 1954.

"near record sale" ... NEWSLETTER, 1947.

paintings hung ... "Partial Exhibition Record, Myra Albert Wiggins," compiled by Sharon Baerny.

Argent Gallery ... "Catalogue of Exhibition," September 30 to October 12, 1946; "Three at Argent," *Art Digest* 21 (October 1946) [p. 16-17]; Howard DeVree, "Among the New Exhibitions," *New York Times,* (10/6/1946) [sec. 2, p. 8].

"Fish with Metals" ... Miller, "Half a Century an Artist."

Knox Manning ... NEWSLETTER, 12/17/1947.

Alfred Stieglitz ... Sue Davidson Lowe, *Stieglitz: A Memoir/ Biography* (New York: Farrar Straus Giroux, 1983).

write his address ... Myra Wiggins wrote down two addresses and phone numbers for Alfred Stieglitz: 489 Park Ave, Plaza 2765 [his Intimate Gallery housed in the Anderson Galleries], and 38 Ea. 58th, Regent 1847; Wiggins recorded Johnston's address as 65 University Place, N.Y., and Mrs. Toedt's as 158 W. 58 Circle.

achieving acclaim ... NEWSLETTER, 12/17/1947.

Fifty-fifth Annual ... "Women Artists Put Best Feats Forward," *Art Digest* 21 (May 1, 1947) [p. 13].

her woodcuts ... *In Valiant Quest,* a collection of poems by Washington poets published by Ethelyn Miller Hartwich of the Seattle Branch of the American Pen Women.

Orton Collection ... NEWSLETTER, 1947; Worth D. Griffin, "Orton Collection Given to Washington State," *Art Digest* 21 (November 15, 1946) [p. 20]; Orton Collection, Washington State University Museum of Art, Pullman.

"As I look" ... Letter, Fred Wiggins to Myra Wiggins, 8/23/1947, RSBC.

Art Achievement ... NEWSLETTER, 12/15/1948.

fall of 1948 ... Ibid.

Wolcott Hotel ... Letter, Fred Wiggins to Reuben and Mildred Benz, 5/27/1948, from the Wolcott Hotel, New York, RSBC.

"the workingest" ... NEWSLETTER, 1947.

May, 1949 ... Ibid., 1949.

Flash Bantam ... Ibid.; "Kodakery," George Eastman House, Rochester, New York, 10/5/1950.

"I have paid" ... Letter, Myra Wiggins to Fred Wiggins, 6/1/1949, RSBC.

"I have used" ... Ibid., 6/6/1949, RSBC.

Edward Steichen ... Ibid.

Biennial Meeting ... NEWSLETTER, 1950.

Kodak Company ... Ibid.; "Visitor, 80, 'Shot' Her Wedding with Flash Powder," *Kodakery* (October 5, 1950).

sixty-year ... NEWSLETTER, 1950; "Sixty Year Retrospective Exhibition of the Paintings of Myra Albert Wiggins," Elfstrom Galleries, Salem, November 7-20, 1950; "Old Friend, Myra Albert Wiggins, Salem Native, Shows Oils for Two Weeks Here," *Oregon-Statesman* (Salem), 11/6/1950.

Ninfa Valvo ... NEWSLETTER, 1951; Myra Wiggins, handwritten manuscript.

Larson Museum ... NEWSLETTER, 1951.

Phi Delta Nu ... Ibid.

Henry Gallery ... Ibid.

Pen Women ... Ibid., 1952.

"[I] left a call" ... Letter, Myra Wiggins to Fred Wiggins, 4/21/1952, RSBC.

"Tell me *right* away" ... Ibid.

"Father dear" ... Ibid., 5/18/1952, RSBC.

"Finally found your" ... Ibid., 5/24/1952, RSBC.

"Well we surely" ... Ibid., 6/4/1952, RSBC.

"Do be careful" ... Ibid., 7/15/1952, RSBC.

Helen X. DuMond ... NEWSLETTER, 1952.

"rented a suite" ... Ibid.

"Miss New York" ... NEWSLETTER, 1953.

"dream of my life" ... Ibid.

The exhibit ... Ibid.; Kenneth Callahan, "Exhibitions Keyed to Christmas Season," *Seattle Times,* 12/1953.

De Young Museum ... "List of Pictorial Photos by Myra Albert Wiggins," M.H. De Young Memorial Museum file; Henderson, "Took Her Own Wedding Photo"; NEWSLETTER, 1954; "M.H. De Young Memorial Museum," *Architect and Engineer* 2 (February 1954) [pp. 6, 8].

Nancy Craig Show ... NEWSLETTER, 1954; correspondence regarding television show, RSBC.

story about Wiggins ... Sally MacDougal, "Artist a Camera for 60 Years," *New York World-Telegram,* 5/7/1954 [Section two]. Wiggins crossed out a number of statements in her personal copy of the article and penciled in corrections, RSBC; Marshall, "Classic Style Favored, Busy Sixty Years."

Beaumont Newhall ... NEWSLETTERS, 1954, 1955; letter, Beaumont Newhall to Reuben Benz, 2/19/1957.

60th anniversary ... NEWSLETTER, 1954; "My Dear," *Oregon Journal,* 11/21/1954.

"I do trust" ... Letter, Fred Wiggins to Myra Wiggins, 10/10/1955, RSBC.

a deadly freeze ... NEWSLETTER, 1955.

A stroke had ... "Myra Wiggins Earthbound Life Has Ended," funeral brochure; Kenneth Callahan, "Tiny, Energetic Mrs. Wiggins Was Vital, Dedicated Artist," *Seattle Times,* 1/22/1956.

Fred Wiggins ... RB to author; "F.A. Wiggins, Nurseryman, Dies in N.Y.," *Seattle Daily Times,* 5/21/1956.

Setting Sail ... From the Myra Wiggins funeral brochure.

Selected Bibliography

General References

"Art Students League Jubilee Catalogue." 1950/1951.

Bisland, Margaret. "Women and Their Cameras." *Outing* 17 (October 1890) [pp. 37-38].

The Blue Book of Amateur Photographers [Sprange's Annual]. Beach Bluff, Massachusetts, 1893.

Clarke, S.A. *Pioneer Days of Oregon History,* Vol. 2. Portland: J.K. Gill, 1905.

Collins, Douglas. *The Story of Kodak*. New York: Harry N. Abrams, 1990.

Cooley, Winifred Harper. "The Future of the Women's Club." *Arena* 27 (April 1902) [pp. 367-80].

Corning, Howard McKinley, ed. *Dictionary of Oregon History*. Portland: Binford and Mort, 1989.

Davis, Keith F. *An American Century of Photography: From Dry-Plate to Digital.* New York: Hallmark Cards, Harry N. Abrams, 1995.

Doty, Robert M. *Photo-Secession: Stieglitz and the Fine-Art Movement in Photography.* New York: Dover, 1960.

Ferrier, Jean-Louis, and Yann Le Pichon. *Art of Our Century: The Chronicle of Western Art, 1900 to Present.* New York: Prentice Hall, 1989.

Fletcher, Randol Beryle. "The Peoria Party." Self-published, 1978.

Gaston, Joseph. *The Centennial History of Oregon, 1811-1912,* Vol. 1. Chicago: S.J. Clarke, 1912.

Gover, C. Jane. *The Positive Image: Women Photographers in Turn of the Century America.* Albany: State University of New York Press, 1988.

"Hand Held Cameras at the Paris Exposition." *Western Camera Notes* 1 (May 1900) [p. 95].

Hannum, Gillian Greenhill. "Photographic Politics: The First American Photographic Salon and the Stieglitz Response." *History of Photography* 15 (Spring 1991).

Hartmann, Sadakichi. "The Salon Club and the First American Photographic Salon at New York." *American Amateur Photographer* 15 (July 1904) [pp. 296-305].

Helmer, Frederic Flagler. "A Monograph on Monograms: With Examples by the Author." *Craftsman* 8 (April-September 1905) [pp. 349-56].

Horner, John B. *Days and Deeds in the Oregon Country*. Portland: J.K. Gill, 1928.

________. *Oregon History and Early Literature: A Pictorial Narrative of the Pacific Northwest,* 4th ed. Portland: J.K. Gill, 1931 [1919].

Johnson, Sidona V. "Houseboating in the Pacific Northwest." *Pacific Monthly* 16 (August 1906) [pp. 213-28].

"Kodak Manners." *Ladies Home Journal* 17 (February 1900) [p. 16].

Lee, W. Storrs, ed. *Washington State: A Literary Chronicle.* New York: Funk and Wagnalls, 1969 [1941].

Lemagny, Jean-Claud, and Andre Rouille. *A History of Photography: Social and Cultural Perspectives*. New York: Cambridge University Press, 1986.

Michaels, Barbara L. *Gertrude Käsebier: The Photographer and Her Photographs.* New York: Harry N. Abrams, 1992.

Palmquist, Peter. *Catharine Weed Barnes Ward: Pioneer Advocate for Women in Photography*. Arcata, California: Peter Palmquist, 1992.

Parrish, Philip H. *Historic Oregon*. New York: MacMillan, 1943.

Peterson, Christian. *Alfred Steiglitz's Camera Notes.* New York: Minneapolis Institute of Arts, W.W. Norton, 1993.

________. "American Arts and Crafts: The Photograph Beautiful, 1895-1915." *History of Photography* 3 (Autumn 1992) [pp. 189-232].

Pratt, Daniel L. "Through the Wonderland of Alaska." *Pacific Monthly* 14 (August 1905) [p. 190].

Presbrey, Frank. *The History and Development of Advertising.* New York: Greenwood Press, 1968 [1929].

Quitsland, Toby. *Her Feminine Colleagues*. Baltimore: University of Maryland and the Women's Caucus for Art, 1979.

Rosenblum, Naomi. *A History of Women Photographers.* New York: Abbeville Press, 1994.

________. *A World History of Photography*. New York: Abbeville Press, 1984.

Schlereth, Thomas J. *Victorian America: Transformation in Everyday Life, 1876-1915.* New York: Harper Collins, 1991.

Stieglitz, Alfred. "Painters on Photographic Juries." *American Amateur Photographer* 14 (July 1902) [pp. 311-14].

Watson Schütze, Eva. "Signatures." *Camera Work* 1 (January 1903) [p. 36].

"What of the Woman Herself." *Ladies Home Journal* 18 (June 1901) [p. 10].

Wheeler, Candace. "Art Education for Women." *Outlook* 55 (January 1897) [p. 81].

White, Lily E. "From the Log of the 'Raysark.'" *Pacific Monthly* 16 (August 1906) [pp. 160-63].

Publications about Myra Albert Wiggins, Including Reproductions of Her Artwork

Abel, Juan C. "Women Photographers and Their Work." *Delineator* (September 1901) [pp. 406-11] and (November 1901) [pp. 747-51].

"Announcement of Awards of the Youth's Companion's Amateur Photographic Offers for 1903." *Youth's Companion*, New England ed. (December 24, 1903) [p. 655 and cover photograph].

"Annual Exhibition of the New York Camera Club - First Annual Members Exhibition of the Society of Amateur Photographers of New York." *American Amateur Photographer* 5 (April 1893) [pp. 168-73].

"At Work" or "Polishing Brass." *American Annual of Photography and Photographic Times Almanac* (1905) [p. 166].

"The Babe." *Camera Notes* 6 (May 1902) and (October 1902).

"Bedtime Stories Told by the Light of the Moon." *Oregon-Statesman* (Salem), 6/6/1897.

Bellemin, Frank James. *Our Present Day Poets: Their Lives and Works*, Vol. 1. Amity, Oregon: Beaver Engraving, Standard Press, 1926.

Bits from the Kodak Exhibitions. Catalogue of Eastman Kodak Exhibition, National Academy of Design, New York, January 1-15, 1898, published by "E. Kodak Co."

Callahan, Kenneth. "Tiny, Energetic Mrs. Wiggins Was Vital, Dedicated Artist." *Seattle Times,* 1/22/1956.

"Camera Art Studies that Win Express Prizes with some Others." *Buffalo Express* (New York), 12/23/1900.

Camera Mosaics. Camera Series No. 8 (May 5, 1894) [pp. 50, 63, 132, 165].

"Catalogue." First Loan Exhibit, Chicago Society of American Photographers, Art Institute of Chicago, 1900.

"Catalogue." First San Francisco Salon, 1901.

"Catalogue Eastman Photographic Exhibition." National Academy of Design, New York, 1898.

"Catalogue of the Members Exhibition, the Camera Club of New York, May-June, 1901." *Camera Notes* 5 (October 1901) [pp. 143, 145, 149].

"Catalogue of Photographs." Portland Carnival, 1901.

"Catalogue of Prints, The Photographic Section, American Institute." National Academy of Design, New York, 1898.

"Catalogue of the Tenth Annual Exhibition of the Photographic Salon." London, 1902.

"Catalogue of the Toronto Camera Club." April 1-5, 1902.

Chicago Times Herald, 11/11/1900.

Clark, Muriel Thurber. "Art Museum Notes." *Capitol Hill Times* (Seattle), 12/19/1953.

Clute, Fayette J. "The Western Workers of the United States." *Photograms of the Year, 1904* [pp. 167-68, 171].

Davie, Helen, L. "Women in Photography." *Camera Craft* 5 (August 1902) [pp. 130-38].

Die Kunst in Der Photographie. Achter Fahrgang, 1904.

"The Edge of the Cliff." In Sidney Allan. "A New Power of Artistic Expression: The Pictorial Movement in Photography." *Smith's Magazine* 6 (January 1908) [pp. 657-58].

Fairman, Charles, E. "The Western Exhibitors at the Philadelphia Salon of 1901." *Western Camera Notes* 3 (December 1901) [pp. 223-28].

Funk, Goldie Robertson. "Mrs. Wiggins of Toppenish Wash—One of the State's Most Remarkable Women." *Seattle Times*, 3/9/1930.

"The Gathering Mist" and "List of Exhibitors." *Camera Notes* 4 (October 1900) [pp. 107-08].

Hartmann, Sadakichi. "The Photo-Secession Exhibition at the Carnegie Art Galleries, Pittsburgh, PA." *Camera Work* 6 (April 1904) [pp. 39, 47].

"Head of the Grand Court." *Leslie's Weekly* (New York), 11/1/1900.

"Heimweih." *Photograms of the Year, 1902.* London, 1902.

"The Heinn Specialty Company's Contest." Brochure, 1899.

Henderson, Janet. "Took Her Own Wedding Photo." *San Francisco News*, 1/1954.

"How the Studies Were Made." *Library of Practical Photography*, Vols. 3 and 5 (1909), and Vol. 3 (1911).

Hull, Roger. "Myra Wiggins and Helen Gatch: Conflicts in American Pictorialism." *History of Photography* 16 (Summer 1992).

Humphrey, Marmaduke. "Triumphs in Amateur Photography." *Godey's Magazine* (March 1898) [pp. 257-65].

"Hunger ist der Beste Koch." *Photo-Era* (Christmas 1899) [p. 526].

"Illustrated Lecture, Mrs. Myra A. Wiggins Gives the Second of Her Entertainment to Good Audience." *Oregon-Statesman* (Salem), 12/17/1904.

"The Knot." *American Annual of Photography and Photographic Times Almanac* (1904) [p. 194].

"Kodak's Marvels." *Mail and Express* (New York), 1/1/1898.

"The Lacemaker" and "Editorial Notes." *Photographic Times* 32 (February 1900) [pp. 68, 90].

"Leading Pictures by Western Workers in the 2nd San Francisco Salon at the Mark Hopkins Institute of Art, Jan 9 to 30, 1902." *Camera Craft* (January 1902) [pp. 89, 115, 145].

"Looking Seaward." *American Annual of Photography and Photographic Times Almanac* (1901) [p. 167].

Maxwell, Ben. "Wiggins Who Sold First Car Here Still Active at Age 81." *Capital-Journal* (Salem), 6/14/1950.

"Members Exhibition of Prints" and "Hunger ist der Beste Koch." *Camera Notes* 3 (October 1899) [p. 79].

Miller, Queena Davison. "Half a Century an Artist." *Seattle Times*, 11/24/1946.

"The Mother." *Oregonian* (Portland), 2/2/1902 [p. 21].

"The Mother. "*Photo-Era* (October 1901) [p. 133].

"The Mother." *Plastigmat Art: A Souvenir*. 1901.

"Mrs. Wiggins Defends Oregon's Building at St. Louis World's Fair." *Oregon-Statesman* (Salem), 7/5/1904.

New York Herald, 4/15/1894.

"Oregon Amateurs Win in World Competition. *Oregonian* (Portland), 1/19/1902 [pp. 20, 24].

The Phelps Family of America and Their Fnglish Ancestors, compiled by Judge Oliver Seymor Phelps of Portland, Oregon, and Andrew T. Servin of Lennox, Massachusetts. Pittsfield, Massachusetts: Eagle, 1899.

"The Photographic Contest." *West Shore* (October 4, 1890) [pp. 115, 124].

"Photography Outdoors Edition." *Photo-Miniature* 1 (July 1899) [p. 167].

"Photos at the Carnival." *Oregonian* (Portland), 9/26/1901.

"Photo-Secession Notes." *Camera Work* 4 (1903) [p. 55].

Rau, Carl. "Impressions of the Chicago Salon." *Western Camera Notes* 3 (November 1901) [pp. 208-09].

"Roll of Artists of the Pacific Northwest, Compiled by Mrs. Harry Paul Pierce, Chairman of Fine Arts, Washington State Federation of Women's Clubs, 1924-1926." 1926.

"Shadows." *American Annual of Photography and Photographic Times Almanac* (1907) [facing p. 63].

Stieglitz, Alfred. "The Joint Exhibition at Philadelphia." *American Amateur Photographer* 5 (May 1893) [pp. 201-02].

"Three at Argent." *Art Digest* 21 (October 1946) [pp. 16-17].

Todd, F. Dundas. Preface to "Souvenir, Chicago Photographic Salon." *Photo-Beacon* (September 1901).

"Two Amateur Artists—Mrs. Wiggins and Mrs. Gatch Win High Honors." *Oregon-Statesman* (Salem), 6/6/1901.

"Two Kodak Exhibitions." *Camera Notes* (April 1898) [pp. 97-99].

"A Useful Present." *Oregon-Statesman* (Salem), 4/19/1900.

"View of a Windmill." *American Annual of Photography and Photographic Times Almanac* (1903) [p. 151].

Ward, Catharine Weed. "Women in Photography." *Photogram* (April 1905) [p. 122].

Widrig, Charlotte. "Dean of Northwest Painters." *Seattle Times*, 12/13/1953.

Youth's Companion 4th Annual Exhibition of Amateur Photographs. 1899.

PUBLICATIONS WRITTEN BY MYRA ALBERT WIGGINS

Albert, Myra. "Amateur Photography through Women's Eyes." *Photo-American* (March 1894) [p. 134].

Wiggins, Myra Albert. "Alone in Holland." *American Annual of Photography and Photographic Times Almanac*. New York, 1903 [pp. 227-31].

________. *Letters from a Pilgrim*. 1904.

________. "Trials and Triumphs of an Amateur Photographer." *American Magazine of Art* 17 (September 1926) [pp. 481-85].

Wiggins, Myra Albert, and Wilena M. Knight. "Catalogue, Myra A. Wiggins and Wilena M. Knight." c. 1899.

Index to the Artwork